TOO PRETTY TO LIVE

THE CATFISHING MURDERS
OF EAST TENNESSEE

DENNIS BROOKS

D1303353

DIVERSIONBOOKS

1

The largest cities in the United States can average a homicide a day. Such frequency can make them hardly newsworthy, killings rendered into brief asides in the local papers and evening broadcasts.

On the opposite end of the spectrum are the small towns that seemingly materialize from a Norman Rockwell painting.

Mountain City is one of those towns. It is the lightly populated county seat of Johnson County at the northeastern tip of Tennessee. Around 18,000 people live there in a small community nestled between the mountains that border Virginia and North Carolina. It's a place that recalls the quaint hometowns of past generations. People know one another, and as for the strangers who wander in, residents cheerfully make them feel welcome.

And the vast majority clutch their Christian faith close in their daily existence. Hardly a single living room lacks decor of a religious variety.

For most of my adult life, my main interaction with the town was as a high school football referee. Always gracious and generous, the people of Mountain City were the most welcoming of any location in our region. A piping hot dinner always awaited us after games, and words of gratitude were always provided, rather than the jeers and boos rendered elsewhere. It was a long drive up the valley, but no one ever griped. The people were too pleasant for complaining.

However, my day job involves dealing with unpleasant people. I'm a prosecuting attorney for the state of Tennessee. Thieves, drug dealers, drunk drivers, and violent offenders occupy the dockets of my four-county district.

In seventeen years on the job, I've seen a lot of bad things. I have prosecuted over a dozen people for murder with solid results. Most of those crimes occurred in Johnson City, two counties over from Mountain City but almost a world apart. More urban and home to a large university, my home county of Washington has more drug activity and more violent crime, murder included.

Every few years, if even that often, Mountain City experiences a homicide case. It's usually a couple of men in an argument that went awry, or a domestic situation that spiraled too far out of control. Either way, killings are rare. The criminal dockets are light. On the other end of the state, Memphis has over 100 prosecuting attorneys. Mountain City has one.

But on January 31, 2012, Mountain City had a high-profile mess on its hands. A young couple killed in their home, before daybreak, for no apparent reason at all. The mother, clothed in her pajamas and dead from a bullet through her head, passed away while clutching her infant in her arms. The father was found on his bed with a bullet wound to his face and his neck sliced from one end to the other.

And it was all over nothing.

Folks in big cities may not believe it, but the Internet is alive and well in rural America. People in small towns far away from shopping malls have smart phones. They have laptops. They have e-mail accounts. And they love Facebook.

Isolated people perhaps become more dependent on and addicted to social media than their big city counterparts. An online existence can become their only significant source of interaction with the outside world.

Unlike any murder case I had ever seen, this Mountain City matter featured social media gone awry. Its massive volume of written communications and complex legal issues had required that the case get extra attention. Hence my involvement.

I'm in my mid forties. For a prosecutor with plenty of miles left, I've compiled results of which I am proud. One double murderer on death row. Around twenty jury convictions for murder. I've done this kind of thing long enough that on my first meeting with the family of a homicide victim, I know what they're going to say before they say it. No matter what, I know they have a deep-rooted fear that the killer will get away with the crime, and inevitably will be in their presence as they check out at the grocery store, laughing it up, taunting them with the darkest memory of their lives.

I have learned another fact over the years. No matter how solid the case is, all murder trials present challenges. They last multiple days, and they almost always present enormous pressure.

Yet this Mountain City matter was especially challenging. In this case, I prosecuted people for murder when they had not participated in the act of killing. I prosecuted people who acted with others who, come to find out, were fictitious people. I prosecuted accused people who had not the slightest violent blemish on their criminal records.

And in this case, our prosecution team convicted them all. This is our story.

2

The defense attorney, hair perfectly coiffed, clothed in a form-fitting designer suit with cufflinks, sauntered to the podium to question potential jurors. His client sat behind him. She was his opposite— an utterly forgettable young woman with dark-rimmed eyeglasses, a homely white blouse covering a tall and gangly frame. Being shy, her face revealed a state of mind that she was ready to dig a hole in the courtroom floor and escape.

She was on trial for two counts of first degree murder, killings that, even by the state's proof, were committed without her even being present.

"When you look at my client, what one word would you use to describe her?" asked the attorney.

"Scared," answered the first juror.

"Ordinary," said another.

"Worried," said a third.

Other jurors echoed those descriptions.

I couldn't fault those labels. These jurors did not know the woman. They were describing their first impressions.

As I sat at the prosecution table, my mind wandered to what words I would use to describe her. "Vengeful," "manipulative," "devious," "hateful," "unusual," "pathetic," "lonely," "helpless," and arguably "insane."

She was the most unusual person that I had ever encountered. For the past two years, I had invested a large portion of my life into getting her charged and brought to this moment. As a prosecuting attorney for two killings, I had staked my reputation on the notion that this woman should be imprisoned for the rest of her life.

Yet I was prosecuting a case that had neither a blueprint nor field manual for how I was to proceed toward my goal. I was writing the guidebook as I went.

She was all of those one-word labels and maybe more. I knew her better than anyone. I knew her motivations, her schemes, and her desires. My job was to present what I knew in such a way that twelve jurors agreed with my labels. My theory of prosecution, however, held within it a premise so unusual, so insane, that I often doubted my ability to pull it off.

This one woman had conjured up a fake identity as a federal agent, tricking three people into going along with her childish game against girls for whom she possessed a fierce jealousy. Her game had led to two killings that our trial judge later reflected were the most "bizarre" and "senseless" killings he'd ever heard in his forty years in the criminal justice system.

3

It began with a phone call. It was an ordinary fall day in 2012 at my office in Elizabethton, Tennessee, the hometown of the Dallas Cowboys' Jason Witten and the Overmountain Men who fought the British at King's Mountain. The day winding down, I picked up the phone to answer a call from my junior cohort Matt Roark. I was a fourteen-year veteran as an Assistant District Attorney General for the First Judicial District, and Matt was a far younger one. "Can I come talk to you?" he asked.

I always liked giving Matt advice. When I was his age, I wore the older attorneys out seeking their guidance. Matt was one of our only newer attorneys who would do the same. I saw a lot of myself in him. He, like I, was green in experience but bountiful in exuberance.

I had no idea what he wanted.

An hour later, Matt came marching up the steps to my office with a banker's box full of stuff. Papers. CDs. DVDs. "Can you help me with this," he said. "With what?" I asked. "The Potter case," he replied.

Oh.

I was no stranger to working murder cases. I had my first within three years of graduating law school, and several trials and a death penalty conviction later, I had proven myself worthy of such cases. There is nothing like the exhilaration of a jury quietly filing into the jury box, the judgment being written on a paper that is slowly read by the foreman. The joy, or should I say relief, of a victim's family as they tearfully hug the prosecutor who fought for their loved one.

I had enough murder cases pending. I knew I didn't need another.

"What do you want me to do with it?" I asked. The look on

Matt's eyes answered me better than whatever came from his mouth at that point. He had made a complete copy of the case file. I saw a lot of paper, but what really had me curious was that tall stack of recordable media. A single DVD could only contain two minutes of recorded conversation, or it could contain an encyclopedia of information.

I wondered which extreme applied.

"Well, I'll look at it," I said. My wife for years had complained of me taking on more than my share. Yet here I was, never having the better sense to turn down a new challenge.

With a relieved look, Matt left the box with me, and minutes later, I headed home with my new possessions.

I had heard about the Potter case when a man and woman had been discovered dead in their home in early 2012. The local media went nuts, showing the family portrait again and again until it was ingrained in everyone's memories. The twist that engaged everyone's interest was the fact that the woman was found shot in the head and her infant son—still alive—remained in her arms until they were discovered. Then two men were arrested, and the story was that the victims had unfriended one of the men's daughters on Facebook. The media had made it sound like the unfriending was the motivation for the killing, which is a nice hook, true or not. Soon the story was picked up by national media outlets, which was probably a first for tiny ole' Johnson County.

But then, as all sensational stories around here go, the attention waned away. What remained were legal headaches and lengthy delays, which was the status of the case at this point, a little less than one year after the men were charged. Matt briefly explained to me that the men's attorneys had filed suppression motions that were coming up soon, and he hinted that the legal issues were weighty. If so, the case was certainly too much for any single prosecutor to handle amidst his or her regular caseload.

So I agreed to help.

I stuck the box in my car and headed home with a growing curiosity about the case. Certainly a home invasion killing would be something that I'd find rewarding to work. But why in the world would these people have done this? Most of our homicides are like most others around the country—drug deals gone bad and overblown domestic situations. Obviously this matter would be different, but surely the media had it wrong when it said this was over a social media unfriending. What an unusual reason to kill a person. Or two.

I had no idea how unusual, or how crazy, the case really was.

4

Jenelle Potter liked dogs. Cute dogs, fuzzy dogs, long-legged dogs, floppy-eared dogs, and, in particular, bulldogs.

She was the little girl who never grew up. Born in 1982 as the second of two children, Jenelle was extremely protected and shielded by her parents, Marvin and Barbara Potter. Jenelle grew up on the outskirts of Philadelphia, and by the time she was an adult, her parents picked up their lives as well as Jenelle and moved to Mountain City, Tennessee, in 2004, to better tend to Barbara's elderly mother.

Barbara Potter had power of attorney for her mother, and since Marvin (known better as "Buddy") had relatives in the area, it made sense that they would migrate to Johnson County. Yet the Potters likely never felt that it was home. Instead of the more urban existence of their previous residence, Mountain City had a mere three grocery stores and a Dollar General. That was the extent of the commercial choices for the Potters. While Johnson County featured some nice outdoor opportunities—from beautiful Watauga Lake positioned within the tree-filled mountains to three days' worth of hiking on the Appalachian Trail cutting through the county—the Potters likely perceived themselves as having too many physical ailments for such activity. More leisurely locations did not exist in the county. No movie theater. No mall. Choosing to avoid the small couple of banks in Mountain City, the Potters chose to hold their accounts at the bank in Boone, North Carolina, approximately a thirty-minute drive away, a larger town that featured Appalachian State University. Trips to Boone were likely a real treat compared to the uneventful dullness of their new home.

Buddy had been a Marine, and he was one of those types that liked to remind the world of the fact. He wore the ball caps to prove that status. He had a wall at home with all his military pictures, medals, and decorations prominently displayed. He signed up for the service at age eighteen, secretly signing his papers and not telling his family back in Pennsylvania until he was at boot camp in Parris Island, South Carolina. His family disapproved. Yet Buddy was proud to wear the uniform, and he served in the Vietnam War. Following that, he suffered a debilitating back injury at work, which resulted in his collecting disability. Barbara helped out by getting a job while in Pennsylvania, but by the time they moved to Tennessee, neither Buddy nor Barbara were working. They settled into a quaint, ranch-style brick home on Hospital Road, just a few minutes from downtown Mountain City.

Jenelle was the Potters' second child. The first, Christie, moved out of the home after getting a two-year associate's degree. Christie's relationship with the other three was strained. Jenelle, six years younger than Christie, was born with an auditory disability. Jenelle was classified into special education classes as soon as she entered kindergarten, and she remained at that status until she walked across the stage to receive her diploma at Kenneth High School in Kennett Square, Pennsylvania.

Upon her becoming an adult, Jenelle began receiving a social security disability check due to her many issues. She was a diabetic and had anxiety issues. She had continued auditory handicaps that affected her ability to clearly hear communications. She stood nearly six feet tall. Socially awkward, Jenelle clung to her parents far beyond the age when most children seek to break their bonds. Her voice had a meek, almost squeaky sound. Even as a grown woman, her closest friends were probably the stuffed animals that filled her bedroom.

However, as Jenelle grew into adulthood, the Internet had become a greater communication medium for everyone—even in rural areas. For Jenelle, the tether to computerized communication became particularly strong. She talked on Internet chat rooms. She had an active Myspace page. As the Internet developed further,

Jenelle jumped into Facebook with gusto. It was her way of reconnecting with old acquaintances and making new ones. And for posting pictures of cute puppies.

When Jenelle went out, her parents usually accompanied her. Her social graces were not honed. Locals were taken aback when she tried to hug them or talk as if she already knew them. They politely returned the attention. Soon they invariably received a Facebook friend request from Jenelle. And often, that Facebook association spelled trouble as others found her eventual statements and actions to be off-putting. Thus online conflicts began.

Years later, when Buddy Potter visited Sheriff Mike Reece at his office, reciting yet another online conflagration involving his youngest daughter, Sheriff Reece suggested Marvin throw the computer into Watauga Lake. The combination of a computer and Jenelle was leading to too many problems. Buddy dismissed the advice, replying, "Sheriff, my daughter stays at the house all the time, and that computer is all she has."

Buddy should have taken the Sheriff's advice.

5

Billy Clay Payne was born July 10, 1975. His sister Tracy followed a couple years later. They were typical Johnson County kids. Bill grew up to work at one of the only plants in Mountain City—Parkdale Mills, a factory that produced thread. He began working there after finishing high school, and he never left. Tracy worked various jobs, from a position at the local pharmacy to working in the bakery at Food Country. Bill fathered one son, Justin, while in his twenties.

Bill worked hard, and he lived life equally hard. He was a social guy, getting together with family or friends on his time off. They'd all drink, dance, and sing along to recorded music. One video survived Bill's passing—Bill and friends singing along to Johnny Cash's "Dirty Old Egg Sucking Dog." Bill knew how to enjoy himself, and he was no stranger to the opposite sex, playing loose up into his thirties. He also knew how to pop a pill or two. Like with many Johnson Countians of his age, painkillers were a popular recreational drug. While on no law enforcement agency's radar as any kind of drug dealer, Bill used and exchanged pills with his circle of friends. By the time he got into his late thirties, Bill began seeking treatment for opiate usage, getting a prescription for buprenorphine, also known as Suboxone, to quell the desire for narcotics. His son Justin had moved to Florida with Justin's mother, making it difficult for Bill to assume a fatherly role in the boy's life.

In late 2009, Billie Jean Hayworth began working at Parkdale Mills in a cleaning capacity. Bill would have to leave his machine to go back to the area where Billie Jean worked, and he developed a quick fancy for the attractive brunette in her early twenties. They soon began a serious relationship. Billie Jean moved into the home where Bill lived, which was the house of Billy Ray Payne, Sr. During the fall of 2010, Billie Jean became pregnant. On July 11, 2011, she gave birth to a son, Tyler.

Bill made a turn for the better. The drinking sessions grew fewer, and he recognized that the pills were a hindrance to him being the best father for their new son. Friends said they partied less often with Bill once Billie Jean came into the picture. She frowned on such activity.

For Bill Sr., known as Paw Bill to most people in the area, life had to be a joy. He had his son and new grandchild at his home, and his son was happily with his true love. Life was good.

Yet their bliss came to a crashing halt on January 31, 2012. The night before, Paw Bill had said goodnight to his son. The next morning, Paw Bill rose to get ready to go to his job in Boone and he saw Billie Jean up getting a bottle ready for Tyler. She asked about his arm, which had been hurting, and Paw Bill went on to work. It was a normal day. However, minutes after Paw Bill left, intruders entered the home and put a bullet through both Bill's head and Billie Jean's. Bill's throat was also slashed. The assailants then left, leaving everything in the house undisturbed except for the two young lives they took.

When a family friend, Roy Stephens, happened into the house later that morning, the bodies were discovered. Roy found Tyler, still alive, still grasped in his mother's arms. Billie Jean's blood was smeared on the child's forehead. Tyler was six months old.

The killings stirred up shock and sympathy not only in Johnson County, but throughout Northeast Tennessee. A person's home was a refuge from the evils of the world, but this crime was an affront to that concept. That a baby would be robbed forever of his two biological parents shook Johnson County to its core. In fact the entire region was abuzz, the crime dominating the local television news programs for days. The professional portrait bearing the attractive faces of two beaming parents posing with their infant son was an image that the people of Northeast Tennessee had burned into their collective consciousness.

6

I huddled down with my new box and got acquainted. Learning a new homicide case always began with a similar routine: (1) finding the investigator's summary of facts to get an overview of the case, (2) having a glance at the autopsy to see the number and locations of gunshots or stab wounds, and (3) perusing crime scene photos. None of the above steps gave me any insight into this case. The case defied neat summaries.

I had an immediate interest in any evidence that implicated the Potter women. I was aware that an undercurrent of popular opinion existed that the Potter women, Barbara and Jenelle, had caused these murders to be perpetrated by the men. But the public's Internet message board rants and uneducated opinions do not equal a conviction. Or probable cause to arrest. And so far, several months after Marvin Potter and Jamie Curd had been charged, these women were still free. A mountain of evidence had been compiled, but no one as of yet had absorbed, categorized, or theorized how it might equal any charge, much less murder, against the women.

Correction. Barbara Potter had been charged with the crime of tampering with evidence. Apparently, when a search warrant was executed on the Potter residence, an investigator observed Barbara tearing up a series of photographs that were deemed relevant to the case. Thus her charge, which was a low-grade felony, was the lone accusation formally lodged against either woman.

The killings had occurred on January 31, 2012. One day later, Agent Scott Lott of the Tennessee Bureau of Investigation and Chief Deputy Joe Woodard of the Johnson County Sheriff's Department visited the Potter residence and interviewed Jenelle in the presence of her parents. They questioned her about word in the community about an ongoing feud that she had with the victims. Nothing from that interview led to any evidence useful in linking any of the Potters to the killing, other than confirmation that indeed they had a past history of harassment allegations with Bill Payne, Billie Jean Hayworth, and Billie Jean's close friend, Lindsey Thomas.

Soon after that interview, Jamie Curd spoke to investigators at the Sheriff's Department, confirming a past series of conflicts but divulging nothing incriminating.

The investigation then ground to a slow crawl. Other persons were looked at as suspects, but quickly dismissed as logical targets of the investigation.

By February 6, the investigation picked up steam again. Curd agreed to submit to a polygraph examination, and the polygraph examiner deemed that he had practiced deception on key questions. Watching the resulting interrogation was beyond painful. For what seemed like many hours, Curd sat there, looking through his heavily shaded eyeglasses at investigators who bore into him with a prying fury. They smelled blood, and like sharks circling a capsizing boat, they were not going to let the opportunity slip away. Curd mumbled meager responses as his interrogators sensed avenues to get him to fess up.

Interrogations, particularly involving the Tennessee Bureau of Investigations (TBI), involved this same routine. Interrogators did most of the talking, searching for some semblance of mitigation or understanding as to why a person would participate in a heinous crime, wearing down their subject's defenses until resistance withered away.

With Curd, his tormentors stuck to the script. They sensed that Curd likely was an accessory, or aid, to Marvin "Buddy" Potter. Thus they broached the possibility that Curd was forced into being involved—that he was afraid of Buddy and given no other choice. They suggested to him that perhaps all he did was cut Bill's throat after Buddy shot the man, and that since Bill was going to die anyway, possibly his actions had not led to Bill's death. They searched for all sorts of possibilities that might make it easier for Curd to start talking, but mostly they were answered by grunts and begrudging nods from Curd.

Eventually the interrogators pieced together enough grunts and yeahs to compile a written statement that Curd was reluctant to sign. That statement would point to Buddy as being the gunman. But before Curd was finished in the interrogation room, he made one little slip. It was a slip that would forever taint any defense his lawyers could muster for him.

"Is the CIA here?" That was the question Curd asked. With an incredulous look on his face, Agent Mike Hannon quickly answered, "No." Hannon and Lott then asked Curd why he would ask about the CIA. Curd then muttered something about Jenelle having this brother named Chris. Curd said Chris was mad about things. The investigators knew nothing of what Curd was talking about. Neither did I as I watched his interrogation the first time.

Chris? CIA? Not knowing where these facts would lead, the investigators didn't pursue that line of questioning any further.

Little did they know that Curd had just blurted out the key to the case. But for now, that revelation was lost to all concerned.

Next, Agent Lott set up to have Curd call Buddy. "You want to help get Buddy?" Lott asked. Curd didn't really answer, but Lott pressed on. Curd was supposed to be at work at this time, at the Parkdale Mills plant where he worked the same machine as Bill Payne had, so Lott wisely arranged for Curd's call to come from the plant instead of the Sheriff's Department.

For his call, Lott requested Curd ask Buddy if he had gotten rid of the gun and knife used in the killings. Meanwhile, the call was to be recorded. Curd called, and Barbara Potter answered. Knowing that Curd was to be at the Sheriff's Department for questioning and possibly a polygraph, Barbara asked how it went. Curd said it went fine. Barbara replied that "Chris" had sent a message that Jamie had just been booked, and that she had said he was just listening to "Adam," and people just "hear what they hear."

What the devil Barbara was referring to, neither the investigators nor myself understood. But again, with this simple and cryptic comment, Barbara had slipped up and revealed the key to the case.

"And they just let you go?" Barbara asked. "Yeah," answered Curd, lying. "And your lie detector test, you passed?" Barbara inquired. "Yeah," said Curd, lying again. "Well, that's wonderful," Barbara responded. "We've been praying our hearts out. Jenelle even saw an angel today, come in the computer room."

She then let Buddy get on the phone. Less verbose, Buddy asked if everything was going all right. Curd answered that people were pointing fingers. "Pointing fingers?" Buddy responded. "Jiminy Christmas."

Curd then got to business, in his own special stuttering and stammering way: "Yeah, I just, uh, wanted to, you know, call and uh, let you know, just, uh, you got rid of everything that was from Bill's, didn't you?"

"Uh-huh," Buddy answered.

"Ok. That makes me feel better," Jamie replied.

"Yeah," Buddy affirmed.

Going on with the party line regarding the killings, Buddy attempted to reassure Curd that he would be alright. "They ain't got no reason to point no fingers at you or nothing," Buddy said. "Because Jiminy Christmas, all the shit [Bill] was in. I've heard more stuff about gangs and things there in the last few days and stuff that he was involved in in Johnson City. Everything is crazy, and I still think it's a drug deal went bad."

Knowing that he was headed to jail, possibly never to come out again, Curd had little more to say to Potter, ending the call soon after.

Thus, as Curd was headed to the Johnson County Jail for two counts of first degree murder, Lott prepared an arrest warrant for Buddy Potter as well as search warrants for his home and truck. His evidence against Buddy at that point consisted of an ill-defined motive and an "uh-huh" and "yeah" in response to Jamie's question. That was it.

The name "Chris" was nowhere in either arrest warrant for the men. Who "Chris" was and how he was connected to the January 31 event—those mysteries were still unsolved.

7

It is not a news story when a man in Northeast Tennessee is found to own dozens, perhaps hundreds, of guns. Ever since the mountains and hollows of the Appalachian Mountains were settled in the late eighteenth century, men held their guns to be necessary possessions. In more modern times, Tennessee politicians who dared stand in the way of completely unfettered access to firearms did so at their own peril. As one of the first states to allow legal-carry permits in the 1990s, many Tennesseans proudly believed that carrying a gun was their best protection against those who would do them harm.

Buddy Potter believed that theory so much that he carried two. All the time. Even when mowing the yard, he wore a gunfighter's gun belt like in the old cowboy movies. It had a pistol holster on each side, and bullets plugged into the tiny loops along the length of the belt. He had the matching cowboy hat and vest too.

Thus, when Agent Lott and Chief Deputy Woodard set out during the wee hours of the morning on February 7 to arrest Buddy Potter, those guns were firmly in their minds. If a man had been willing to gun down Bill Payne and Billie Jean Hayworth, surely he'd be just as willing to gun down officers to prevent his arrest. Minimizing that risk was a priority. So as to have Buddy expect their presence at his house, a call was placed to give Buddy the notion that Woodard was coming to talk to him about something other than an arrest warrant.

His guard down, the officers entered the Potter residence and told Buddy that he was under arrest. They saw him make a quick motion with one arm, and they pounced on him and his arms, preventing him from making any attempt to pull a gun. They then shuttled him out to the sheriff's department, where he would take Jamie Curd's spot in the hot chair. Agents Lott and Hannon would handle his interrogation while Woodard and his investigators conducted the search of the Potter home.

It did not take long into the interrogation to tell that Buddy would be a harder nut to crack than Curd. More confident and less meager, Buddy could deny involvement ad infinitum. While acknowledging issues he and his family had had with Bill Payne and his associates, Buddy firmly denied any involvement in their killings. He was firm enough that the investigators did not even try the polygraph angle. While polygraphs are inadmissible in court lest jurors give too much weight to their unproven results, they are a useful investigative tool. Deceptive answers can lead to deceivers giving up their lying ways. That's what had just happened with Curd. Buddy was going to be tougher.

Thus they pulled out their best ammunition—the recording they'd just made of him saying "uh-huh" and "yeah" to Curd's inquiry. The investigators knew that Buddy had disposed of the evidence. They had that admission on tape, so they played it for him. Hearing this for the first time, the color went out of Buddy's face. His confidence took a direct blow.

Buddy was visibly shaken for several minutes. His face revealed his guilt, but the words weren't present. Still not admitting to anything, Buddy eventually got his feet back under him and stated that he must not have heard what Jamie had asked. The investigators weren't going to buy that, but it took a long, long while to break him. They tried different angles and most didn't work. They tried such tactics as, "This is Jamie trying to throw you under the bus," or "I know you're not a monster because you spared the baby's life."

Yet they finally touched a nerve when they suggested he had only acted to protect his family. Buddy was vulnerable to that approach. He loved his wife, and he loved Jenelle. With enough of that suggestion, Buddy's defenses weakened.

"The only reason you did it was because you were scared for your family, and you love your family," said Hannon.

"Yes," mumbled Buddy.

"Is that why you did it?" Hannon pressed. No answer.

"This world is going to shit," the agents suggested.

"Yeah, that's the truth," Buddy replied.

"That seven-hundred-pound gorilla is on your back and you want him to get off bad, right?" asked Lott. Buddy nodded.

"This was the only way you knew how to take care of the situation," suggested Hannon. Buddy nodded.

The interrogators closed in on their subject, as they do when they sense they are near a breakthrough, leaning into Buddy's personal space. Then Buddy opened up with a flurry of emotion, his voice cracking, holding back tears. And what he said was nothing short of bizarre.

"When you hear people plotting to take your—cut your daughter in a restroom and take her out the back of the store and they want to take her and get her so sick in field and murder her, and they wanted to rape her because she's a virgin and just so much shit and…."

"You had no other choice," said Hannon, trying to finish Buddy's sentence.

"No," answered Buddy, his head shaking. "Especially when you hear somebody's put a $3,000 bounty on her head, on my wife, and me. Me, I didn't care about."

Suggesting that Jenelle could not protect herself, Hannon was met with Buddy's agreement, "No, she can't."

The interrogation then shifted to an attempt to get the Potter women embroiled in the mess. After all, the investigators were on a roll. A mere several hours ago, their investigation was adrift without any charges, and now they had two avowals of participation. Might as well try for two more.

Thus they offered to allow Buddy to call his family and let them know what he'd done. Better to hear it from him. And so Buddy unwittingly went along with it, placing the call home on a phone line being recorded. He told his wife that he'd done it and that he'd told the investigators the story. Barbara said nothing in reply that would directly implicate her in the killings. However, she did strangely offer up herself as an alibi witness for him, suggesting that he was at their home the whole time. "I saw you," she said, in a manipulative tone. "I saw you."

"Yeah, I know you did, but…" Buddy countered. Jenelle even came to the phone and, sounding upset, also suggested that he was home the whole time.

Barbara took the phone back and continued suggesting that Buddy was without sleep and without his oxygen. Thus he wasn't in his right mind. Buddy would have none of it, eventually sharing with her that Jamie had talked. "What?" answered Barbara, finally sounding shocked. Buddy said yeah, but that Jamie had lied about parts. Without going into details, the call ended. In fact, the interrogation ended, because by talking to his wife for fifteen minutes, Buddy got the strength to tell the investigators that he wanted a lawyer, thus legally ending the interrogation.

In all of that lengthy interrogation, Buddy never mentioned "Chris."

8

"You can't see the forest for the trees." That's the old saying, one that symbolizes the difficulty of taking complex sets of facts and condensing and summarizing them into an overall narrative that's simple and makes sense. Some prosecutors are good at looking at the trees. Some are specialists at analyzing the forest. I had always thought of myself as the latter. I could condense any case down to a simple, five-minute narrative, and spin it back to a jury.

So in dealing with complex murder cases, I had always preferred partnering with a prosecutor who was my opposite. Someone who could worry about the trees while I pontificated on the bigger themes.

However, this case had a lot of trees. Tens of thousands of them, in fact. These trees were e-mails, close to a thousand of them, plus eight megabytes of Facebook data and hundreds of text messages. Turning them into a visible forest looked practically impossible.

I had met my match. This would be one case that could never be summarized quickly.

In going through the box for this case, I was getting nowhere in learning exactly why Buddy Potter, a sixty-year-old man without a violent criminal record, would partner with Jamie Curd, a thirty-eight-year-old man also without such a criminal record, and commit one of the most shocking killings in our district's history. They didn't have the background for this kind of crime. The interrogations didn't really explain it. At least, they didn't make sense. The crime scene photos didn't help. Neither did the autopsy. Or the crime lab results. Of all the "things" that I might typically consider in putting together a homicide case, none of them illuminated the motives or compulsions of the killers.

There had been some history of pills and the like being sold out of the Payne residence, but their prescription drugs were left undisturbed following the killings. All of their valuables were still present—television, coin collection, cash, debit cards. There was nothing overturned or spilled, which might have indicated a heated argument turning into a physical confrontation leading to death. This wasn't a robbery; it wasn't a drug deal gone bad; it wasn't any of the things I would normally see in a murder case. It was a preplanned, execution-style hit.

With the normal routes to understanding a killing leading to a dead end, I looked for other avenues. I turned my attention to the email evidence.

When Curd had been interrogated, the investigators' dealings with Curd had led to his car. In it were clues leading investigators to become interested in three e-mail accounts: Curd's at sleepiingbear@ yahoo.com, Barbara Potter's at bmp9110@aol.com, and Jenelle Potter's at bul2dog@aol.com. Agent Lott issued search warrants to AOL and Yahoo for whatever e-mails still existed on their servers for those accounts. Those e-mails came back in electronic form, either organized by subject headings or by convoluted computer-generated numbers. In order to get any feel for what value they might provide, I would have to search through them one by one.

From that point on, every evening after my regular prosecutorial duties, I'd cuddle up with my computer and read e-mails. Sometimes the e-mails had no relevance whatsoever to the case, but some did. I started seeing references to the victims, Bill and Billie Jean. I also saw mentions of other characters—Lindsey, Tara, Christie, Tracy, and many others. Without the messages being organized in chronological order or by subject matter, it was horribly confusing to keep up with what was being discussed.

But I met "Chris." That mysterious and unknown character who had been mentioned in passing by Jamie Curd during his interrogation and by Barbara Potter during that phone call—here he was. In print.

Chris wrote to Jamie and Barbara through Jenelle's e-mail

address. Apparently, he also had access to Jenelle's Facebook account, where he could further converse with Barbara. He never used any online account of his own. Always Jenelle's. There was a litany of e-mails going back and forth between those three characters, Barbara, Jamie, and Chris. The e-mails covered a span of one year or so.

It didn't take long to determine that Chris wrote like he was a homicidal maniac. He used the most vile, revolting language imaginable. He hated people. He killed people. He killed them legally, though, because it was all part of his duties as a CIA agent. At least that's what the e-mails said. That's why the CIA exists, right? To kill people?

Despite his supposed federal employment, it was clear to me from the start that whatever the educational requirements for being a CIA agent, Chris must have forgotten practically everything he was ever taught in grammar school. He misspelled words. He transposed letters. His writings were a mess. Yet in the world of 2012, words were abbreviated and language hacked for the sake of speed as one e-mailed, texted, or tweeted. So in and of itself, the grammar and spelling issues did not immediately register to me as being important.

Except for one issue. Over and over, I noticed a tendency of Chris's to forget to drop the "e" in words where he added an "ing" at the end. Such as, "takeing," "loveing," and "careing." This error was repeated constantly. It was not a mere typo. It was not a mistake for the sake of speed. It was, simply, a sign of ignorance.

Thus, surely this person did not work for the CIA. And wasn't it odd that Chris the CIA operative would have such a fascination for and preoccupation with all things concerning Jenelle Potter? Everything he ever wrote was Jenelle-centric. Her problems were his concerns. Her foes were his enemies. What she liked, he loved.

I cannot remember how long it took me to realize it, but it was obvious that there was an extremely high likelihood that Jenelle Potter *was* Chris. Jenelle Potter's educational background was such that one might expect repeated grammatical errors, and who else would be repeatedly writing about how "pretty and kind and sweet" Jenelle Potter was?

As odd as the idea that a person might pose as a CIA agent and author inane writings, it was odder still to see the responses from Barbara's and Jamie's e-mail accounts. They wrote back to Chris like they believed he was real. The obvious clues that Chris was not who he said he was were completely ignored. Jamie wrote as if he confided with Chris about his relationship with Jenelle. Barbara wrote long, detailed, and oftentimes rambling e-mails to Chris. She even called him "son." Barbara would write to him and ask to be able to see him. She wanted to have him over for dinner. Meet him somewhere. Anything. She loved him, and she wanted more than just be his pen pal.

Yet that's all he was. A pen pal. Not a son Barbara could hug. Nothing from these e-mails indicated she ever saw her "son" in the flesh. And nothing from Jamie's e-mails indicated a reference to hanging with his bud, going out for drinks, or talking on the back porch with Chris. Nothing.

Barbara and Jamie had been catfished.

9

I became aware of the term "catfish" when my wife and I received a movie from Netflix with the same name. In that movie, a young, hip guy from New York made a documentary about his search for a person with whom he had developed an online relationship. Over the course of many months, they had met on online forums, exchanged e-mails and texts, and became very close. So close that the guy was arguably in love with this female, who lived in another part of the country. Pictures were exchanged and phone calls made.

To make a long story short, the fellow made the long journey to find his online love only to discover she was a middle-aged, unattractive woman who was not as advertised. He had been catfished.

A television series on MTV resulted from the movie, in which the same guy went around helping others who wanted to meet their online friends or lovers. Usually they'd find that the real person was, again, not as advertised.

People could be whomever they wanted to be online. If you were ugly, you could be pretty. If you were unsuccessful, you could have a real career. If your life was uninteresting, you could spice it up. The Internet was a canvas on which to recreate oneself. For some, the fantasy life created online could become too real.

And so it was that Jenelle Potter saw fit to create her own fantasy. The shut-in, late-twenties female who had never lived away from her parents, never had a driver's license, and never held a job, had a very boring life.

The only noteworthy aspect to her life was the sheer enormity of how unfulfilled she must have felt. Whatever physical or mental ailments she possessed, Jenelle still had typical yearnings. She wanted to feel worthwhile to the world. Or to other people. She wanted to love and to be loved. She wanted adventure. She wanted to be popular.

She wanted to matter.

But she couldn't be any of those things. She was tall for a female—six feet tall, to be exact. When she walked she had a lanky, awkward gait, shoulders sort of forward, a walk like she was hunchbacked. Her face could look almost attractive in one picture but fall well short of the bar in the next. She was too socially awkward to make many friends. She wasn't invited to parties. She was unnoticeable in a crowded room. And perhaps most importantly, she was too protected by her two loving parents to have any substantial relationship with a man.

Those facts, plus unlimited time on a computer with broadband access, could be a recipe for disaster. And a disaster it was.

From the e-mails I was reading, Jenelle Potter had created various online personas. Chris, Matt Potter, Dan White, Tim, Brian—all men. They were men who cared deeply about Jenelle. They believed she was pretty, kind, and sweet. They hated anyone who disagreed. They were fiercely protective of her. They were the older, protective brothers that Jenelle had probably always craved.

Yet they didn't exist. There were no indications from the TBI file that investigators had found these persons. No one had ever talked to them. No one had ever seen them. These characters only revealed themselves through the online accounts of Jenelle Potter.

Chris was the primary character. He often appeared authoring messages from Jenelle's account, and with enough perusing of the e-mails, it became apparent that the "Matt Potter" who posted public online rants about Jenelle's enemies was actually Chris writing under that pseudonym. Or should I say, Jenelle writing as Chris who was writing as Matt Potter, for those keeping score.

Chris had the adventurous life that Jenelle lacked. He traveled the world. He had an exciting job. He was important to his country. He had been married to his true love, but alas, was now widowed.

He was too busy for a love life. But he was happy, traveling the world killing bad people with his three Great Danes and small Yorkie in tow. And he was a good-looking dude.

From what I gleaned, Chris had gone to school with Jenelle. E-mails suggested they were born a minute apart on the same day at the same hospital in Pennsylvania. They both shared similar physical ailments. They grew up as close friends, but apparently it never blossomed into a full-scale romance.

In one e-mail, Barbara pleasantly noted the coincidence of Jenelle and Chris coming into the world almost simultaneously at the same place. The absurdity of Chris's life as it was written was completely lost on Barbara.

Despite his growing duties as a CIA agent, Chris stayed in touch with Jenelle. So much so that he would come to Johnson County from time to time to observe the goings-on of Jenelle's enemies. He would follow them, even try to kill them. He would confront the local police officers about issues that concerned Jenelle and, when necessary, he would kill them, although he never mentioned such officers by name. He'd just write, "I got one, mom."

From the many e-mails that passed between the two, Barbara obviously believed Chris was real. That his job was real. That his concern for Jenelle was real. From everything I could see, Barbara felt love for this fictional character.

She was catfished. What made this all the more amazing is that she was catfished by someone in her own house. Using the same computer.

Chris wrote bad things. He wanted this person or that person to die. He even mentioned wanting to kill a baby a time or two. Not once did I find an e-mail from Barbara admonishing him for such thoughts. Nothing he said could shock her.

Instead, Barbara would just play along. She was familiar with Chris's lifestyle all too well. After all, she was the wife of a former CIA agent.

10

Around 2007, over four years prior to the killings of Payne and Hayworth, Buddy Potter paid a visit to Mike Reece, Sheriff of Johnson County. In a rare instance of Buddy not wearing a gun, he came there to discuss a matter as a courtesy to the sheriff.

"I normally carry a gun, but out of respect to you as the sheriff, I won't do that in here," Buddy stated in the patrol room next to the sheriff's office. Buddy went on to explain to the sheriff that he had a history of working for the CIA and was expecting to be re-activated in their employ at any time. He was just waiting on the paperwork on where to report.

He also stated that he had killed people in the past. Legally, of course.

Sheriff Reece tried to gracefully finish the conversation and move on to regular work.

This was not the only instance of Buddy talking of his CIA exploits. He mentioned it to regular people too. Barbara bragged about it. Even Jenelle spoke of it.

As the case wore on, we discovered more information about Buddy's supposed CIA involvement. One person close to him explained that while he was in Vietnam, supposedly he had participated in a CIA-led mission that wound up destroying a village that shouldn't have been touched. Since it shouldn't have happened, the event was wiped from the government files. Thus the medal Buddy had supposedly earned during the event was in fact never granted. It vanished from the books.

At least that was the story. In actuality, Buddy was prosecuted in federal court in Pennsylvania for claiming military honors he did not possess, thus creating some credible proof that Buddy was prone to exaggeration. What Buddy did or did not do for the CIA was never verified by anyone during the investigation. Agent Lott made contact with the local people for the CIA, and they knew of no Marvin Potter being affiliated with the organization. They also were not aware of a "Chris" operating in the Johnson County area.

But, of course, the CIA was a secretive bunch. Who could really know?

Perhaps a year after getting into this, I was having a discussion with a local lawyer who was no longer involved in the case but had been privy to the investigative findings. He said something that stuck with me: "Whoever did this crime in the Payne house, they've killed before." The killing precision was that of a professional, he thought.

Indeed, one well-aimed shot to Bill Payne's face, just below his left eye, was all it took to take him out. Likewise, one shot to Billie Jean Hayworth's right side of her head, just above the ear, sent a bullet in one side of her brain and out the other. In and out. Surgical precision.

Was Buddy trained in the CIA arts? Or was he just a wannabe, a person who liked to *think* of himself as that type of badass? It could be as simple as him wanting to fit the delusional image his wife possessed of him. Barbara practically thought she was married to James Bond.

In one of her earliest writings to Chris, in January 2011, Barbara wrote to him, letting him know she understood the difficulties of his work, having been married to Buddy:

> And, as long as you are doing the right thing for mankind, then you will not be judged badly. If it is like Buddy did, you are helping others by getting rid of the bad. I understand what you do fully if it is like Buddy did. I worry about when you retire though...don't let it ever get you down Chris.

From Barbara's writings, Buddy's interest in CIA work wasn't just in the past—it was in the present and future. Repeatedly, she wrote to Chris asking that he convince his superiors to give Buddy a

CIA identification. And just as often, Chris would reply that he was working on it.

For example, on the morning of March 1, 2011, Barbara wrote to Chris:

> HI CHRIS. Bud was wondering When he would be contacted to meet and pick up his ID you spoke of some time ago. Just for YOUR info, He IS home every day now (as I am home), he can come alone bc Jenelle can be w/ me. HE is Actually wondering IF there is an ID or not! They call him, he'll put in his 'code' & meet wherever. We will stay at home… not a problem. Are they just saying this or what?!?....Much love & many blessings your way, Barbara (Would love to see you.)

Chris's reply, dated the evening of March 1, 2011.

> I'm so sorry I didn't even write back to Jenelle I have been busy they had me in Nashville for a few days and that place is crazy like Here lol. But Yes I saw the ID they have not gave it to him yet??? That's what makes me so mad they say they will do it and they have not called him. I even TOLD my BOSS about it and he said yes and that he would get Tonmy to talk to him. I don't understand them I will say something for Buddy b/c he does have it and I have seen it and its just like ours. UGH damn guys.

And so the exchange went on for months in an almost daily routine, Barbara asking on Buddy's behalf for the ID, and Chris replying that it was stuck in the bureaucratic channels of the federal government. Chris would go as far as saying that Buddy "was in the computer."

The preoccupation and delusion of somehow being involved with the CIA was of a pathological nature for all three Potters. Their constant self-deception was convincing evidence of very sick minds.

11

It goes without saying that convicting a person for murder is not easy when the person wasn't present at the killing. DNA or fingerprints won't point their way. Likewise, there will be no taped statement from the person talking of how they killed the victim. And if you don't have the actual assailants pointing the finger toward the people who put them up to the killings, exactly how the heck could one expect a prosecutor to make his case beyond a reasonable doubt?

Certainly, there was a popular consensus among the public that the women were responsible. However, that was worlds away from proof in a court of law. Fact was, the citizenry's assumptions were based on misleading information rampant in the media reports. Facts that could look convincing on a one-minute evening newscast could crumble to dust in the face of a skillful criminal defense attorney in a courtroom setting. Cross-examination has a way of tearing down preconceptions. Sometimes all it takes to exonerate someone is to put them on the stand and have them explain the facts away.

Thus, looking down the road, my mounting a case against Barbara and/or Jenelle was going to take more than a fleeting look at ill-informed polling data. After all, what the public knew about the case—or thought they knew—was that these killings occurred simply because Billie Jean and Bill had unfriended Jenelle on Facebook. Misinformation was being perpetrated by the media that this was the "Facebook unfriending" case, but even the slightest analysis of the e-mails showed that explanation to be false.

Unfriending was indeed a part of the storyline. Billie Jean and her friend Lindsey Thomas had unfriended Jenelle at one point.

However, the e-mails made it clear that Jenelle simply did not like

Billie Jean and her friends Lindsey and Tara Osborne. That dislike predated the unfriendings. Jenelle possessed a seething contempt for all of them. Why was not immediately apparent. Yet through her writings as Chris or Matt, her hate dripped from the pages.

The worst of the spiteful writings had been posted to Topix, an online site that assigned separate forums by cities. Many towns in the United States had Topix forums that were seldom used. But in some of our more remote small towns, those Topix forums could be quite lively. People could use whatever name they wanted and talk trash about their neighbors, their teachers, their politicians, or simply people they did not like.

Jenelle's enemies got plenty of it. For instance, in an e-mail containing Topix postings copied through Jenelle's e-mail account, there were these kinds of examples, this one from Matt Potter during April 2011.

> All 3 of these's girls are no good whores and sell drugs and Drink and If you ever hit Jenelle Linsday your ass better watch out. She dont even know you and you all always have to pick on her and hurt her and her family. She has a great name and you all are so unhappy with your dumb little lives and you guys do is sleep around and make ppl lives hell. Why dont you go bnackto fucking Hell where youcame from. Keep on fucking with Jenelle. She has alot of friends that will back her and know whats really going on. all you fucking sluts know what to do is to hate on someone elseb/c you all are not happy with your damn lives. Fucking Lindsay better watch your damn fucking back Bitch. you ever put hands on Jenelle you have to answer to us. you have no clue what your fucking dealing with none of you do. And why are her house and trying to Brake in to it??? HMMM we got pics dumb fuckers. Now go one 3 of you and lives your damn lives and leave Jenelle's alone and LInsday your never be Jenelle so get over your damn self.

From "Kelly" in the same thread:

Right Matt?? They are whores no good ppl and that have nothing else to do. They are nasy sluts and dont Linsday ahve HIV is what i heard. Small town and i know this is true what guy would want that Bitch. she is so ugly and she is mad b/c Jenelle is so pretty and sweet and nice. They are trying to hurt Jenelle all the time like they have other girls. Its so sad matt. i went to school with her and she is a BITCH. Nasy ass she was HVI now and she will give it to alot of guys now. they better get tested. i agree with you and i will always back Jenelle. Thank you for puting it all out there.

From "Dan White" in that thread:

Wow Matt and Kelly. I new she was bad but i had no clue she was off on the deepend. She is crazy that's for sure. Sounds like all of them are. I know Billie that Bitch has lived with more guys and have sex with 80% of Mtn City and Lindsay i would say Half of Mtn city Then you Trade and Butler and then you have Doe and then Johnson City and then Kings port she has been all over and she does have HIV this is all around town. and Tara she will give it to anyone her poor Husband he's a nice guy but he never wants to be home with her. I think when his baby is 18 he will leave her dumb ass too. She is a whore too. I agree with you both. and this girl Jenelle I do know as in Passing but she is a good girl and was brought up right you can tell everything is your welcome and Hello and thank you and she just a sweet girl. I will be praying for Jenelle. As far as the other ones go there no good whore sluts and that is carrying something and giving it to everyone. Damn girls. They live in high school still and they need to grow up.

There was a lot more of this stuff. A litany of unknown "men" contributing insults and threats toward girls who, on the surface of the messages, posed a grave threat to the peaceful existence of Jenelle Potter, a girl who was simply "pretty and sweet and nice."

Saying that someone is an HIV-riddled slut may be in poor

taste, but that does not make Jenelle guilty of murder. I kept digging. Then I came across this, an e-mail directed from Chris to Jamie, dated October 25, 2011.

> [S]he really loves you man she has never loved anyone like she loves you i see it all over her. and you are very blessed for sure. and you have a great girl and these's mother fuckers just want tomake her life hell and i hope she dont think about killing her self. she has you to live for. and her mom and dad.

"[I] hope she dont think about killing her self." I stopped abruptly on that sentence. Those nine words told me what I needed to know. If indeed Jenelle Potter was posing as this Chris guy, and through Chris's communications was trying to make Jamie believe that she might commit suicide due to the perceived torment she was experiencing from these girls, then was she trying to manipulate her boyfriend to commit murder?

My opinion was yes. That sentence stepped over a line. That wasn't simply a shut-in female playing make believe. Right there, my feeling was that I had something I could prosecute her with. Surreptitiously compelling her boyfriend to do her evil bidding by killing her enemies? That's pretty low, and it's exactly what I thought she was doing by suggesting the possibility of suicide.

And so I got on board with the notion of pursuing Jenelle Potter as a conspirator in these murders. More analysis of the e-mails was in order, of course, but I was sold.

Two days later, on October 27, 2011, this gem of a message popped up, from Jenelle's e-mail address to Jamie's (important parts underlined for emphasis):

> Hi Jamie. It's Chris, I wanted to say hello and I thank you for being there for Jenelle and Her Mom and Dad. They are good people and what others say about them is wrong. I know you have taken up for Her family and her. It means a lot to me... Thank you for being the one there for her. She need's you in more way's then one. she is a

wounderful sweet careing girl. She would do anything for anyone before her self. But i know you know this about her. She is a good person. These's girls are just driving her so crazy and you know they are crazy. But what they are doing is still fucking wrong and hurting her like they are. There is no reson for it. Just b/c she is sweet and very pretty prettyer then them. They need to get over it. They just love to pick but from what i know ... <u>something will happen to them in time. With you and Buddy I hope you all can get them. I hope it all works out great. I hope that you will pray about it and Buddy is and that you known what you are all doing is great. Your going to help the town. I wish i could kill them but right now i really can't.</u> But anyways I'm so happy that you and Jenelle are happy together and love each other so much... But pray for Jenelle i know she is having a very hard time and she just needs someone like you and i'm so happy and blessed she has you. Well take care dude and I love ya. You are my brother and thank you for being a true blessing to my Sister. Take care and God Bless. Chris

Suddenly what Jamie Curd had said in his interrogation made sense. "Is the CIA here?" He actually bought the notion that the CIA was interested in this nonsense. He probably even thought the CIA was going to bust through the door and tell Agents Lott and Hannon to leave him alone. After all, he had helped the town. He had done a great thing.

At least, it was great in Chris's eyes. Or Jenelle's. Surely Jenelle's efforts to cloak herself as a CIA agent promising official sanction or backing to Jamie Curd's actions had somehow emboldened or motivated him to act. Why else would he have asked the investigators about the CIA being around?

I vowed right then that I wasn't just going to pursue Jenelle Potter as an outside conspirator. I was going to convict her as the primary culprit.

Problem was, how the heck was I to present this in court? How was I to prove Jenelle Potter wrote this?

I had no idea.

Heretofore, every time Jenelle Potter had been called to the floor for her actions, whether they be anonymous phone calls from her home to the vitriol produced at her keyboard, she denied them all. Every time. "I got hacked," she'd say. "I don't know who these people are," she'd cry. "They spoofed my phone number," she'd explain. She was going to deny every single word written on her e-mail account.

Our investigation was a thousand miles away from anything near a confession from Jenelle that she was indeed Chris. No admission to anyone whatsoever.

We had nothing but conjecture. A theory.

And theories aren't facts.

12

One of my earliest thoughts once I vowed to start on the road toward convicting either or both of these women was this: "It sure would be nice if Jamie Curd would cooperate." Codefendants who cooperate in multi-defendant cases such as this can make things so much easier. Stories get better developed. Proof gets easier to introduce. And it could be your only chance to have a person from the witness chair point at defendants with proper indignation.

The trick for a prosecutor is picking which conspirator is the right one with whom to negotiate a plea deal. Pick the wrong conspirator, and suddenly you're plea bargaining the worst guy in the group just to get a person lower on the scale of evil. You don't want to make that mistake.

Jamie looked to be the likely target for a plea negotiation. The word I was getting from some people in the community was that Curd was thought to be a completely harmless individual prior to him hanging around the Potter family. Many people who knew him were shocked that he could be involved.

I had no personal opinion of Curd at the time other than what I'd formed watching his interrogation the first time. He looked to be a meek, meager, quiet man. A leader he was not. Buddy was the much stronger man of the two—emotionally and intellectually. At least that was my initial instinct.

One thing I wondered was whether Jamie could shed some light on Jenelle's authorship of the Chris e-mails. Problem was, if he actually was catfished and thought Chris was a real person distinct from Jenelle, exactly how much help could he provide on that question?

The only way to know was to kick the tires. Prosecutors can't just go down to the jail and start asking a murder defendant questions. In the movies, they do. We cannot. Curd had a team of lawyers from the public defender's office. So I had to broach the idea of cooperation with them. I quickly learned, or assumed from their response, that they'd been there and done that. They had tried to kick the tires themselves, and their efforts came up way short. They speculated that he still loved Jenelle.

Following his booking, Curd had a chance to collect his thoughts. Regroup. And the next day, he recanted his confession. He said he didn't know anything about what happened at the Payne house. He wasn't there. He had no part in any of it. The cops tricked him into signing a statement, and they lied when they told him he failed his polygraph examination. That was going to be his strategy henceforth.

Inmates all over the country have their phone calls recorded. Both the inmate calling and the callee get a prerecorded message at the start of the call letting both parties understand that their conversation is subject to recording and monitoring. So anytime we get hold of a serious case, there's a chance an investigator or myself could track down those calls.

Curd had made lots of calls to family members. It was all deny, deny, deny. Things like, "Those investigators don't have shit on me." Cussing and ranting, he sounded unlike the weak little guy cowering in a chair as two agents hovered over him with their prying questions and accusations.

One call stood out. It told me what I needed to know. "When that prosecutor comes and offers me a plea bargain, I'm gonna tell him to shove it up his ass," ranted Curd.

I took it that he was talking about me.

I figured I'd need to keep searching. Curd wasn't going to give Jenelle Potter to us.

13

Expert witnesses have it made. They work on a case, rest in nice hotels, testify about their findings, and then travel home thousands of dollars richer.

There is an extensive industry of court experts for hire out there—psychologists, toxicologists, reconstructionists, and a hundred other examples. They charge extravagantly, but they give lawyers the specialized testimony our lawsuits need to thrive.

Most of our witnesses are fact witnesses. They testify about events they saw or words they heard. However, evidence law greatly restricts what *opinions* they may testify to at trial. For instance, an eyewitness can say he saw a defendant hit a person with his fist, but he cannot state opinions such as why the defendant hit the guy or his conclusion that it was done without provocation. Simply put, the witness can say what he witnessed, but it's the jury's province to assign opinions to the situation.

To pursue Jenelle Potter for her criminal liability, I needed someone with an opinion. Someone who could take the stand, talk about the e-mails and convince the jury that Jenelle Potter authorred these messages.

Internet Protocol addresses would provide a valuable clue. "IP address" for short, such information is generated by internet providers, assigning a unique numerical label to each device participating online. The TBI had tracked down IP addresses for Jenelle's bul2dog@aol.com e-mail account, and it appeared the Potter house's IP address matched the America Online records. The IP address also matched Barbara's account at bmp9110@aol.com. Pursuant to the search warrant for the Potter home on Hospital Road, one computer—a

Dell desktop—was found and confiscated in a small bedroom that was used as a computer room. Thus both Potter women were sharing that computer. There were no other devices.

With their past history of complaining about being hacked or spoofed, I knew I had to prove Jenelle was Chris. Not just suggest that she was Chris. I had to prove it.

Obviously, e-mails do not have fingerprints or DNA attached to them. Anyone can sit at a keyboard and type and try to be whomever they want to be. Back when people always wrote by hand, prosecutors could match handwriting styles. Or when they typed on typewriters, the unique features of the typewriter used could shed clues as to the origin.

This was going to be trickier. More troubling to me was the fact that I had no idea who in the world could help me with this challenge.

So I did what had become a habit for me whenever I didn't know how to do something. Whether it's repairing a lawn mower, finding a good grilling recipe, or diagnosing what's wrong with my dog, I turn to Google.

Blindly entering search terms, I finally came upon a branch of forensic expertise that I was previously unaware existed. "Forensic linguistics" was a growing field. Such experts were available to testify about trademark violations, what might be meant by words in a contractual clause, and most useful to me, authorship identification.

I continued my quest by looking for available forensic linguists who could analyze the Chris e-mails and help me prove Jenelle was the author. I examined the web pages for a couple of such experts until I ran into the page of Dr. Robert Leonard.

Dr. Leonard was a professor of linguistics at Hofstra University in New York, where he led the forensic linguistics program, the only one of its kind in the United States. His website indicated that he had aided law enforcement agencies around the country and testified for many companies, including Apple. He had been featured on television shows and helped solve all sorts of cases.

Honestly though, what further drew my attention to him was his being a founding member of the vocal performing group Sha Na Na, which opened for Jimi Hendrix at Woodstock. I grew up watching Sha Na Na on television as a kid, and I always remembered the tall, skinny Bowzer with the slicked-back black hair and goofy expressions.

Apparently Dr. Leonard left the group in 1970, opting for the academic life over the world of rock 'n' roll.

So on November 13, 2012, I found his e-mail address and sent him a quick inquiry, telling him just a little of what I was seeking. I even posted a link to a Huffington Post article published when our crime happened, hoping it would pique his interest. One of those sensationalized "Facebook unfriending leads to murder" articles. I doubted I would ever hear from him.

Two days later, I did. He e-mailed back to me, saying, "This is precisely the type of case we handle. Please let me know if you want to discuss the case."

I called him right up. I let him know what analysis we needed and got his compensation rates. He sounded very enthusiastic about helping me. I told him a little about some of the things I was seeing in these Chris messages, and he agreed that they sounded very significant for the type of work he performed.

I got off the phone and drafted the biggest funding request I'd ever written to our conference in Nashville, begging the folks in the fancy office for the money to pay for Dr. Leonard's work. His hourly rate was $250, which was his reduced law enforcement billing standard. Apple paid much more. More concerning to me was the amount of time he would have to spend on the case, picking out details and comparing writings, then working up a detailed report. We did not have unlimited resources, and I feared the request could be rejected due to the estimate being too high. Therefore, in my written request, I stressed that his analysis was critical in assembling murder cases against uncharged persons.

To my relief, our conference approved the funding on November 21.

Now I could begin to see a pathway to bringing Jenelle Potter to justice. A long, long pathway, for sure, but it was time to begin the journey.

14

The search warrants and interrogations had taken place long ago. The bodies of Bill Payne and Billie Jean Hayworth had been laid to rest almost ten months prior. Dr. Leonard and I got to work. I sent him computer files and any papers I thought might help him. Everything I could send went out via Federal Express.

Yet there was something I did not have.

Dr. Leonard had to educate me how to go about the case. It was not unlike doing a handwriting analysis. In those cases, the expert often gets a handwriting exemplar from the subject, where they have them write all kinds of things so that they can be compared to the questioned documents.

Speaking as he did, what was important at this point was having "K docs," documents "known" to have been written by Jenelle Potter. We would then analyze those documents for their peculiarities and habits. With what we learned from those K docs, we would begin parsing through the "Q docs," the writings of Chris, Matt and Dan, to determine whether those same characteristics were present. Thus we had to have a witness testify to knowing that Jenelle Potter had written such K docs before we could get off the starting blocks on the Qs.

Well, that's easy, I replied. "We have lots of letters that Jenelle wrote to her father and Jamie after they went to jail," I said, adding that I had seen her leave that "e" at the end of words when adding the "ing" there. I knew I had her. I just needed an expert to voice the opinion. "Are the letters typed?" Dr. Leonard asked. "No, they're handwritten," I answered.

Not good enough. He explained to me that whatever analysis

we could make from her handwritten K docs, the other side might counter us rather effectively that people have different tendencies when they type versus when they pen their words by hand. He could do the work with handwritten letters, but his work would be flawed and easily attacked.

Another issue we discussed was the possibility of Jenelle, as Barbara's thirty-year-old daughter, having distinctions about her writing that were in fact distinctions shared by her mother. After all, she could have learned those from mom. In fact, the more I studied Jenelle, the more I recognized learned traits that she developed from her mother's style. We also had an issue of whether it was possible that one of them could have written a document but then the other one proofread or corrected it.

Ideally, we needed known written documents by Jenelle where someone sat there and watched her write them. So how in the world would we get that?

At this point we could have just gone to Jenelle Potter and asked her to type up some writings. That would be easy, if she went along with it. I doubted she would, based on what I'd gleaned from the initial investigation. During calls between Barbara and Buddy following his arrest, Barbara said that investigators had wanted to talk to Jenelle again, but she wasn't going to take Jenelle to the sheriff's department. At this point, I assumed cooperation was still unlikely.

Even if she did agree, I imagined even she would have been smart enough to wonder why we were asking for her to write long passages in her own writing. Suppose she tried masking her writing style to fool us? What if she said no, realizing we were on to her and thus preventing any further possibility of getting proof from her? At this point, she surely thought she was going to be in the clear.

With those issues running through my head, I took my homework assignment and shared it with the others in the inner circle of the case. My co-counsel, Matt Roark, was enthused about what I'd discovered about forensic linguistics, and Agent Lott seemed relieved that perhaps there actually was a way to make the case on Jenelle. I asked them about finding some K docs for Dr. Leonard to look at.

They pointed me to Chief Deputy Woodard, who was the point man for the case for the Johnson County Sheriff's Department. I spoke with Woodard, and he said Jenelle had written out complaints in his office—and in his presence—regarding harassment she had alleged against others. However, those were hand-written complaints. We needed something typed.

Sometimes a random break aids the course of an investigation. A serendipitous and unforeseen event. Sometimes, though, I think that perhaps the breaks come from a higher source, a higher power, just when an investigative team is bumbling along at its worst. We needed the help.

And so it was, when Woodard got back with me later. He let me know that Barbara and Jenelle had contacted him about more harassment or vandalism that they were alleging against people up in arms about Buddy's alleged crime. People were throwing things onto their property and making them feel endangered. They wanted Woodard to do something about it.

So both Barbara and Jenelle were going to come to us, to the Johnson County Sheriff's Department, on June 6, 2013. Just when we didn't know how to proceed, we stumbled into a way.

I hatched a plan with Woodard. He would make them an appointment to come in and give full statements about what was going on. He would ask them to sit at his computer and type their statements as he watched, encouraging them to write every little thought that came into their heads so that he could investigate the matter to the best of his ability. They would type and unwittingly give us what we needed.

Meanwhile, I would go through Jenelle's Facebook writings, circling postings that Woodard would then ask her if she authored. Of particular interest to me was the long introductory statement she had about herself on the "About" portion of her Facebook page. This idea would be trickier to execute. We'd have to come up with a convincing scheme to keep her from becoming suspicious.

I asked Woodard to tell her that since she had alleged so much hacking going on with her Facebook page, it would be helpful if we knew what she had written and what she had not written. After all, if these people were hacking and harassing her, the Sheriff's Department needed to identify exactly how they were doing it so that it could properly investigate them.

I hoped Jenelle would not be insightful enough to question such an unusual request.

When the time came for them to appear, I was wearing Woodard out with texts asking how it was going. Eventually I heard back. Woodard told me they typed lengthy statements for him, and he was going to send them to me right away. As for the Facebook writings, Jenelle and Barbara had looked at him quizzically when asked about checking off the circles I had secretly placed next to the writings I wanted her to authenticate. Properly suspicious, they asked if they could call their lawyer about whether Jenelle should do so.

At that point, Woodard figured the Facebook circles were a lost cause. However, they called their attorney and got the secretary at the office of Randy Fallin, who was representing Buddy in his murder case, and the secretary said it sounded fine to do what Woodard was requesting. Just get a copy of what you do, she said.

So Jenelle then looked over the documents, checking my circle next to the long summary of herself, plus another sentence or two. Then she thought better of it and said they should probably talk to Fallin before doing any more.

Good idea. Too bad we already had what we needed.

With a collection of typed K docs in hand, we sent them off to Dr. Leonard immediately. He could finally supplement the work he'd begun with the handwritten K docs, but now he could verify his findings by comparing typed K docs to the typed Q docs. That Facebook posting Jenelle checked as her writing was a treasure trove of little things that sounded just like Chris, who repeatedly told others how "fun and caring and loving and sweet" she was.

Most eveyone know's me in some way or another. I'm a very sweet caring person. I'm from Kennett Sq PA but I have been living in East Tennessee for going on 9 years. I do miss a lot of my friends that are pretty much everywhere now. I love life and I love to make others laugh. I'm fun and caring and loving and sweet. If anyone needs anything they let me know. I'm a little shy sometimes and most of the time out going and I love to make new friends or talk to just about anyone. I love my Family so much. My Mom and Dad are my world and some of my great friends mean the world to me. I love them all to pieces. I'm a good Chrisitan girl and have always done my own thing and my friends and family know where I stand. I guess that's all for now. You can e-mail or IM me anytime. I do not praty or drink or smoke at all. Thank you for reading this.

And that long, typed statement she pecked out on Woodard's computer:

Doing the month of May My Mom and I were in Mtn City Phar.We were meeting with the Pharmacist and picking up my new Prescriptions re my Brittle Diabetes. and i was standing at my mom's right sholder trying to listen to the Pharmacist and Janie Henry came in and saw me and give me looks then she walked in back of me and said she was going to meet me outside and "kick my ass" and then i got really upset. At that point a guy starting talking to me about my upset at that point my mom walked to the front door and Jaine was siting in the car waiting for me and then this guy went out and looked as well and said she was still there . At this point Mom Barbara called 911 to help us get out safely. Well the town cops had-ken Lane-Joey Norris come and i had went out to the car with him and he was geting my info and then this girl in a blue shirt came out of the Pharmacy and she was pissed because she siad that janie has to use the bathroom and janie said that she was scared of me and that she didnt do anything to me. And i told her it was none of her business and to go away . But then she new Ken Lane and i walked back in to the Phar. and sat down and then Joey Norris was looking at the tape still and i was waiting but then we got all my meds and left but Ken Lane was still out said waiting to see if we were safe and i told him thank you. Then Mom and I got in the car and went home from there.

After the Phary. I have gotten threats sence this has happened from Janie Hanery, Tracy Greenwell, Tara and Brad Osborne,-__? Allen he is in his 50's and said he was going to rape me and he would like to see me dead. Steven Dugger, Nicky Church Yelton, Lindsey Thomas, Jason Greenwell and Clay Greenwell, Tim Anson Christie Kay Groover Potter, my so called older sister. And Husbands and boyfriends and also friends i dont know names. They all have said i killed Pal Bill but he had cancer and other things wrong. And Tracy also has said he wants to kick my Ass and they have broken in to my phone and left me text meg. Tracy and Janie Henry have been up my road and then Tracy has been there. More then once. Yesterday i got her on tape going up my road she was up to something and then when i was over in Va the other day to see my Doctor at the Hosptial they left stuff in my lane. and Yesterday a 2 guys in a black Ford truck threw a bullet and caseing in my lane at me while i was geting stuff out of my dad's truck in to my Mom's car and they called me a Fuc**** Bitch. and they went so fast down the road. My Mom was staning on our front Porch and saw this. Then about 12 Am Tracy was parked in the down belong lane in out mexcains lane. Jessica Teaster came in to Randy Fallin's office and said she didnt want me there and i was a bitch and hope i get Killed.

Jenelle Leigh Potter signed that statement on June 6, 2013, at 6:26 p.m.

From the above, one could tell a lot of things about Jenelle besides her writing quirks. She was paranoid, obsessed even, about people whom she perceived as aligned against her. The simple act of a person driving by her house could send Jenelle into a conspiratorial tizzy. It was also difficult to comprehend a person walking into an attorney's office and announcing that she hoped their client's daughter would be killed. There was hardly anything she alleged that a reasonable person could find plausible. Possibly, her intellect and ability to perceive and understand situations was greatly diminished compared to an average person. Or perhaps she simply had a propensity to exaggerate in order to gain attention.

The more I studied her mother's writings, the more I understood the source of all Jenelle's strange psychological characteristics. As the old saying goes, she got it honest. Jenelle had learned many traits from her mom.

15

My decision to pursue criminal charges against Jenelle Potter did not take long. Assuming she was the author of all things written by Chris and Matt Potter, her e-mails showed a constant preoccupation with the activities of the victims and their friends. She wrote hateful, spiteful thoughts toward them. Moreover, as I was beginning to suspect, she would author fake threats from Billie Jean's friend Lindsey Thomas. Then she would copy and paste those threats into e-mails to Jamie and her mother. Messages that promised doom toward herself. Since she was also suggesting, as Chris, that the torment and harassment from her enemies could very well end her life, I believed that by doing this she was needling her father and Jamie to believe the killings were necessary since Lindsey appeared to be threatening her harm.

One thing I needed to do was determine whether that harassment was real. Was Jenelle really a victim of anything?

There had been allegations and charges thrown back and forth between the Potters and their tormenters. Those events were referred to repeatedly in the e-mails between Barbara and Chris. In one lawsuit, Tara Osborne had filed for an order of protection in early 2011 against Jenelle, but that case was thrown out due to Tara not being qualified to get the order as she was not a relative of Jenelle. Tara's motivation for taking out the charge was her allegation that she had received many annoying phone calls from the Potter residence.

A second court case was a bigger source of concern in the e-mails. Lindsey Thomas swore out a charge of phone harassment against Jenelle Potter after Tara's suit failed. Lindsey also alleged a great many phone calls. That case dragged out through the summer and was finally tried in Johnson County General Sessions Court on November 30, 2011. Sessions Judge Bliss Hawkins ruled that Lindsey had not proven Jenelle guilty beyond a reasonable doubt and dismissed the case. References to this ongoing court saga were aplenty in the correspondence between Barbara and Chris. Often the messages spoke of the fear of Jenelle going to jail over it, and her inevitable death should that happen.[1]

If those e-mails were to be believed, Jenelle was the one aggrieved. The Potters lived in fear of multiple people, convinced that Jenelle would be greatly harmed should the opportunity arise.

The best way to analyze this situation would be by talking to Lindsey directly. A couple of phone calls later, I arranged for her to meet me at our Mountain City office.

First, I needed to be prepared with the writings I suspected Jenelle had falsely created as being written by Lindsey. There were aspects of the writings that screamed out Jenelle's authorship, at least to my untrained eye. Sensing this could be the first time Lindsey had ever seen the writings, I wanted to see her reaction when I handed them to her.

One of the e-mails was entitled "this is from linsday from c" sent from Jenelle's e-mail account to Jamie's, dated October 9, 2011:

> Your a fucking Bitch and you know your fucking ass is going to jail and Bill is going to kill you he has said that and i hope he does. None of us want you around nor living. Your a wasit of air and time on everyone. You are nothing. You really think you are sweet and smart HAHA yeah right your dumb and your very ugly no one wants you. Billie thinks your fat and Bill Me Fucking linsday i just hate your a live. you will die bitch and i cant wait to see it. go to Hell bitch.

---

1   One of Barbara's traits was to instantly react to anyone in conflict with her by saying that the person wanted her dead or wanted to kill her. This strange philosophy transferred to her daughter. If someone wanted Jenelle convicted of a crime, surely they wanted her dead as well.

One from April 21, 2011, entitled "what linsday said" sent from Jenelle's account to Barbara's, was especially strange:

> **Jenelle i will get you no good bitch … I'm fucking Linsday remember that.**
>
> **I know everything you talk about on your e mail to someone named Chris who is that your fucking bitch?**
>
> **You cares what i have and i can use it if i want too your ass is mine your a fucking bitch remember that i can get you and will. your daddy cant do shit to me. I'm above the law dumb fucking bitch.**

Was Jenelle writing these things and sending them to Barbara and Jamie, hoping they would believe that Lindsey and her gang were going to hurt her? It seemed possible.

Lindsey met me at our appointed time. Tall and slender, she was an outgoing young woman. It didn't take long to tell she had a little bit of country in her, but like most young people in twenty-first century Appalachia, cable or satellite television and the Internet had greatly bridged what cultural gap might have previously existed between a rural kid and those in large cities elsewhere. She seemed a typical young, American adult.

I asked her about her association with Jenelle.

"I didn't really know Jenelle," she began. "Billie Jean had accepted a friend request on Facebook from her. We knew of her."

Following Billie Jean's acceptance, Lindsey accepted a friend request from Jenelle as well.

"One day Billie Jean told me that Jenelle had talked bad about us on Facebook," Lindsey said. "So I confronted her on Facebook. But she didn't stop. Then I called her at her house, and she said she hadn't wrote anything. She said she didn't know what I was talking about.

"Then I started getting calls from her. She'd call me twenty-seven times or so a day. Then she'd send something from a Bob or people she'd make up."

Amidst allegations from Jenelle that Jenelle was the victim of

Lindsey's harassment, Lindsey stated that she was working twelve hours a day at the time, manufacturing needles at the Phoenix Medical plant. She said she had no reason at all to bother Jenelle.

"I was getting all these calls from their house, and her dad would be a part of it," Lindsey said of Buddy. "He'd get on and say to quit calling, and I'd tell him, 'she's the one calling me.' Her dad said to me that he'd kick my ass. Then my boyfriend would get on the phone and say something to them."

After this routine went on for some time, Lindsey said she'd had enough.

"I took a lot from her until I went to the next level," she said. "I never threatened her. I just told her to stop."

"Ok," I said. "What was the worst thing you ever said back to her?" I considered this question important, because country people I know will only take so much. Eventually they bite back.

"I told her if I ever saw her out, things might not go so well," she answered. "I probably said that online. I don't think I ever made an outright physical threat. I'm not aware if I called her names, but I can't remember doing that.

"I probably said more to her in helping out Billie Jean because Billie Jean wasn't a confrontational person. Billie Jean was getting more harassment online than I was."

Lindsey became close friends with Billie Jean around three years before Billie Jean's death. They had known each other in school, but since Lindsey was older, they only got to know one another better later in life.

"I even got a phone call from a cop in Pennsylvania that Jenelle wanted to press charges against me there because Matt wouldn't do it," Lindsey said, referring to my counterpart Matt Roark.

The e-mails talked extensively about Lindsey driving by the Potter house. Was that true?

"My parents lived about a mile from them," she said of the Potters. "I would drive on that road, but not up to their house. I've never stopped and communicated with her. My only communications with Jenelle were either online or on the phone."

Several of the e-mails referred to a confrontation that Lindsey supposedly had with Jenelle at Food Lion, one of the three grocery stores in Mountain City.

"There was a time Jenelle was with her dad at Food Lion, but Jenelle started on me. I just walked away," Lindsey said.

Did she ever hear about the CIA being involved in anything?

"The first I ever heard about the CIA was either on Topix or Facebook," she said. She thought most of the talk had been on Topix.

Anytime that drug selling might be relevant to a homicide investigation, the police have to be informed about it. Determining a list of suspects is the first order of business, and it is an unfortunate fact that drug activity can lead to homicides. What can make the law enforcement officer's task all the more difficult is when witnesses hold back that information to protect themselves or the victim's reputation.

Since Lindsey valued finding the killers over protecting anyone, including herself, she felt she had to be truthful to the investigators when they questioned her early on about why her friend might have been killed.

"I told Scott Lott and Joe Woodard about the drugs," she said. "I thought that could've been a motive for the murders."

In her original statement to investigators, Lindsey had mentioned visiting Billie Jean the day before the killings. She told them that Billie Jean had been selling Lortabs for someone unknown to her, and that Billie Jean had asked her if she knew anyone who'd want to buy them. Lindsey said that Billie Jean was selling on the side so as to buy baby supplies.

However, learning that nothing had been stolen out of the Payne house—money, drugs or otherwise—she figured, just as the investigators had, that drugs had nothing to do with the killings.

For that matter, the Johnson County Sheriff's Department drug officers had never heard a word about drugs being sold by the victims or from anyone in their home. As a general rule, if anyone in a jurisdiction was moving any quantity of dope, officers would catch wind of it. Particularly in a small community like Johnson County. If Bill and Billie had indeed sold pills or Serboxyn strips, they likely did so on a very small scale.

Lindsey was very accommodating in sharing information. I decided it was a good time to ask her about the questioned e-mails where it was made to appear that she had made threats against Jenelle.

One by one, I handed the documents to her. It was clear that she hadn't written them. Her facial expression was that of a person who had never seen such writings, incredulous that any such things existed.

"I didn't write these," she firmly stated. "For one thing, my grammar isn't that bad. They can't even spell my name right."

I was convinced based on her reaction that she hadn't written a single one of those messages. They were made up.

It was even clearer to me now what I was dealing with: Jenelle, despite whatever intellectual issues afflicted her, had gone to great lengths to pit the people who loved her against the people she loathed. She had harassed Billie Jean and Lindsey to the hilt, got the desired reaction as Lindsey had bit back and thus caused her parents to think Lindsey hated Jenelle, and then Jenelle upped the ante by concocting false threats against her so that her parents and boyfriend would react.

I told Lindsey that it was a wonder she was alive, that the Potters seemed to have hated her as much or more than the ones they had killed. I asked her if she and Billie Jean had fully perceived the level of hate and contempt the Potters had toward them.

"I just thought of it as something silly," she answered. It was more a nuisance to her than a life-or-death conflict. "When Bill and Billie Jean got killed, I didn't even think of the Potter family at first. It was such a stupid bunch of stuff with them."

Hence the reason Lindsey mentioned the pills at first, when investigators were looking for their initial clues.

Likewise, Billie Jean likely didn't perceive that her life was in danger over their conflict with the Potters. After all, the Paynes always left the door to their house unlocked. Even the morning they died.

16

With Dr. Leonard churning away toward linking Jenelle with Chris, we were feeling good about our pursuit of Jenelle as a participant in the homicides.

Barbara Potter, though, was more elusive.

When she wrote a letter or e-mail, Barbara always wrote a lot. In her hands, a simple letter could turn into a book. Because of her tendency to write long passages, any linking of her participation in the killings was likely buried in an avalanche of words. While the Jenelle/Chris passages revealed themselves to me as criminal acts, Barbara's took longer. For sure, there were mentions of Bill and Billie Jean in Barbara's writings from her bmp9110@aol.com account, but piecing together criminal liability was akin to assembling a doctoral thesis.

I digress here to explain the concept of criminal responsibility for the conduct of another. It's a statutorily-based law in Tennessee that one is criminally liable for the crime(s) of another when they have "solicited, directed, aided or attempted to aid" the other in committing the crime with the intention that the crime be completed.

Other states have such laws on their books. Charles Manson has spent most his life in the California prison system due to such a law. He is reputed to be a notorious killer when in fact he has killed no one. He had others do it for him.

Often the cases in which we employ the criminal responsibility statute are on theft crimes. Perhaps a burglar entered a home while his cohort stood guard outside, never entering the home. By our law, both would be equally guilty of burglary.

In homicide cases, our typical scenario in utilizing the criminal responsibility statute is that the accomplice aided the principal criminal in some way. For instance, the accomplice held the victim down while the principal stabbed him. Or the accomplice drove the principal to the scene of the crime and then drove him away. Either way, the accomplice is guilty of first degree murder just the same as the one who did the actual killing, if they also intended the killing to occur.

Sometimes the assistance of an accomplice only occurs after the crime has been consummated. When that happens, in Tennessee the crime is called accessory after the fact. This is a low-grade felony rather than being treated equally as the principal. Examples of this include hiding the killer in one's home or lying to the police about facts pertaining to the crime so as to aid the killer in eluding detection or capture.

So, to convict the Potter women of murder, we had to have proof beyond a reasonable doubt that they solicited, directed, aided, or attempted to aid in the murders of Payne and Hayworth. And that they did so with the intent that the victims be killed.

Nowhere in any of the e-mails did there exist an outright solicitation of murder. There was no, "I want you to kill them tomorrow," type of written exchange. More troubling was the fact that no evidence existed that the primary killer of the victims ever used the computer. By all accounts, Marvin "Buddy" Potter was computer illiterate. Any urging or pleading with him to kill the victims had to have occurred away from the computer, so what we had in proving the Potter women guilty of murder was a circumstantial case. That is, unless Jamie Curd was going to tell us the whole story. Which wasn't going to happen.

Our challenge was to piece together enough writings to convince a jury beyond a reasonable doubt that such an exchange most assuredly *had* occurred at some point, and thus led to the homicides. From a legal standpoint, it seemed horribly challenging.

Circumstantial evidence gets a bad rap from the public sometimes. "All the evidence was just circumstantial," we might hear from naysayers. Unlike direct evidence, such as a confession or eyewitness account of the crime, circumstantial evidence can sometimes require a prosecutor having to overly prove his or her case before a skeptical jury. After all, no one would want to go to jail simply because they owned a car that matched the description of the getaway vehicle or because they owned a similar weapon to the one that was used in a crime. Perhaps because one simple piece of circumstantial evidence could generate a case against any of us in a crime in which we were totally innocent, there is a healthy level of suspicion any time a case is built on circumstantial evidence.

However, I was picking out statements from Barbara that were valuable to me. Trouble was, I didn't know if it was direct evidence or circumstantial evidence of guilt. It was more like she was the cheerleader on the sideline yelling out cheers for her side, suggesting that her sweet nothings in the ear of Buddy Potter were of the sinister variety. Hidden in this long message to Chris on April 12, 2001, I found some key references that I underlined:[1]

> **Hello Chris fr Barbie, Tues, 4/12/11, 2 am ——PART 2**
> On 4/7 ... George,atty, told us loudly after judge was done, court done, "you have to talk to the magistrate & mayor and let them know what is happening to you, your property, harassment. he needs to know." ...And Mike told them all plainly in front of Bud last Tues.4/5 that they were to leave us all alone & to turn Tara away, no more false reports unless she has proof - so that is what she is doing now - making up emails galore(had some w/her lasst week in court,but no one wanted to see them).She complained bc some man is calling her but Jen doesn't know who that man/men are. She's stupid for a nurse! Jen is only on her own facebook but her friends have told

---

1   To explain some of the references in this message, "Mike" is Sheriff Mike Reece, "Chr" is Barbara's older daughter Christie, "Tara" is Tara Osborne, who had tried taking Jenelle to court for an order of protection in 2011, and the matter in federal court involving Buddy was a charge of him boasting of military medals that he had not earned. The Potters always asserted that Buddy was falsely accused and had in fact earned such honors.

her that they have seen the fake one & fb does not allow one to have more than one fb at a time... and Jen's had this one for at least 5 yrs. when it came out...they need to back off. Bud is sooooo mad &I'm 100% behind whatever happens. You guys meet when you are ready Chris. <u>Maybe Bud will have ID by then & can use CIA guns, etc. for his protection - get the jobs done. ya know. They all need to go & the ones left need to be given a big scare as they watch & wonder "am I next?"</u>....

<u>Whatever/whenever you want to do whatever, contact Bud. Did you tell your bosses/guys work w/you? Prob. not do that bc he h as no ID.ya know. Bud knows this area well & will help you he said. He is fed up & ready. Shame they had to push him to this bc he is a very patient man, but once you push him to hard too long, its over. He won't take it. Good you hve a list, but don't let anyone see it. I'm sure you have it memorized. Keep scaring up these 3 girls w/guns,etc. &breaking their cars, Chr's too. Make things hard for them bc they are making life hard for us. Thanks Chris.</u> Son, you take care. I am praying for you & for us. Its getting scarier now. Oh my goodness. Keep telling the cops to stay away from our house/road checking on Jen&Bud &Why???are they? grr Bud is mad about it bc has seen them; Mike needs to know this.Bud&Jen do nothing wrong,illegal nothing. They are good like me. Now I'm going to be getting our some; have driven against yest.& did fine other than worry about cop harassment. I drive Bud's truck usually now. (I agree w/your statements bout getting them all....all th way - they aren't going right by m.cty.,let alone us)

Well Chris, I hope that you are starting to feel some better. I can't imagine how badly you are bruised up inside & out plus a broken arm, hurt back and neck . grrr &Mike is the reason. Well, he can be taken care of too by you all- huh? That was mean & dirty-not good at all bc he wants You dead! proved that much. Take care. Hope to hear from you soon. I/We love you son... and praying for your healing & rest, asking God to hear your prayers also. I'm glad you & we are Christians, something no one can take away from us...! Byeee for now! :) hang in there. Love you. Mom.

The above passage revealed several things. Most importantly, she was apprising Chris of Buddy's intentions. There were a multitude of messages between Chris and Barbara concerning Buddy getting a CIA identification—Barbara wanting Bud to have it, and Chris responding that it was in the works. Here Barbara sounded like whatever plan Buddy had concocted for their enemies, he hoped to have a CIA ID and CIA support behind him. Barbara was almost offering Chris Buddy's assistance in any mission Chris undertook against their tormentors. Barbara was also responding to Chris's messages detailing his efforts to watch Billie Jean, Lindsey, and Tara. He even mentioned attempting to tamper with Lindsey's vehicle so as to make her crash. Here, Barbara seemed to endorse such actions.

While that e-mail did not include an overt statement implicating her in a crime, in my opinion, it did confirm that Barbara's whispers to Buddy at night were of a criminal nature. She and Chris talked via e-mail, she passed on the information to Buddy, and then she followed up with more correspondence with Chris. Message after message, Barbara reported to Chris what Buddy said or what Buddy planned, and Chris answered. While Barbara was never explicit that Buddy planned to kill, she was clumsily cryptic, talking about them having "a list" or her being behind "whatever happens."

By the end of 2011, Barbara had become more deranged, dangerously paranoid, and obsessively preoccupied with the movements and plans of her family's foes. On December 6, 2011, she wrote a long, rambling diatribe to Chris. I underlined the most pertinent parts:

Tues. 11 am 12/6 Hey son, thanks for writing. Yeah, glad gave you all that info about the house - U needed to know. Wow! isn't it something?! But yeah, <u>bill never acts along.</u> <u>we know of some he's been in on killing and girls being</u>

raped there..its no secret. So they may as well accept the loss and go on w/their lives bc they are Not going to get Jenelle. there is no way. Between our heavy quantities of ammo and protection of her at all times and your all's they are going to get the surprise of their lives. and as far as J[1] goes, he's safe and he knows it. He don't want to be messed with and he is heavily armed and ready thanks to dad. lol so let them try to get to him....he is ready and dad & you guys + trade gang are just a phne call away.. you know;..the relatives of 'the Bloody Three which dad is the grandson of the leader. They don't' want to mess w/ buddy - not only does he have the strength and training, but he learned lots from his grandpa Enoch in trade.[2] grrrr ..so if someone wants to bring it on, they will All die, including the baby. —Yeah we know that Lindsey is the one pushing this along but Bill , Billie, Tara-all their mean buddies - are enjoying it & he can't act or think alone; he has to have his gang you know....well they may as well stay at home bc there is no getting Jen, no way no how. We are not afraid; she is not either. She knows how to protect herself and she has guns at her access at all times here in the house too. they better think twice if they want to live any longer-all of them. Justice was served assholes: accept it! -I'm glad you are saying what you want Chris bc you know we tried 3 times to tell you or whoever it is to stop talking about bill and being a bad dad and Billie erased it! the bitch-she wants bill all worked up all the time & its a shame. Yes, he lied to dad about keeping Lindsey away. Billie is a satanic, mean, manipulating liar,&she has him right where she wants him & as long as he don't see that she is the one who pushes him around and tells him how to think and do—how stupid is that!?, then he is like her puppet.LOL ...too bad for Bill bc he could have had a better life but he chose bad ... His poor daddy, Bill, Sr., could get

---

1   "J" presumably was referring to Jamie.
2   Buddy did have a grandfather named Enoch from Trade, a small community in Johnson County that borders North Carolina.

caught up in all of this shit and its too bad, but that's life. too bad..bc we like him a lot and he likes us. He has no idea what his son is into to at all but its time he did... bill is a lot of talk and he can't and won't act alone but he gets his buddies to do for him..that's him. He is not strong and not willing to fight man to man, one on one, with Buddy like He stepped back the other night.[1] Bud was going to fight & kill him, had it in his mind plan-ready to go- & you know all the training he has; he was ready and wanted to so bad, but bill back down afterall...too bad-thsi would be over... So you think that it will be ina week or so - things will be happening - we are thinking different/sooner..and ready....well we will see - it may be sooner than anyone thinks. *Yes, we've had enough and we want peace and no one here wants to kill anyone, but we will. Yes, you ppl reading this... time to step back ppl and think about what you are doing and saying....

And dare they come after Jen w/me around (& I'm always around when we're out), well that will be all they wrote in this world. And if they don't think I'll shoot their asses when I'm out, they're wrong. I carry 2 guns, lots of ammo-more than 75 rounds and I'm ready, clips full - sometimes have the shotgun too. I will do whatever I have to do to save my kid or myself - whether bud is around or not. I have no way to call you, but can call bud or jamie, but you need to give j. a code to get you if they get to me and jen...think about that. But most likely once I call, it will be all over anyway..like the other nite at food lion=-she thought she was going to grab jen—jen is fast and smart and then they thought they'd wait for me and her? ha ha —no way—they would be waiting for death!...I was so pissed and then Bud came and he looked everywhere for her ass and her buddies. Those guys are no good to her. We don't care about them; they better leave us alone ...

---

1   This referred to a confrontation between Bill Payne and Buddy at a store near the Payne residence following Lindsey losing her harassment case against Jenelle.

And when he called me a 'mother f——-g bitch, when I saw the look on dad's face, I knew then there was no going back! he got soo mad—that anger came from a place I haven't seen since he was in wartime & wow! bill was goiong to die for sure..but bill don't want to push that button with dad! no way...bill is lucky he got to walk away at all! really. Bud is trying to be patient for the 'right time' but now, he says the Time is Has Come-whenever now! -and If they want jen so bad they can't stand it, then come on! and they will breathe their last breath..bud is soooo ready, we all are..and you're right, dad is not Bill's friend or his druggie dealer at all. Bud is Cia and bill knows it but likes to poke fun at it—bc he has no idea what that entails or what all buddy has done in his life-40 yrs.. Well he don't know anything about that kind of life but he only knows m.Cty which is a hick town with little boys who play mean boy scouts all the time...he hasn't really seen what Bud can and will do with no thought at all—it's a normal reaction for him to kill if approached in wrong way - & I'll tell you, I wouldn't want to be on the other end of Dad's training and him using it - it likes Vietnam here to him now and he's ready for the enemies - with or without a weapon, he is ready at all times...so they better back off while they can. Bill can call him fat ass, mr cia, whatever, but he don't want to be on the other end of buddy! believe me-I've seen him in action... its not pretty. But if Bill thinks there is not enough room in this town for Jamie and for our family, then they are going to see who is going to be leaving... not us for now..this thing has to be over.. -And Bill won't get jen into round 3 yelling again bc of the Plan they have...thank you very much for that info.. Billlie is a woose and she just backs down anyway, has no strength and won't even look any of us in the eye, she is sneaky bitch, coniving, & Lindsey & bill 'fights' dirty & uses knife, kicking, etc. and she is going to get Bill hurt real bad and/or killed.... we don't call 911 anymore. We are ready to take care of this ourselves, espec. Bud and

Jamie are super ready all the time..Now you know that
Dad could do it alone, but whatever they want to bring
on, bring it on. Wish that Lindsey would just come on and
try for Jen here out in the yard-just one more time! - that
would be so good and she'd be gone...she says that she
is going to come after her wherever, so come on bitch!....

I did tell B&J you said their backs are covered well and
that all is good—but dad knows that but says that he will
do whatever it takes no matter whose around, but all is
okay anyway& thanks...we never know if you hear all, see
all or not, but we're all ready. They are glad cia is around
but they say that they will be able to handle it all but good
to know. & thanks....

Jenelle, sweetheart, knows (God lets her know) who
is good and who is not and she did not want Bill ever.
She and Jamie are friends w/All of us now and that is it.
He cares about Jen's health (bc he's experienced taking
care of his mom so long) and he cares about me & my
probs. BUT he is Not romantically involved w/jen! for the
umpteenth time! bill!)

By late 2011, Barbara's writings had become a deranged stream
of consciousness. Sometimes her lunacy was almost comical. For
instance, during that message she described Jenelle as having learned
"2nd degree black belt Philippine killing karate."

Barbara's delusions were profound. She had totally bought into
the idea that there was a man named Chris from the CIA who cared
deeply about her paranoia. She believed that Lindsey, Billie Jean, and
Bill were downright evil. Billie Jean was satanic, she said. She feared
leaving Jenelle alone for what these people might do to her.

And what about the insinuation from Barbara that Bill had
once wanted Jenelle in a romantic way? That seemed very unlikely.
However, one wondered what Jenelle had reported to Barbara,
especially in light of all the Jenelle-penned tirades on Topix talking
of how Billie Jean was ugly, how Billie Jean was a whore, and how
Jenelle was so much prettier. Perhaps Jenelle was the one who

wanted Bill. But couldn't have him—hence the real reason why Jenelle's hatred ran so out of control.

Once these messages were placed in order and read in context, I concluded that Barbara Potter was not only a participant in the killings of Bill Payne and Billie Jean Hayworth, but that she might have been the biggest instigator of the criminal conspiracy.

And that conclusion was all the more firm when analyzed in light of Jamie Curd.

17

Before he met Jenelle Potter in his mid-thirties, Jamie Curd never had a girlfriend. He dropped out of high school and went to work to help his family with their finances, and he stayed with his parents as each of them died. He even cared for his brother, who passed away in 1997. He never lived away from home, and he saw very little of the world beyond Johnson County.

When investigators first started looking into the case, some people in the community described Jamie as Jenelle's boyfriend. Such was their perception.

Their actual relationship was complicated.

Barbara and Buddy were extremely protective of Jenelle. Socially isolated herself, Jenelle caught Tracy Greenwell's attention years after the Potters moved to Johnson County. Tracy, who met the Potters while working at a Mountain City pharmacy, felt sorry for Jenelle and tried to be her friend. As Tracy told me, in order for her to be allowed to take Jenelle to the mall in Boone, she had to come visit the Potter parents at their home and let them get to know her, similar to how a teenage boy might have to meet a girl's parents before being allowed to take the girl to a movie. Tracy passed their inquiry.

From that point on, Tracy became good friends with the Potters. The computer taken from the Potter house had numerous photographs of Tracy with Jenelle and/or Barbara. Jenelle was around Tracy enough that she met Bill Payne, Tracy's brother.

At some point, Bill and Tracy introduced Jenelle to Jamie Curd. Tracy told me that they thought it would be a good idea for Jenelle and Jamie to get together. Both were very available. Yet, Jenelle and Jamie were unable to have a typical relationship. People in the community perceived that Jenelle was prevented from it by her parents, who felt Jamie was not good enough for her.

Thus their relationship as boyfriend-girlfriend was conducted in secret.

When Agents Lott and Hannon interrogated Jamie, they asked him if Jenelle was his girlfriend. He said no. When Lott and Woodard interviewed the Potter family the day after the killings, they asked Jenelle if Jamie was her boyfriend, and she said no. Buddy and Barbara interjected that Jamie was a good friend of the family. That was all.

They apparently didn't know about the nude selfies Jenelle had sent Jamie.

The pictures were of the self-shot, pornographic variety, taken of Jenelle and sent to Jamie. Lots of them. Pictures involving every part of Jenelle's body. And if someone flipped open Jamie's cell phone, its screen background was a shot of him posed with Jenelle, both fully clothed.

Inside Jamie's car, investigators found cards or letters from Jenelle indicating the two were in love. And indeed, their e-mail correspondence and texting histories, found via search warrants, indicated a serious relationship. Jenelle would call Jamie "my husband" and herself "your wife."

By all indications, Jamie and Jenelle had to keep their love away from the peering eyes of Jenelle's shielding parents. Barbara's long diatribe from December 6, 2011, indicated as much, apparently denying an accusation from Bill that Jamie and Jenelle were an item, saying "for the umpteenth time" that Jamie was not romantically involved with Jen.

In his e-mails with Chris, however, Jamie made multiple references to his frustration at having to be secretive about his love for Jenelle, and to his fear of what would happen if her parents discovered his true motivations for being so willing to come over to the Potter house when they called.

On October 30, 2011, Jamie wrote this to Chris:

i hear ya bro

jen means the world to me an it hurts me so much she cryies i wont to be there to dry her tears make her feel better an let her know everythings ok in i know i will ask her mom about going to JC and im worried about them bill and all of there shit is hurting jen and the whole family more than they let on i like her mom but she intemadates me idk an when im aroun jen every one can see that something is there an you know if they knew idk what would happen her dad hasant said anything but i know he knows i like her i wont jen happy an the happyest ive seen her is when she is with me with her non an dad its like walking on egg shells an im afraid they will see something or say something an if they try to come in between jen an i i afraif to think what jen would do.

Actually, there was evidence from Barbara Potter's writings that she had been aware of Jamie's interest in her daughter. How Barbara's attitude toward Jamie had changed over the course of 2011 was one major piece in deciding to pursue her as being criminally responsible for the murders.

Jamie had been introduced to Jenelle more than two years prior to the deaths of Payne and Hayworth. According to Tracy, they became involved quickly after the introduction.

One early e-mail from Barbara to Chris, dated December 29, 2010, made reference to Jamie while addressing the reality that Chris did not want Jenelle in a romantic way:

I never forget you & Jen doesn't either. She knows that you don't want her anymore but she says she understands. Life is hard you know. Bud and I are worried about her after we die -what will happen to her then? She can't live on her own at all. She needs a good person to take care of her and be good to her. These guys down here are trash and we threw the last one out last year in Jan. – jerk Jamie Curd. He took advantage of me,& was dirty, muddy, and walked in the house any old time, even when Jen was in the hospital one time! He did not have good manners and smelled too. He used to hang out with Billy Payne, the 'maybe' father of Billie Hayworth's baby, not sure yet, and he is running a whore house you know. We would not let her go out in the car with him bc he had a trap for a car and we did not have a trust with him. she did not want to go out with him either. She is such a good person.

In contrast, by the end of 2011, Barbara was acting almost motherly in her e-mails to Jamie, just several months removed from him being "smelly" in her mind. In an e-mail on November 1, 2011, from Barbara to Jamie:

Hi Jamie - I just wanted you to know that I saw all that junk on topix and am highly pissed! grrr. guess you are also. I mean I don't get angry easy, but that is hurtful, lies and mean...but good ol Chris went after them big time as "Matt Potter" and he tells them off something awful... Anyway just wanted to thank you for calling last night. I was sick in bed but bud told me and jen was upset. I saw that on Saturday starting, but I didn't tell her bc the least amt. of time she is upset about them the better. I am upset and it eats at me, but I don't want to put it on her at all. I guess its making me sick; I really don't know. I pray a lot.

Anyway, I guess you got my other email. I hope that you had a good night at work and things went well.

You do know that the real Matt Potter and his sister that work down there are bad news don't you? Well they are. They hang out with Lindsay, billie, bill, tara and the whole bunch and party drugs you name it... its bad. so listen w/your ears at what you can hear... they like to talk shit. Chris is listening and taping them all the time at bill's house & thru their phones so they can't say anything or do much that he don't no about. its an awful way to live, but hopefully someday, things will get better. I feel bad for you bc how they run you down, its terrible. You are not the bad person they lilke to say you are...they even told the police last year that you were in trouble & bad & to keep you away from our house! .so you see? Can't trust bill or any of them. I feel bad for you. Know this. <u>You are Not alone</u>. We are here and we care bout you a lot. When my health is better we can get together more...I just never know when I'm going to be sick. I was sick again last night and in bed when the topix thing came out & I heard about it. I knew but told Jen just to not care or worry bc its lies and it is. some of her friends, it looks like, are taking up for her too. but topix is a shit place to talk anyway and we don't talk or usually go on there. its just for the past year or more they have been talking/running down Buddy, me and Jenelle. They run me down under one of Jenelle's 5 names they have put on there and talked so bad about me - the cuz's in pa are involved also -that is, and the meanies down here. They dont'know me at all! and they will never.

Anyway, God Bless you Jamie. I'll talk to you later. You can call, I'll call you or you can write to me. I'll check back later. Hopefully I'll have a better day. This all is getting to me! grrr. Wish they'd just break in and I could have the pleasure of shooting them...but that will never happen bc they work on the edge of the law as you know....the Evil ones.

I know they think that I'm a little sweet lady who won't do anything but just smile and be nice to them, never carry a gun, but they are dead wrong....I hide my anger and readiness well....my dad and buddy have trained me well...even b4 I met buddy, my dad & i hunted, fished together & he spent lots of time talking to me, teaching me things of life. I had a great dad..really. I miss him so much. My mom is mean to me in Doe and she is 81 now. I don't go around much anymore bc she she loves Christie more than me & treats me bad most of time or uses me. tho I'm Poa for her, I pay her bills and do all kinds of things, I can't relax w/her bc of /Christie and my brother who has turned bad w/drug dealing, Randy Phipps, who lives in Oxford, PA. I mean he don't say anything about me on internet or anything; and acts like he loves me, but he does not know I know what I do about him. I hate it for

him bc he will get caught w/christie and will pay one day .
I love him still but can't call or see him anymore. Oh well,
that's life. We have to stay w/good ppl and close to God.
That is the only way.

Well, I will go for now. Have a good day dear.
You take care and hang in there
Love, Barbara

Note how Barbara reported to Jamie about Chris having listened and taped conversations at Bill's house. Such was the content of Chris's writings to Barbara, which represented that the CIA was intercepting the Payne bunch's evil plans. Most importantly, by November, Barbara was commiserating with Jamie about perceived slights that came his way from Bill and his gang.

Whether or not Bill was really saying anything against Jamie, I had no idea.

The important thing at this point, however, was Barbara's manipulative change of heart evident in the e-mails. Within a year of calling Jamie "ignorant" and saying he "smelled," she had done a complete one-eighty and was treating him like a son, commiserating over Chris's reports of the awful things Bill supposedly said about Jamie. Moreover, there were numerous photographs found on the Potter computer showing Jamie at their house during Christmas in 2011. While Jenelle's parents might not have condoned any romance between Jenelle and Jamie, they were not adverse to allowing Jamie into their home in the months leading up to the killings.

Other e-mails from Barbara to Jamie were important as well. One existed where she coyly told him of their intent to go to the "movies" with Buddy and the others as well as one almost overtly asking for Jamie's advice on a plan of action, since Buddy was stuck on what to do.

I had a feeling that the Potters knew exactly what they planned to do—they were just pulling Jamie Curd into their plan.

So not only was Jenelle scheming to draw Jamie into her conflict, but so was Barbara. They just took different angles to the same problem.

18

Being the daughter of Barbara Potter had to be a life-long curse. While children crave nurturing, love, and guidance from their mothers, what the oldest daughter of Barbara Potter received were delusions, irrationality, and obsessiveness.

Christie Groover was Barbara and Buddy's only child until she was six years old. Then Jenelle came into the world, and Christie's life changed. Instead of being the focus of her parents' attention, that attention was then shared with her younger sister. As it became apparent that Jenelle would have special needs, Christie perceived that her parents were more immersed in her sister's demands.

As she grew into her teen years, the inevitable tensions between parents and child arose, and Jenelle still commanded their attention. Christie's relationship with her mother suffered. Following high school, Christie stayed at the family home as she obtained a two-year degree from a local community college, and then off she went.

Throughout her adulthood, Christie periodically tried to reconnect with her immediate family. But each attempt ended badly. At the time of the Payne-Hayworth murders, Christie had no contact with Barbara, Buddy, or Jenelle.

Sensing that Christie might be a cooperative source of information about the Potter family, Agent Lott had sought her out during his investigation. Likely wary of the possibility that a child of Buddy Potter could tell him to take a hike, Lott was pleasantly surprised that, in May of 2012, Christie was willing to talk to him at length about her family's history. She even signed a statement.

I had yet to consider Christie as a potential witness for the state. As a general rule, I did not like pitting family members against one another unless the case demanded such action. Years ago, I had a particular distaste for when a divorcing parent would drag their adolescent child to court and want the kid to testify against the other parent. I'd usually refuse to go along.

Of course, this case was different than a weak misdemeanor case in general sessions court. Quite a bit more serious.

I felt comfortable that Dr. Leonard's work would allow us to present a solid case against Jenelle. We had a solid collection of known documents written by her, and her grammatical tics were so unusual that I figured any jury would be easily convinced of Chris being her online alter ego.

But now I was turning the state's guns toward Barbara as well. Which meant we probably needed to do some forensic linguistic analysis of her writings in addition to Jenelle's. I figured that both women would dispute for eternity that they wrote any of these e-mails, hiding behind the claim they had been hacked by persons unknown. Framed, even.

Any linguistic study of Barbara would differ from one of Jenelle. Barbara's grammatical quirks were less obvious. Since she was brighter than Jenelle, she knew better how to spell and punctuate and was more conscientious about writing properly. We would need more documents known to be authored by Barbara. All we had at this point was what Woodard had obtained in getting that one typed statement from her in his office.

However, some things about Barbara's writings would be simpler. For one, she never pretended to be someone else. On her e-mail address of bmp9110@aol.com, Barbara always signed off with her own name—"Barbara," "Barbie," or simply, "Mom." Also, her writings meandered aimlessly at times and thus inevitably included many references to facts in her life that would not be commonly known.

It was because of the need for further known writings that I searched through the TBI records for Christie Groover's phone number. I reached her, and she agreed to have me meet her at her home in Southwest Virginia.

During the hour-long drive, my mind raced through the possibilities concerning this meeting. Sure, Agent Lott got a statement from her, but could I develop enough of a rapport to extend that to her testifying for me?

Whether she was estranged from her family or not, I fully expected to be cursed and thrown out on my ear.

Christie lived in a townhouse apartment. She answered the door and invited me in. She was alone, except for a well-trained poodle that sat with her on the couch. She had a very clean and orderly home, which was a contrast with her parents' house.

I tried easing into the conversation, asking about her background and that of her family. Hopefully I could get a feel for where I might be able to head if I listened long enough.

She told me, as I knew, that she had moved out of the family home early in adulthood and gotten a job in graphic design in Pennsylvania. She had made a good income there and gotten married.

She told me a story about when she had tried to introduce her fiancé to her parents, and how Jenelle threw a tantrum and created a distraction. Dejected by her parents' apparent disinterest in her upcoming marriage, the gulf between them widened.

The marriage ended years later, but Christie kept her married name after the divorce. She was in no rush to be linked to her immediate family.

However, Christie did have a strong, nurturing relationship with her maternal grandmother. As her grandmother became elderly, she needed someone to look after her on a continuous basis. With a recent layoff from work and her divorce, it was a good time for a fresh start somewhere else. So Christie moved into her grandmother's Mountain City home. There was no job market for a graphic designer in Johnson County, so she got employed with the rescue squad in neighboring Washington County, Virginia.

After she moved near her parents and Jenelle, the same old problems arose. When Barbara visited her mother, conflicts were the norm. Arguments were constant, and bad enough that when Barbara visited her grandmother, she called ahead, and Christie made herself scarce to minimize problems.

At one point, Christie filed for an order of protection against Barbara. While her grandmother was hospitalized, she said that her family had entered her grandmother's house and threatened her. Christie said they beat on the windows for several minutes before she cracked open the sliding glass door to ask what they wanted. When she did this, Barbara forced the door open and the three entered with Barbara, trying to get Christie to hit her.

Christie said she called the police, and Barbara tried to get Christie arrested for driving with Pennsylvania tags while living in Tennessee. When they later appeared for court, Christie said that Barbara told the judge that Christie had hit her and wielded a knife.

According to Christie, her relationship with Jenelle was nonexistent. She told me about how Jenelle was different from the average person. Doctors diagnosed Jenelle early on with a hearing disability. As Christie described it to me, where someone normal · might hear a person kiddingly say, "I'm going to kick your rear," Jenelle could not discern the non-threatening tone and instead literally believed that the person intended to commit the act.

That statement hit home with me immediately. Could it be possible that at some point Bill Payne or Lindsey Thomas had gotten frustrated with Jenelle's antics and said something they didn't mean literally? Suppose Lindsey got tired of the phone calls, dialed up the Potter home, and told Jenelle something in colorful language that Jenelle wrongly interpreted as a threat. It was entirely possible.

Before her grandmother passed away, Christie moved closer to her work in Virginia and maintained her distance from her parents. She told me of the numerous conflicts that Barbara had with both sides of her family. Barbara's brother Randy had issues with her, and practically every single member of Buddy's family wanted nothing to do with her.

"Barbara and Jenelle have always been victims," she told me. I noted the peculiarity of her calling her mother by her first name. As she elaborated, she told me that Barbara always had a conflict going on. Barbara often believed an individual to be a good person and friend, but at the first sign of disagreement, Barbara's opinion would transform into believing the former friend was an awful, perhaps even evil person.

That sounded familiar. Barbara's writings often brought up perceived failings in others.

One source of tension within their family was that after Barbara married Buddy, Barbara's brother married Buddy's sister.

I could tell that Christie loved her father. She said her father was a completely normal dad as she grew up. Yet when she became an adult, Jenelle began accusing Christie of various unfounded malfeasances. Buddy took Jenelle's side. Moreover, as their marriage continued, Buddy stood up to Barbara less and less until he eventually went along with anything his wife suggested.

Since Jenelle had special needs, Christie said her parents gave her younger sister an inordinate amount of attention. Barbara accused Christie of being jealous of Jenelle. Christie denied that. Instead, she felt they had done Jenelle a disservice by babying her too much. Whatever Jenelle wanted, Jenelle got.

While Jenelle had some level of mental disability, Christie said she was smarter than their parents thought. She said that when Jenelle was little, she would often act like she could not perform some task. Thus her parents would do it for her, but once they were gone, Jenelle would do it for herself and giggle.

One interesting fact that could not be gleaned from e-mails was Christie's description of Jenelle's temper. She said that if Jenelle was confronted over a lie, she would scream and writhe, similar to a child's temper tantrum.

Christie's grandmother had been a conduit of information for Christie about Barbara, Buddy, and Jenelle. One of Jenelle's ongoing problems was her DKA condition. Diabetic ketoacidosis (DKA) occurs when cells are unable to get needed glucose because of a lack of insulin. It is a life-threatening condition. Jenelle was routinely hospitalized for her DKA, since her need for insulin and fluids was so severe.

Christie believed that Jenelle caused a lot of the DKA incidents, eating inappropriate food and driving her blood sugar numbers to inordinate levels. She did it to gain attention, Christie said.

When her father was arrested for the murders, Christie said she found out through her grandmother. The news shocked Christie. She was unsure if Jenelle had anything to do with it or not.

The fact that she wasn't sure made me comfortable in sharing my next statement. I had heard enough to say it.

"Well, I wanted to meet you and hear what you had to say about your family, because I have studied at length what your mother and sister have written, and I intend to have them charged with murder themselves," I said. "I fully believe they are the cause of these killings."

To my surprise, Christie had a look of relief.

"It may sound wrong of me, but I am glad," she said. "Because if my father has to be punished for this, if Barbara and Jenelle are responsible for it, I don't believe he should be alone. I do not believe my father is that type of person. He had to have been manipulated into doing it."

That was all I needed to hear.

"Would you be willing to look over some writings of your mother and verify for me that she wrote them?" I asked.

"I will," she answered.

I explained to her that we had many letters Barbara had written to Buddy while he was in jail, and that we could use someone who could testify that they were familiar with Barbara's writing and thus authenticate the letters as having been written by Barbara. Christie said that she was very familiar with her mother's handwriting.

Christie also provided information about Barbara's writing style that I found familiar, such as her taking many sentences to say goodbye, and that she wrote long, meandering letters.

I shared with her the challenges we had in proving Jenelle's guilt. About how she had posed as Chris from the CIA to manipulate others.

Christie piped up when I mentioned Chris. "There was some story about how Jenelle was going to marry a Chris but it never happened," she said. Since Christie was not close to her sister during Jenelle's teenage and later years, she did not know about whether a Chris actually existed.

And the CIA thing had been a recurring subject. Had Buddy been in the CIA?

"I think he had some involvement while he was in Vietnam," she said. "Like he'd gone on a mission, but I'm not aware of anything beyond that." She added that in her childhood years, he never seemed to be gone for extended periods.

We talked about Jenelle's claims of being harassed by certain girls. Christie said that she was confident that, if Jenelle had been harassed, then she had caused it. Jenelle put on a sweet front, but deep down she was mean and temperamental.

Another thing Christie disclosed was a history of girls thinking that Jenelle was "too pretty."

That sounded familiar. Jenelle had repeatedly written of her striking beauty.

Christie said that when Jenelle was in middle school in Kennett, Pennsylvania, a girl attacked Jenelle and caused her serious injury by striking her in the head. After Barbara and Jenelle went to court against the juvenile, they explained to Christie that the girl said she hit Jenelle because Jenelle was too pretty.

The "too pretty" claim was probably a learned trait from Barbara, according to Christie, who had heard her mother complain about being unable to find a church in Mountain City because she was prettier than the other women in the churches. Ugly women shunned her.

Even though Christie had a lot of insight into her parents, her estrangement likely left her unaware of how her parents' coddling of her sister had descended into psychological depravity.

One interesting topic of conversation was Jenelle's love life. Christie said Barbara and Buddy had been extremely watchful over her association with boys. If Jenelle developed a relationship with a boy and wanted to break up with him, Christie said Barbara or Buddy would be the one to deliver the news to the jilted male.

Christie did not know Jamie Curd. She was aware, however, of her parents' disapproval of any relationship between Jenelle and Jamie. They believed Jamie to be unworthy of their prized daughter.

She told me one story that summed up how sad Jenelle's life had been. In 2010, not long after Bill Payne introduced Jenelle to Jamie, Christie got the strangest wake up call of her life.

At 6:15 in the morning, Barbara called her mother's house inquiring about Christie's whereabouts. Christie's grandmother said she was in bed, but Barbara wanted proof. Barbara stated the Johnson County Sheriff's Department had called and said they found her daughter roaming the county roads late at night and had her at the station.

That had to be Christie, Barbara assumed.

Christie took the phone, heard her mother's panic-stricken story, and calmly explained to Barbara that the story must not be true. Christie was at home, after all. On the phone, in fact.

"Have you checked Jenelle's room?" Christie asked.

Incredulous at the mere suggestion that Jenelle would do anything so wild, Barbara answered no.

With her mother on the house phone line, Christie used her cell phone to call the Sheriff's Department and inquired whether Jenelle was at the station. The official's reply was yes, that an officer had found her wandering down Cold Springs Road in the middle of the night. She was filthy and tired.

Christie asked the officer if they were certain it was Jenelle, and they were. The officer replied that Jenelle had admitted to sneaking out of the Potter home late at night to rendezvous with her boyfriend so they could elope. Only he never showed.

Christie then told her mother to go get Jenelle, but by then Barbara had checked Jenelle's room, only to discover, to her horror, that her youngest and frailest daughter was not there.

"She was freaking out," Christie reminisced.

Later that day, Barbara called Christie's grandmother and explained that Jenelle's blood sugar had dropped, and Jenelle did not even remember leaving the home. Yet she had packed a bag with her clothes and medications.

She was leaving home.

Christie said that, days later, she heard that Buddy had called the boyfriend—Jamie Curd—and told him that Jenelle did not love him and to not come back to the Potter house. He was no longer welcome there.

"That was the first time that they didn't have complete control over Jenelle," Christie said.

This story from Christie made sense of one particular passage written by Barbara to Chris on January 5, 2011, during the period of time in which Barbara had been voicing disapproval at the mere mention of Jamie's name:

> Billy Payne has been in our home a few times, but not since Nov.2009, he brought that guy, Jamie Curd, up here to get Jenelle,& it made us mad bc he was not good for Jen at all. He told Jen to run away from home 5:30 a.m. in the morning last Feb.& he'd pick her up, but he didn't show...and Deputy SeanBrown 'bit' picked her up, frozen, mixed up, a mess, and they called us to come up & get her. Then we had her call Jamie & tell him to not come around anymore, but it took some rough treatmt fr us to get rid of him; he wouldn't stop! Finally by end of March, I told him off good,Bud warned him for the last time, &its over. The guys down here are basically no good...and she has finally found out. I don't know much about him,but he lives back in the holler,Jen would not survive long over there w/his old grouchy sick mom. She would have been alone most of time,tried to be a nurse for mom. But! She was so sorry she did that;he had her brainwashed & so scared& mixed up. Now she is so thin, it is scaring me. The cuz's picking on her didn't help-she thinks she is ugly, fat, needs plastic surgery bc they said it. We told her better.mean girls... Mom's & dad's worry about their kids,can't help it.

But by the time the year was out, Jamie was right there in the Potter house, wearing reindeer antlers and posing for pictures with Barbara, Buddy, and Jenelle at Christmas. He had gone from being trash to practically being a member of the Potter family.

The reason for Jamie's increased standing with Barbara was of a sinister nature, as I would later figure out.

19

There was one subject I was reluctant to touch when talking to Christie that first time. Christie was likely unaware of the extent of Barbara's negative attitude toward her eldest daughter.

Barbara and Chris had engaged in a long, convoluted conversation about Christie. Barbara told Chris about all of Christie's drug dealing, lying, cheating, stealing, and possibly violent conduct. She even told Chris that Christie had beat her.

Chris fed Barbara's delusional thinking about Christie. Jenelle had lived her life learning which people drew her mother's ire the most. By Jenelle's adulthood, Christie was at the top of that list. My theory was that in order to get her mother's attention, Jenelle used Chris as a vehicle to trash people Barbara did not like. Christie was one of those people. Barbara eagerly devoured any information that validated her low opinions of others.

In early 2011, Christie was the primary target of the Chris-Barbara correspondence. As the year wore on, Billie Jean, Lindsey, Bill, and Tara took her place. But for that early part of the year, Barbara craved any information Chris could provide on Christie.

The correspondence we found began with this message from Chris on January 1, 2011 (note his explanation for not being able to see Barbara—that he might be recognized):

> Hi Barbara
>   How are you? I hope you are well. Yes this is Chris AKA Cody. I'm so sorry to hear all of that is going on. I wish there was away tohelp you all. I cant come up there and

see you if someone saw me it would not be a good thing.[1]
I hope to get out and talk tho. Yes what i found on Chrsitie
was true and she is a in a mess. You cant help her its to
late. She was up here today runing her whole and no one
pay anything mind to her. But she needs to learn that you
cant get up in a cops face either....

She needs to grow up. I have been in S A[2] and also
all over the world its very pretty and neat . I got rid of
a few family memebers in ruisa and then NY and some
others. I have shot a lot of ppl in my work with them. I
got toa point where they were bad ppl and i new it was
us or them so i had to kill. But i love to shoot now. and
Killing does not borther me at all... I will try to meet you
all i really will... I'm no longer scared of Chrsitie. I can Kill
her at anytime and your family in PA i have has each one
of them inmy sights and i can get to them anytime. I just
might. I hope that God Understands my Job and i'm still
beliveing in him.

The e-mails progressed, explaining that he was watching Christie
and monitoring her movements. He was closing in on her, he said,
and at any moment she would be held accountable for her actions.

Chris reported Christie's transgressions at length. In another
early January 2011 message to Barbara, Chris wrote to Barbara that
Christie wanted to kill her:

I know Billie hayworth and Linzsay and Bill and Bill has told
a few of us thathe told them more then once to stop. and
leave Jenelle and you all alone. But it didn't stop intill i had
to say something. They are just mean girls lol. Chrsitie is
also friends with Linzsay and that's someone that awful to
even know. Her brother is injail for stelling and also doing
drugs and selling big time drugs and aslo Meth soshe has
no room to talk about anyone. She has done the same

---

1   Notice the explanation for why Chris could not meet Barbara. This
message likely followed one where Barbara pleaded for her "son" to
meet her and Buddy.

2   Saudi Arabia?

thing. She just crazy. But Chrsitie is who you need to look out for. she is after you all a lot. and after what i saw in the court room she wants you dead and out of the pictrue.[1] I'm so mad Barbie i dont know what to do. But if anything happends to you. She is gone for good or maybe before.

Before the day was over, Chris sent another message to Barbara:

I'm so sorry about your house and your truck and your car and Chrsitie doing nasty thing behind your backs. Yes she has asked guys for Sex and blow jobs for money. and they have not. they say either they are married or they dont want too. Also your Mom is no Angel. She is going behind your backand talking about you to friends and also family[2]... I have to get back to work . They are calling me from the spot i'm in.

The typical mother would be taken aback by such messages, particularly that the CIA was watching members of her family and her oldest child wanted to kill her. Most mothers would find those messages to be ridiculous. Yet instead of pushing Barbara away, they drew her in. They excited her.

How this talk massaged Barbara's active imagination spoke loudly to Jenelle's knowledge of what topics interested her mother. Inheriting her fair share of her mother's estate was important to Barbara. Seeking revenge for Christie's ongoing rebuke of her parental authority—that was a goal close to Barbara's heart. Jenelle knew these things, and she exploited them.

A gullible Barbara wrote back to Chris late at night on January 1, 2011:

Hi Chris. Just wanted to know. WoW!! I never knew how much I was hated or how much I am in Danger at all! Thank you so much for all of the information hon. I am

---

1 A reference to court proceeding for Christie's request for order of protection from Barbara.
2 Chris informed Barbara about her mother's plans on dividing her estate, giving portions to persons other than Barbara.

<u>going to print this and delete it, tell Buddy about it, and</u> <u>he will take action as needed</u>[1] and wait to hear from you if you want to meet, etc. ya know... oh my! I am not really so upset as thinking, "I knew it!" My mom has turned on me since Christie moved here about last Oct. 2009 and she has always been the pick grandchild&mom never had any use for Jenelle at all, &she keeps telling me that I'm fat, need to do something w/my hair, etc. insulting me since young girl-sz9-12! I always wondered if I was her kid. Maybe not. Because she also says, "You don't look like me, but you look like your father's family!" She is mean to me at times and other times, sneaky quiet, too quiet. I am scared to go over now, not alone for sure and yes, I will be carrying. I guess my 380 is not going to be enough. I just told Buddy that I want to go target shooting again. I really need this shit. I don't. My brother is in on it? He isn't doing me right either. And I have always been the responsible, good kid, gave up my life as well as Buddy, to stay bymy mom (&dad), and when dad died, moved down here to this Godforsaken place, hole inthe wall we are so wanting to get out of but can't financially, so we're stuck right now, but oh my goodness. I came her to be near my mom and what good did it do me. None. Christie will Never go to work if she gets rid of me; she has it made and they have a plan it sounds like. I can't believe my own so called 'loving mother' is doing this also and is on it.

From that message, it appeared Barbara had bought the notion that Christie was spearheading some plan to kill her. Following Chris's initial updates on the activities at her mother's house, Barbara offered suggestions to Chris as to the best place to put a listening device in Christie's room. On January 5, 2011, in an e-mail to Chris

---

1   This was a critical insight into the Potter family dynamic. Not being a computer user, Buddy would not be able to see Chris's messages. Thus Barbara would print them, delete them from her e-mail account (which at times she might have forgotten to do so), and then show the printouts to Buddy.

that referenced the botched elopement between Jenelle and Jamie, Barbara instructed:

> About the 'piece' you're going to put in Ch's room. She sleeps in the 1st bedroom on the left w/bath across from it..big queen bed & she is on computer/phone there a lot-stays in room most of time my mom says-says she has headaches all the time.b ut gets on phone/computer. (She also sits at end of sofa or loveseat where the lamp/footstool are & plugs in computer there most of time when out in living room.)

In that message, Barbara even asked Chris if Christie was dealing methamphetamine at the fire department and whether she was using the drug. Both questions were utter nonsense.

Chris wrote back later on January 5, 2011, reporting:

> I'm 1000 yards away from your mom's house I see everything Perfect. I have also been around your mom's house and I know where the rooms are. When they have not been home. I guess you are wondering what my Job is for the CIA and also ICE over sea's that's keeping girls from Trading and also for CIA I just KILL and I Enjoy that a lot. I get to shoot all the bad guys. And with NICS well I work with some marines over sea's and do things with them and also go on walks and know what's going on there. There is a lot I'm in but they seem to want me all the time. I don't know if it b/c I'm Skinny and long or b/c I can do things faster then most . Not really sure. I'm a Sharp shooter also would tell you carry a gun with Hallow point so it would blow them away. Make sure you carry please.
>
> And you might want to make sure Buddy is with you or around. He will get a call if anything we here that they say they will kill any of you and he will not be in the dark. There are so many of us here they don't know what to do the cops LOL. We got them out today doing there job. Well this is short but I need to get hold of Mike and I few other dumb cops on some papers I found and they are fake.

Ugh got to love all the lies from these's cops.

LMAO I'm happy I'm smarter them them.

Love ya mom. Take care and write back later. Just be careful Drugs and I know Ch. has some type of gun I'm working on that. Tell you later what it is when I find out.

The reference to working with Marines was noteworthy. Christie told me that the plan Jenelle had growing up was to be a Marine like her father. Her disabilities prevented any such possibility, but the preoccupation lived on. The bul2dog@aol.com address? Christie explained that the bulldog was the mascot of the United States Marine Corps. Jenelle's Facebook page was full of cute bulldog pictures.

Christie had also mentioned to me that law enforcement officers fascinated Jenelle. If she ran into one, and they said hello, she'd act like they were good friends. One facet of Chris's e-mails to Barbara was repeated references to local police officers. For instance, the "Mike" referenced in the January 5 e-mail was Sheriff Mike Reece.

That a CIA agent specializing in the art of killing was watching her mother's house from a thousand yards away did not take Barbara aback. Instead, the idea was titillating. Before she went to bed on January 5, 2011, Barbara wrote this meandering diatribe against her family:

Hi Chris. Great to be hearing from you again. I'm glad you didn't have to go, but then again, I think you were looking forward to going - right? Someone outrank you? lol :)[1] No, I understand. You said you wanted to stay here and do the job you are doing and I thank you for what you are doing for us. Ya know? I'm scared & if you get orders to 'do it' to them, the cuz's & whoever else, including Ch., do it. enough is enough! I'm scared of her, Mike,his dad,& the cuz's&Smokey too-he emailed me mean emails on aol!& Paula, Randy's wife's girl, 51 in MD is mean & wants Bud

---

1   This statement references Chris stating that he was going to "be called out but the other guy is going to go. He told me he would take it. I really needed some sleep."

dead, then us..they all do.

I never thought I'd say that and I've asked God to forgive me, but she does not mean me any good at all....

I'll tell you-Barlow, the neighbor watches mom's house and tells us when someone is around or we are seen there... he said he is the road watch man and more than 1 of the neighbors saw Ch arson mom's out bldg. in April 3rd, but sheriff's and State Farm would not investigate, so my mom is getting lots of money for a lot of things she is not replacing - about$15-20,000 or more - it keeps coming. Ch.worked for fire co when they were having all the arsons in Downingtown, Coatesville area,& when she was gone and went back for a vist, as soon as she got there, the nest day there was a fire set again...all house were lost and some ppl died I think. It finally ended, but she knows how-she told me that much. That makes me afraid she will get our home. I am so sad that she chose this way. She knows better. I can't do anything for her now. She is killing my love; most mothers would have walked away long ago, but Christmas nite did it for me and Bud-she would not speak and went to her room. She is mean to her parents/ no respect at all for anyone in fact.&hates Jen of course.. and lies on us all. I know you've heard it all.

Later in the e-mail, Barbara expressed further fear of Christie, referencing Chris's mentioning of him killing mob members, citing how "mean" they could be while in the same breath expressing her own homicidal delusions about family members:

And getting rid of the Mob is a good thing too. I guess someone has to stop them bc they can be so mean, as you know well. I am afraid Christie will get Mike or his dad to order someone to come down & kill me,Jen,Bud or one of us anyway. She wants me dead...don't know why. It's sad. But I don't want to be/feel afraid like I do & its sttessful; it gets tiring for me. I carry my gun, but it won't save me if they are waiting for me somewhere.

Barbara signed off, asking Chris to warn her of any imminent doom and hinting that she was sharing these communications with Buddy:

> Hey, if I go over mom's Sat. to see her & work, etc., Ch may be there, so I will have my gun on..but if she has one, she will come out of her room & prob. shoot me. Please let me know what you find out if you do find out what she has & if she has the nerve to kill me. I hate to hear that. I know she would like to plant drugs on me then call the police about it. I'll watch for that. I 'm sure she has that plan.
>
> Well Son, I'll talk to you later. You hang in and I'll be watching for you to drive by me sometime or getting together or calling for Bud anyway, if not us. You will see me at mom's I am sure and around town. Gotta go for now so tired -will get some sleep. Take care, be safe. Prayers and blessings for you.. Love you always, Mom ;) & dad - Barbie and Buddy (Jenelle says "hello-hope you are ok.")
>
> (I'll try not to worry.) Bud says to tell you that he has a Son that has kept him pretty informed thanks to you, and we'll keep an eye out for drugs, etc. Thank you Chris. Good night! :)

Could Barbara really have felt the need to wear a firearm to visit her mother, lest Christie kill her? One theory I had was that Barbara's mental condition, as unhealthy as it was, surely had a deleterious and harmful effect on the people around her, mainly Buddy and Jenelle. She was the rotten apple that spoiled the rest.

Continuing through the e-mails Barbara wrote Chris, Christie's perceived misdeeds were a common theme. There were times when Barbara gleefully offered her own assistance to the CIA effort. At one point, she did her own surveillance on Christie, sneaking into Christie's bedroom and prowling around as Jenelle snapped photos. Barbara sent those photos in an e-mail to Chris on March 23, 2011.

Next came a series of embedded pictures with captions. Taken when Barbara and Jenelle had snuck around Barbara's mother's home while Christie was not present, the photos depicted important things for Chris to take note of. The first was of a computer keyboard, monitor, transparent tape dispenser, computer modem, and pen holder on a desk. Next was a photo of Christie's bed with some bags present. Then a snapshot of a multi-photo picture frame Christie had on the wall. It had pictures of her with friends as well as one of two small children—her known associates. Next was a photo of an unknown object wrapped up and positioned behind a couch or chair in front of what appeared to be a curtain-covered picture window in a living room, the caption stating:

> Not sure what is in this wrapped up/locked 'tarp' but it is in the 'front room' at mom's behind the sofa between sofa back and draperies... hidden well she thinks... (Assuming that bc her car is in shop, she is driving mom's so had to get the 'goods' out of her car & into the house temporarily???)

While the final picture was totally worthless, since it was entirely dark except for an indiscernible tiny light in the middle, the caption was illuminating, as Barbara referenced the presence of possible drug activity, using the street drug term "dime bags" to describe what she found:

> This is very hard to see (w/o flash), but this is a 'candle like' light left on at all times on the night stand next to Christie's bed. Besides it are numerous small, what I might call 'dime bags' of 'something' - don't want to say what bc don't know... It sure looked fishy and like Christie is getting very sloppy, knows mom knows and won't say anything, or that maybe mom is making money too. :(I don't know but mom is very protective of Christie's 'things' room, etc. ya know...
>
> But, I will be the one to take the pics next time Chris and I'll get the best I can.
>
> I WILL GET BACK THERE SOON FOR PICS.
>
> MOM SAID THAT A CERTAIN PARTOF HER ENGINE BROKE IN CAR AND IT WILL COST HER $400 OR MORE TO

GET IT FIXED SO HER CAR IS SITTING DOWN AT EXXON IN
TOWN FOR NOW AND SHE IS USING MOM'S CAR.
  Barbara

That last part was important. The CIA needed to know what car
Christie was driving, which wasn't her own. It was her grandmother's.

There were so many writings between Chris and Barbara that
cataloging and organizing them would have been a wasted effort,
as they had no direct relevance to the deaths of Bill and Billie Jean.
However, they did help to further reveal how twisted and demented
Barbara and Jenelle were.

But how to deal with Christie seeing any of this? Would she
be able to handle it? Somehow I could not imagine my own mother
taking surveillance photos of my bedroom and sending them to the
CIA. Or thinking she had.

I was surprised by her response. Christie took it well enough.
She prefaced it with mentioning that many years of therapy had
allowed her to better handle her mother's treatment of her, but that
picture of the unidentified item wrapped up in tarp and hidden
behind the couch?

"That was a ceramic penguin," Christie messaged back to
me. "Here's what it was," she wrote, attaching a picture of a cute
penguin figurine.

20

Charge someone with murder, and expect a stack of motions to be filed on their behalf. Defense lawyers seem to gauge their effectiveness as attorneys by how thick their motions are in the court's file.

Jamie Curd's attorneys had filed a lot. If the common national perception is that public defenders are substandard defense lawyers, those folks have not seen ours. Jeff Kelly, our elected public defender, had always been the most conscientious defense attorney I knew, always ever-consumed with his responsibilities to a client facing serious charges. His newest assistant, Melanie Sellers (who, a short time ago, was one of my coworkers as a prosecutor) was as sharp as any attorney in the area, and she had gone on a mission to prove her worth by hurling arrow after arrow at our investigation.

Being new to the case, I was riding backseat to Roark on the motions work. Curd's motions were to be heard soon. While Roark focused on that, I was immersed in constructing the road map to pulling the Potter women into the case.

Still, I attended the motions hearing. Special Judge Jon Kerry Blackwood presided, having taken the case on his limited docket when one of our sitting judges had fallen ill.

It was at this hearing that I got my first look at Jamie Curd in the flesh. He was a crumbled heap of a beaten man, sort of bent down as he sat expressionless though the hearing. He had on his prescription shaded glasses, which he'd worn during his fateful interrogation. Many defendants during hearings are very involved in their cases, taking notes, conferring with their attorneys, sometimes trying to confer to the point where they are a hindrance to the lawyer. Curd was none of these things. He looked disinterested.

In their motions to suppress, the public defenders had little to go on in getting Curd's confession tossed, but they focused on the ensuing searches. They got a win when they challenged the search of Curd's vehicle following his statement, as Judge Blackwood agreed that the warrantless search was improper. That was not a huge setback for us, as we would lose only some love letters and such from Jenelle.

Of greater concern was Sellers's motion to knock out the TBI search warrants for Curd's e-mails. When Agent Lott had written the search warrants for e-mails, he had gotten Johnson County General Sessions Judge Bliss Hawkins's signature authorizing his access to the materials. Sellers pointed out in her motion that Judge Hawkins had no authority under state law to order searches in places outside Tennessee, which was the case for AOL and Yahoo servers.

Between Roark and I, we spent hours looking for ways to get around this motion, but it was to no avail. I even contacted our state attorney general's office for guidance, and they provided nothing helpful. Obviously, this issue was going to be vital to any prosecution of Jenelle and Barbara. We had to have those e-mails, and they had to have been received pursuant to lawful authority.

Searching for another mechanism to legally obtain the e-mails, Agent Lott made contact with the proper people at the home offices of AOL and Yahoo, who put him in touch with the local law enforcement officers, who commonly issued search warrants signed by judges local to the Internet companies. That way, the search warrants were being signed by judges with the lawful authority to order the materials to be produced. After a great deal of coordination, Agent Lott was able to reacquire the same e-mail data. This time, though, the defense attorneys could not cry foul over the judges' jurisdictions.[1]

---

1   After the Potter-Curd case ended, we discovered the U.S. Code provision empowering state judges to order search warrants of electronic data held in other states. Generally, state prosecutors like us don't know federal law much at all, as this story attests.

Yet for all their motions and finely tuned arguments, the public defenders had accomplished little toward improving Curd's case. His simple acknowledgement of being present during the killings, as well as his written communications with Chris and Barbara, were going to be more than enough for a jury to convict him. Particularly when that jury heard about Billie Jean dying with Tyler in her arms.

Curd wasn't getting out of culpability. His only shot at the system showing him mercy was for him to stop fighting and come clean. He needed to cooperate and aid us against the Potters. Our pursuit of Jenelle and Barbara was a sworn secret at this point, but I again tried to feel out Kelly and his other assistant, David Crichton. Although they acted like their opinion was that Jenelle was responsible for these killings, they had little confidence that Jamie would turn on her. He loved her still, they thought. His cooperation wasn't going to happen.

Buddy Potter had his motions as well. He had retained the leading criminal defense attorney in Johnson County, Randy Fallin, an older attorney who had practiced for many years in Florida. Fallin was an adept trial attorney, and had enlisted the aid of the younger but bright David Robbins to assist him with the case. Their stack of motions was much lighter than the stack Curd's lawyers had filed. Their main motion was to suppress Buddy's statement to Agents Lott and Hannon, wherein Buddy had admitted his guilt.

The thrust of the motion was that because of his medical conditions, the prolonged nature of the interrogation, and the late hour of night at which it took place, Buddy's statement was not the product of his free will. In other words, without his medicines, without his oxygen, and without rest, he was not in his right mind, and his interrogators had overborne his will to the point where his confession was coerced.

At the hearing, Judge Blackwood first heard Agent Lott testify about the interview, and the circumstances behind them arresting Buddy late at night following Curd's confession. Roark then played the video recording of Buddy's interview, which lasted for nearly three hours before his eventual call to Barbara and Jenelle.

Roark then closed our proof.

Defense attorneys are never required to call witnesses, either at trial or at motions hearings, and if they do intend to call one, in Tennessee they are not obligated to tell the prosecuting team the identity of their prospective witnesses. Sometimes, in a motion to suppress a confession, the defense attorney will call his or her client to the stand for the limited purpose of testifying as to the defendant's state of mind or circumstances around the statement. Whether Fallin and Robbins intended to call anyone at this hearing, we had no idea.

I noticed Barbara in the audience before the hearing started, her blond hair being fixed just right, dressed like she was going to church. She sat quietly during Agent Lott's testimony, and she listened intently to Buddy's statement as it was played. To my disappointment, Jenelle was absent. I had hoped to get a look at her mannerisms in person, as opposed to making assumptions based on her many selfies with stuffed animals.

When Robbins stood to call their first witness, my breath was taken away when he said, "Barbara Potter." Not only was I going to get a read on her mannerisms, but we were also going to get a full dose of her speech, reactions, and what might make her squirm while in the witness chair. Assuming we could make her squirm.

My pulse quickened at the opportunity to cross-examine a woman for whom I was seeking a murder indictment. This was a rare chance for me to play investigator. However, I knew I was woefully unprepared. I had not seen this coming. I was merely prepared to take a back seat as Roark performed the bulk of the work. Whatever I'd be doing in cross-examination, I would be winging it.

A mere twenty feet away from me, Barbara sat in the witness chair. Robbins went through his questioning of her, eliciting background information at first.

Barbara testified that she and Buddy had been married for forty-two years. She related that Buddy had sustained life-altering injuries in the 1970s from a work-related fall. He broke his back and suffered a concussion. Since then, he had undergone spinal surgery and developed chronic levels of pain.

It was clear that Buddy's defense was using Barbara to establish Buddy's poor medical condition. Barbara was cast perfectly in her role, being a person prone to exaggeration.

She told the Judge of Buddy having a wheelchair. How wherever he went, he carried a bag of medicine and oxygen. How every day he used his oxygen machine for sixteen hours.

"He's weak and not the man I married," she said.

Barbara stated that Buddy was never off his oxygen for eight straight hours, which was going to be the thrust of their argument that he was not in his right mind. She had seen him when his oxygen saturation was low. At such times, his eyes would roll to the back of his head in the middle of a conversation, and Barbara would have to tell him to put his oxygen mask on.

He was so weak, Barbara said, that he would fall easily because his legs were low on oxygen. His speech would slow, and he might stop talking altogether.

"The longest period I've ever seen him without oxygen was about four hours," she testified. "And he'd needed it. His symptoms were coming."

In the last couple of years, Barbara said her caretaking function for Buddy had increased to the point where she had to help him shower and get dressed. She medicated him and rubbed medicine on his legs.

Buddy had a long list of medications, she said, for pain, diabetes, and thyroid issues. Doctors had prescribed him long-acting morphine to be taken three times a day. 200 milligram doses. He had Valium for muscle spasms.

"He suffered even when he took them," she said.

The defense moved on to when Agent Lott first visited them. She noted that Buddy was not using his oxygen then, but she said the machine was very visible to the investigators during the conversation. I presumed the defense would argue that the investigators should have been aware that he was a man who needed supplemental oxygen.

On the morning of his arrest, Barbara said she awoke during the night and Buddy was up. He had the oxygen on at the time. She said she answered the door when the officers arrived to arrest Buddy. She said his oxygen was not on at that time.

Regarding Buddy's experience in talking to the police, Barbara said he had been an "alternate deputy" in Pennsylvania. She added that he had made police reports regarding people vandalizing their property, and that he had been interviewed by the FBI regarding his military medal controversy.

With a few questions regarding his visits to the Veteran's Administration Medical Center in Johnson City during the week leading up to his arrest, Robbins finished his questioning.

It was time for me to take the lectern.

21

For my parents' generation, the ideal of a great courtroom lawyer was Perry Mason. Every episode, he got down to the truth with his sharp questioning. And it never took more than an hour. Later, Matlock was the man to be admired, a folksy country lawyer with a similar ability to extract the truth. And for my generation, Tom Cruise grilling Jack Nicholson in *A Few Good Men* was a moment of titillating euphoria, as Jack popped his fuse and said exactly what his cross-examiner was seeking.

While I possess enough self-confidence to jump at the chance to question those I am pitted against, I am none of the above. No lawyer is. There are no carefully crafted scripts to follow in the courtroom, and in the real world, not every cross-examination reaps tremendous rewards.

Most of the time we are happy just to score a few points for our side. Totally destroying a witness is rare. So my aim wasn't to get her to confess to aiding in killings. I simply hoped to score points.

My goal as I approached the podium was to get Barbara to acknowledge engaging in correspondence with Chris. After all, that was why we were paying thousands of dollars to Dr. Leonard, to prove she was writing to Chris and that Chris was Jenelle. Getting her to admit her part in that, well, that would be quite the coup. It would almost make Dr. Leonard's analysis of Barbara's writing completely unnecessary.

There was one problem with my goal. A big one. The issue of "Chris" was not relevant to the motion we were hearing. I certainly wasn't going to be able to go line-by-line through her e-mails, asking her, "What did you mean when you told Chris you needed peace from these people, or when you told Jamie that you are were set to go to the 'movies?'" I was limited to questioning her only about Buddy's statement to Agents Lott and Hannon, and whether that statement was admissible. Barbara had taken the stand to establish Buddy's health issues as they related to his ability to knowingly waive his right to silence, understand his right to an attorney, and know what he was saying when he spoke to the officers. The issue of Chris did not seem relevant at all to these issues, and between the two lawyers at Buddy's table, they were sure to cry their objections the second I went in that direction.

So I had to coyly set it up. Somehow. Yet as I pondered my first question, I had no clue how to get there.

I knew one thing from experience. If I hoped to get her to make that ultimate admission, I had to make her feel comfortable talking to me. I couldn't appear to be a bloodthirsty prosecutor. I couldn't be her enemy. No, experience had taught me long ago that people's lips get the loosest when they are comfortable. And I could not give her the impression that I was aiming for her to sit with Buddy as his codefendant.

Not knowing where to start, I began by getting more information about Buddy's mobility. I knew from our witness statements and the officers' observations that Buddy was more mobile and functioned better than Barbara had just described. She had made him sound like he was just this side of being admitted into a nursing home. I knew that was an exaggeration. If his lack of mobility was a stretch on her part, then so was her claim that Buddy always needed oxygen.

I asked her about the times when Buddy went to see his doctors. Would she take him, or did he sometimes go alone? She admitted that sometimes Buddy did go alone, but said he could not walk unaided.

"He had a walker with two wheels on it that the VA gave him, that held his oxygen tank and his bag of medications and papers, whatever he had to take," Barbara said. "They issued that because he was too weak to walk in the parking lot. He always had the walker. He always used the walker."

We had witness statements talking of Buddy being out in the public, walking under his own power. No wheelchair. No walker, I presumed. So I went in that direction, hoping she would concede that he did not always use the walker.

"What about when he would go to the store with you?" I asked.

"He always had the walker with him," Barbara responded. "He didn't always use it. Sometimes. Not every time did he stay in the store very long. He'd get what we needed, come out." Or he would sit in the power chair provided by the store.

I asked, "If we would bring a witness in who said they saw him out in a store somewhere without a walker, that would be true?"

"That could be true," she admitted. "That has happened at times."

"He's been incarcerated since the time of this interview, correct?" I asked.

"Yes."

"Has he had access to his oxygen machine in jail?"

"No. I've asked and asked— "

"And today did you see him walk over to the table? Did he have a walker with him or anything?" I asked this because Buddy had walked in the courtroom without incident, ankle bracelets and all. Surely she noticed.

"No."

"Did you notice the ankle—I don't know what you call them— chains around his ankles?"

"I've noticed how he walks. I don't see him as a man who walks well with or without chains," she answered.

"Have you witnessed him fall down because he doesn't have a walker?"

"Yes."

"Where?"

"In the house. Out in the yard."

"I'm just asking about since his incarceration. Have you been able to visit him?"

"Yes."

"This isn't the first time you've come to court when he's come to court, right?"

"No."

"When you've witnessed him walk with the chains around his ankles and without a walker into the courtroom, has he fallen down?"

"No."

"And have you talked to him on the phone?" I asked. I knew she had. Often.

"Yes."

"Has he ever complained of falling while he's been in the jail?"

"He hasn't complained of falling, but of tripping because he's so weak."

Not only had the defense elicited information from Barbara about Buddy's need for oxygen, they had also touched on his fatigue from being questioned extensively during the early morning hours. I knew from the Potter interview, conducted in their living room the day after the murders, that Buddy had admitted in Barbara's presence to staying up late most nights watching for anything unusual from their harassers.

I wanted her to admit that.

"When you said your husband had strange sleeping habits in the months leading up to his interrogation—"

"I don't remember using the word strange," she said, cutting me off. "But, you know, different."

"Well, staying up all night and taking cat naps in the afternoons is unusual, right?"

"Right. Very."

"Would you characterize that based on what he would tell you, that he just couldn't sleep at night, or did he have a reason to stay up at night?"

"In past years, lots of times he didn't come to bed because he couldn't sleep," she said. "He was hurting so bad. He would walk and sit and walk. We moved down here, it was like that, then we started having vandalism around the house. Like, they broke the garage door. They broke our John Deere tractor. Umm, throwing rocks and bricks at the house. And trying to put sugar in the gas tanks. So he started sitting up."

Completing her sentence, I asked, "On watch?"

"Pretty much on watch," she replied.

"Watching for problems?"

"Mm-hm. And I was up. I never sleep all night. I'm up and down every night. I'd hear something, and he'd look out."

That was easy enough. I got her to admit to their paranoia without the slightest bit of pressing. She was comfortable. Her lips were loose. A plan materialized as to how I could get to Chris, but I needed to be patient, like a fisherman waiting for the hook to set just right before jerking on the reel for fear that the fish would squirm away prematurely.

"In the months leading up to your husband's arrest, would you characterize it that you were both worried about things that might happen at night around your house?"

"Yes."

"And was that a constant worry for you all?"

"A concern. A deep concern."

"But every day you were concerned about that?"

"Yes. I still am."

"To the point where it affected your sleep and your husband's sleep?"

"It didn't affect my sleep because I'm up anyway. But I am on watch."

"And your husband was aware that you were on watch and concerned about things happening at the house?"

"Sure."

"To the point where he would stay up at night watching?"

"He decided that. I didn't."

I changed the subject to that phone call Buddy made to her following his interrogation. The one where she and Jenelle had suggested he had a valid alibi when he knew he didn't.

"During his interrogation, you had the opportunity to talk to your husband on the phone?" I asked.

"Yes."

"Do you remember what he said to you?"

"Not exactly every word. He sounded tired."

Then she flubbed up before correcting herself as to what she had told Buddy.

"I just said, not, not innocent—I mean, not guilty. You're being accused of something you didn't do. He said something about Jamie saying something about him being involved. I said, 'Have you asked for a lawyer? Wake up.' I could tell he was not awake enough to know what he was saying. That was not my husband. All I remember was he said Jamie said I was involved. I said, 'Get a lawyer. Don't say anything else.'"

"Did he tell you that he was going to admit he was guilty of the crime?" I asked, knowing he had.

"The only thing I remember is he was pushed into saying, 'I was involved.' I said, 'Wake up, you were not. You were home.'"

Certain that she had never said these words on the recording, I asked, "You told him to wake up?"

"Yeah. Something to that effect, like, 'Come on Buddy,'" Barbara said as she slid away from perjury. "I was trying to snap him out of it. I know he was completely worn out."

It was time to set up the ultimate question. Back to Buddy's mobility. I started questioning again his ability to walk under his own power, without aid.

"Anybody who has seen him out has not seen him without a cane," she stressed. "For years."

"Tell us your husband's work history."

"He went into the service at eighteen. Four years in the Marines. He went to Vietnam. The longest we were apart was thirty-nine months."

"What did he do once he got out of the service?"

"He looked for a job. He took a job welding pipe."

"Then he had his accident?"

"Yes. He fell seventy-five feet off a building."

That injury led to him collecting worker's compensation and

social security disability.

She was leaving out his long years of supposed CIA service. So, I pressed her.

"Has he ever worked in any form of law enforcement?"

"With the sheriff's department in West Chester, Pennsylvania. He was an alternate. They'd call him in along with other guys who weren't active when they needed extra help for drug busts, deadbeat dads, that kind of thing. It was not often. I usually was working."

"So you didn't go out with him on what he did, right?"

"No," she said, laughing.

The West Chester Sheriff's Department was not what I was after, but I sensed her lips were still too loose for her own good.

"How long did he do that in Pennsylvania?"

"I'm going to estimate five years. I could be wrong. Because we just never talked about it or his other work for the government. That was not discussed."

Bingo.

"What other work for the government did he do?"

Barbara's eyes darted back and forth, perhaps realizing that she had said too much, opening the door to something that was unmentionable. She looked on the verge of being panicked.

After a painfully long pause, she muttered, "CIA."

"What were the years for that?"

"He joined when he was in the service, about 1971. And— it's not something I'm supposed to talk about. Never have. It's, it's government—"

"When did that end?"

"It never ended," she replied, her eyes still darting around like she was fearful about disclosing such a closely held secret. "He actually hasn't gone out for any missions since we've lived here."

It was time to close in on my target.

"Have you suggested to anyone while you lived in Tennessee that Buddy was available to go on CIA missions?" I asked.

"Objection to relevance," Robbins pleaded. Too late.

"Well, we're talking about his physical conditions and this is a question as to what she said," I countered.

Perhaps curious at this point, Judge Blackwood jumped in with me.

"Have you ever said that, ma'am?" the judge asked Barbara.

"I think I've talked with one guy that asked me, and I said he's available," Barbara said, doing as much verbal squirming as a witness possibly could. "I just didn't know if he would go through, because they knew about his health."

With my volume building with each word, I asked, "You acknowledge, though, that in the year 2011 that you told someone named Chris, who purported to be a CIA agent, that your husband was available to go on jobs with him? That's a true statement."

"If I said it, I said it."

"Is that a true statement?"

"I guess it was. Yes."

"You said that in e-mails?"

"I probably did. I didn't speak to a Chris."

"Not probably. Did you? Yes or no?"

Meekly, and in a very dejected manner, Barbara emitted a barely audible, "Yes."

I was done. Mission accomplished. We had Barbara well on her way to being convicted of two counts of first degree murder. She could try distancing herself from her conspiratorial e-mails all she wanted at trial, but she couldn't cherry pick which e-mails she'd written and which she hadn't. Not now. No jury would believe her. I had a mountain of e-mails where she insinuated that Buddy and Chris could get together on an official CIA mission and put an end to Billie Jean, Lindsey, and whoever else threatened the Potters' peace and tranquility.

And undoubtedly, Barbara Potter wrote them.

22

The old saying goes, "A grand jury would indict a ham sandwich." That's not always true. But it's mostly true. Generalities aside, how a grand jury might look at the prospect of charging Barbara and Jenelle with murder when they weren't at the crime scene, I had no idea.

Each of our counties has a grand jury once every two months, so when we had our preliminary report from Dr. Leonard, we had to wait for the next one to roll around in order to do a presentment, which is the mechanism by which Tennessee grand juries can institute charges themselves. We did not want to issue arrest warrants, which would be a quicker way to get Barbara and Jenelle in cuffs, because (1) we wanted to avoid a preliminary hearing, where defense attorneys would get a free chance to nail down testimony in hopes of finding inconsistencies later, and (2) we genuinely wanted common people, not a judge and court clerk, to make the determination of probable cause. After all, if we could not survive the grand jury's standard that these women were criminally responsible for the killings, there was little use in pursuing the issue once the higher standard of guilty beyond a reasonable doubt set in.

Normally, in our district, the prosecuting attorney does not enter the grand jury room. We typically let the charging officer present his testimony, and we are available if the grand jury has questions about the law. Other districts do it differently.

For this case, though, Agent Lott would have to leap hurdles of the legal definition variety, so I intended to be in that room.

We waited until near the end of the grand jury's normal proceedings, then we went in.

The foreman swore in Agent Lott, who began summarizing the case to the twelve grand jurors. We did have the advantage of these jurors being Johnson County citizens, so most of them were familiar with the deaths of Bill and Billie Jean. When baby Tyler's name was mentioned, I saw some painfully sympathetic looks from some of the female grand jurors.

Agent Lott told of the e-mails between Barbara, Jenelle, and Jamie, and he attempted to simplify our theory that Jenelle was posing as Chris the CIA agent and manipulating all persons concerned.

It would not be the first time I saw confused looks from jurors in this case.

I began to interject, adding what Tennessee law provided for when a person is criminally responsible for another's criminal conduct, and Agent Lott seized on that. He explained that with these e-mails, we had proof that the women had in effect persuaded the men to engage in murder.

The grand jury foreman had more questions than anyone, and he seemed stuck on the issue of criminal responsibility. I was not familiar with this foreman, since I had done little work in Johnson County, but usually they are chosen by our Criminal Court Judges and are upstanding members of the community. I was confident he was of such a type. I could only guess as to whether he was genuinely confused, or merely attempting to facilitate his grand jurors' understanding our theory. I hoped beyond hope his aim was the latter—losing with the foreman always results in failure.

I exhausted every possible explanation I could muster concerning criminal responsibility. Meanwhile, Agent Lott poured as much information into the pot as he could.

Almost always, our officers take only a few minutes to present a case to a grand jury. However, when Agent Lott and I exited the grand jury room, we looked at the clock and saw that we had been in there for a full hour. It hadn't seemed that long. Roark and Chief Deputy Woodard asked us how it went, and we both were so frazzled by all the questions and confused looks that we honestly could not answer their query.

We milled around the judge's chambers, where Criminal Court Judge Stacy Street was waiting for any presentment that might result from the deliberations. We had asked him to be available to set the bond immediately, so that the arrests would be expedited.

First, though, we needed a favorable outcome from the grand jury. I paced and paced as the minutes passed, worried that I'd bit off more than I could chew with this case. After all, it was only our side talking in that room. No defense attorneys were there to counter our theories or present their own proof. Yet the vibe I'd gotten from the grand jurors was not that of, "Hurry up and give me that paper to sign so they go to jail." With every minute that passed, my concerns grew.

Eventually, a bailiff walked into the room with papers. He handed them to Judge Street. Meanwhile, I was cranking my neck and upper body in every direction I could to see if he had a Potter paper with twelve signatures at the bottom, which was what we needed.

I couldn't see if we had a presentment or a document destined for the trashcan.

Finally, Judge Street bent over with his pen to write on what he'd been handed, and I could see.

We had it.

He wrote a high bond for each new defendant—Barbara and Jenelle—for two counts of first degree murder and two counts of conspiracy to commit first degree murder.

We had also succeeded in getting Jamie reindicted, so that he would have charges of conspiracy to commit first degree murder, which would hopefully allow us to bring Jamie into the trial against Barbara and Jenelle. Buddy would have to be tried by himself, since we would lose Jamie's confession in a joint trial of the men since he implicated Buddy. For constitutional reasons, we would not be allowed to play Jamie's videotaped statement if Buddy was being tried with him. The accused has the right to confront their accusers and cross-examine them. Buddy's lawyer couldn't cross-examine Jamie's videotape, and if Jamie exercised his right against self-incrimination and declined to take the stand in his trial, then Buddy's lawyer could not cross examine this accuser at all. Therefore, in a joint trial of Buddy and Jamie, we could only proceed by not showing Jamie's video.

Obviously we didn't want to lose Jamie's statement, and we wouldn't if he was tried with the women, since he had in no way pointed a finger at them.

For now, the issue of the moment was arresting the women. And they weren't at home.

Back at the Johnson County Sheriff's Department, Woodard showed off a camera they had installed near the Potter house, which showed in real time what was going on at their home. Interestingly, they had a reason for this, since Barbara had been making constant complaints of people trashing her yard and attempting to vandalize their property. Thus he had installed the camera to obtain proof, if it was happening at all.

For now, the camera was useful to in that it showed us that Barbara's vehicle was not in the driveway. The women were gone. Where to, we did not know.

Fortunately, no one successfully hides in a small community where officers have their ears to the ground. It took a mere several minutes before Woodard got information that Jenelle was likely hospitalized. He checked his sources here and there, and confirmed that Jenelle had been admitted to Johnston Memorial Hospital in nearby Abingdon, Virginia. Barbara was undoubtedly with her.

Woodard contacted the sheriff's department there, gathered up our certified presentments, and went with us to find the women.

In all of my years as a prosecutor, I had witnessed exactly zero arrests other than what might happen as a normal routine inside the courtroom. Handcuffs aren't a part of my tool kit. But there was something about these women that made Roark and I want to see the moment. I wanted to see the shock on Barbara's face when her confidence that she would get away with murder vanished. I wanted to see Jenelle's expression when she realized that we knew what she had done. So we went with Agent Lott, Woodard, and Johnson County Investigator Bit Brown to find them.

While we traveled, I drafted a press release about the

presentments and began queuing it up to send to the local television stations and newspapers. When we confirmed the women's presence at the hospital, I let the television stations know about the looming arrests, and as we pulled up to the hospital, the cameras were already being set up to film the newly accused.

We stopped outside the doors, and Agent Lott entered the building to join the local sheriff's department in leading Barbara Potter out the door.

In her street clothes, Barbara was rushed toward the outside door with her hands cuffed. Ironically, as she got to the door, who should be present but Christie, her wayward daughter, who was on duty for the local EMS.

As she passed Christie, Agent Lott later told us that Barbara muttered something in her direction, effectively attributing this new development to her.

It should have surprised me not in the least that at this dire moment of her life, Barbara would choose to exclusively blame Christie for her predicament. I feared whatever harmful effect this might have on Christie. We had no idea she would be present at the hospital and get caught up in the arrest of her mother.

They walked Barbara quickly past Roark and myself and stuffed her into the back of the local cruiser. Barbara's face was devoid of expression. Jenelle's arrest was less eventful, her being in a hospital bed.

Since they were being arrested in Virginia, the women were at this point in the custody of the sheriff's department there. Later, they would be brought before a Virginia judge and asked if they wanted to waive extradition.

For now, we were a very relieved prosecution team and sought out a celebratory meal of sorts. We settled for fried fish at the Harbor House Restaurant in Abingdon. Agent Lott was getting congratulatory messages from his fellow TBI agents. He was happy enough to buy dinner for all of us.

Meanwhile, my mind was moving on to new worries. We had massive mountains yet to climb.

23

A few weeks later, Barbara and Jenelle appeared in Johnson County Criminal Court, having waived extradition. Buddy and Jamie were there as well, the four of them finally reunited.

I filed my motion to join Curd's case with that of the women, and Judge Blackwood granted it. Hopefully that would allow us to endure only two trials, not three or four. Meanwhile, the public defender's office determined they would have a conflict of interest if Jenelle was a charged defendant. Their office had represented her in Sessions Court over the harassment charge filed by Lindsey, so they were likely privy to too many confidential communications with her to stay in the case for Curd.

The public defender having dropped out, Judge Blackwood decided that two young attorneys, Casey Sears and Cameron Hyder, would be appointed in the case. Sears for Curd. Hyder for Jenelle.

Barbara would be represented by Randy Fallin, the same attorney retained to help Buddy. She waived any conflict of interest he might have in representing both.

I was not surprised that Buddy and Barbara would go down as a team. The chances of any one of them ratting out the others was between slim and none. Barbara and Jenelle had quickly asserted their Fifth Amendment rights to Agent Lott upon their arrest, having learned from Buddy and Jamie that sometimes telling one's story does not work out so well.

They weren't talking. Neither was Curd, who was again expressionless in the courtroom as he sat in the presence of the love of his life, Jenelle, albeit each of them in shackles. And the chances of getting Curd to turn on the others had probably diminished, as

I had much less of a relationship with his new attorney than I did with the public defender's office. This would be Sears's first murder case, and from my perspective, he had his hands full in convincing Curd of anything.

Everyone agreed to the merits of moving the trials to Washington County due to the likelihood of not getting a fair trial in Johnson County. Much to my surprise, there was no criticism at all about sending the case out of Johnson County. Even the victims' families believed it was best, since fewer grounds for appeal better ensured a lasting verdict.

With the trials set to take place in Washington County, Judge Blackwood went ahead and scheduled Buddy's case for trial. He was not the type of judge who let cases be delayed too long.

For me, getting ready for Buddy's trial was going to be an enormous chore. For all the work I put into the case, my focus all along had been in assembling a case against the female Potters. Constructing a strategy or approach to the men's cases had not been my concern.

Now it was.

24

In most places, a man's home may be his castle, but in the South, his truck is his life. As auto manufacturers made trucks more expensive and fancier, trucks became fashion statements in the South. Men needed their trucks, and they needed them big and bold. And should they not be able to afford the newest and best trucks, older ones did fine as well.

Buddy Potter was no different. He had a black, extended-cab Ford F-250 with bucket leather seats. It was decked out with a Rhino Linings bed liner, a bed cover, and stickers from the NRA, Buckmasters, and Marines. He didn't need a truck to farm, to haul materials for work, to pull a boat, or lug a camper, but those things mattered not—he was a man in East Tennessee, and men needed nice trucks.

When it came to prosecuting Buddy Potter for murder, his truck held some valuable stories.

In the American criminal justice system, having someone's confession is not enough to convict them. It was long ago decided by the United States Supreme Court that corroboration of that confession was a constitutionally required predicate to obtaining a conviction. So we needed something to stick with Buddy's eventual moment of sincerity with Agents Lott and Hannon.

The truck held the evidence to give us that corroboration. The TBI search warrant had uncovered a collection of ammunition that would constitute good proof, as it matched certain characteristics of the bullets that killed Bill and Billie Jean. But also there was the trash.

When agents opened the tailgate of the F-250, they found three garbage bags full of shredded papers. Special Agent Miranda

Gaddis at TBI headquarters in Nashville drew one of the worst and most mind-numbing missions imaginable: trying to piece those shreds together. Not knowing if the papers would be relevant to a murder case, she spent a month pulling narrow strips of paper out of the bags and trying to match each up to the others. She taped them onto a sheet of paper once she got enough matches.

It was tedious work, and in fact the TBI never finished piecing together every shred from the three bags. Yet they had assembled many writings, some of which were incomplete, with holes or cuts that eliminated whole portions of text.

However, from what limited portions we could see, these shredded documents looked awfully familiar.

E-mails from bmp9110@aol.com and bul2dog@aol.com populated many of the documents, as well as Facebook messages from Jenelle's account. The documents appeared to have been correspondence between Barbara and Chris. Most of these documents were never uncovered with the search warrant to AOL, likely because the messages had been deleted after being printed. Barbara made many references to her practice of printing and deleting her communications with Chris, so there were unknown amounts of writings that we could not obtain from the e-mail provider.

Unfortunately for the Potters, they had dallied too long in taking their trash to the dump. We had a recorded phone conversation between Barbara and Buddy after his arrest where Buddy made a vague reference to him having intended to take the stuff in the back of the truck to the dump, Barbara adding the word "shred" to the exchange. So he arguably knew she had shredded documents that needed to be discarded.

These shredded documents covered subject matter similar to the e-mails from AOL—talk of Buddy needing a CIA ID, Chris saying the ID was forthcoming, and talk of what should happen to Lindsey, Billie Jean, and Bill.

Since we had no indication that Buddy had ever used a computer in his life, much less written an e-mail, it was unclear if the writings would be admissible against Buddy. They weren't his statements. The rule of hearsay allows the prosecution to enter the statements of the party-opponent, which for this first trial would have been Buddy, but hearsay is a direct bar to any statement of their codefendants in a severed trial. The justice system values cross-examination, and the hearsay rule protects that tool. And here, Buddy's attorney could not cross-examine Barbara, Jenelle, and Jamie's emails.

However, it was critically important to paint the picture of the ongoing, building hate that had emanated from the Potter household. Once Buddy's jury saw the level of evil laced in these words, they would have little problem convicting Buddy once they heard him say, "I did it."

How could I get those e-mails into Buddy's trial? There was a way.

One method of getting around the hearsay rule was that of conspiratorial statements. Our district had a history of rarely prosecuting conspiracies, so using this tool was new—for me. When a group of people conspires to commit a crime, a statement from any of them is admissible against the rest of the conspirators as long as the statement was made in furtherance of the conspiracy.

I briefed the subject with case law to aid Judge Blackwood in making a pretrial determination of admissibility for the shredded documents. And to my satisfaction, he made a ruling before the trial that it was proper to use the documents, although with sizable portions redacted, since many references were not in furtherance of the conspiracy.

We were left with enough writings, though, to make our point. The jurors would see the fire that burned in Barbara and Jenelle.'s minds. One benefit to introducing these shredded documents would be that I could ask Buddy's jurors after the trial about their opinions of the women. In Buddy's trial, we would not get into the issue of who wrote what—that was unnecessary—but I figured the jury would have a good idea.

The contents of the writings were ripe with Barbara and Jenelle's ongoing fantasies.

One of Chris's rants, dated April 3, 2011, was pieced together in its entirety. Chris spoke of his intelligence gathering on the Potter enemies and his fear that Jenelle might hurt herself. He said that Billie Jean, Lindsey, and Tara had all been to the Potters' house the previous night. He ended by saying that he was mad and would kill someone, but that for now he had a broken arm and was crying. Due to the broken arm, he was typing with one hand, but "at least i know how to use a gun and fight. lol."

The shreds featured many references to Buddy getting his CIA ID as well as the Potters' collective belief that the CIA was watching over them. On March 12, 2011, from Barbara (the ellipses denote gaps in the messages, either due to them being incomplete, or edited out by Judge Blackwood):

> We saw the 4 wheelers the other night out back and Bud & I kind of considered them to be you and someone else, but we weren't sure... please feel free whenever you want to drive 4 wheelers on our side/behind our house... if we see you again, unless during day, we will turn on the outside back lights... so glad that you are watching out for us... And thanks for watching our home so well when we are gone or its dark. We just don't know what to expect anymore. So glad that Bud's ID is coming... He certainly needs it.

Barbara wrote this on April 6, 2011:

> [H]e let her know that Lindsay was down here,bragging at how she, Tara, Billie were going to 'get Jenelle' & are planning to come back 2nite- going all over town rounding up help to return tonight w/Tara & Billie to finish the job on the truck, Jenelle, whatever... Buddy is in "Vietnam Jungle Recon Mode" & they don't want to mess w/that... before he got back home, Chris Campbell took Jenelle off his facebook! Some friend huh?

There were several messages from Chris, giving instructions on measures the Potters should take. From April 22, 2011:

> Yes I'm sure it's getting to Jenelle... she is going to die here

I feel with all this crap... Well if he needs to do anything Buddy get Bill first B/c he's really mean and a ass hole. Damn fucker.

And several updates from Chris, this one from April 3, 2011:

I would love to meet Buddy... I'm really trying to find my best to where Lindsay really lives doe or Butler. she's at Bill's all the time. I think se moved in or something. I never see her but her going there or in town or Boone or Johnson City. Damn Whore.

From Chris on April 21, 2011:

And you wait I will get what need done. Lindsay better know God that's all I will say. But My guy is on her tail a lot. Yes they were driving by your house yesterday and I know they were going after Lindsay they stopped her on 421 going down Bill's when she got a ticket. She drives to fast and also a light was broken on her car... will get what's coming to her and so will Billie... they guys do drive by your house and on to them so no worries. I think they all need a life but that's if I let them live it and like I said they don't know God— then they will go back to where they came from HELL. I will put them there... yes I will be getting together with Buddy at some point when I'm all the way back together.

An update from Chris in early May, 2011:

[Lindsey] will back off fast and stop things. But that's if I let her live. I choose that for her boyfriend and Bill and Billie and that damn baby. I will see when I want to kill them... then I'm getting some of the cops. no one would ever miss them... I'm going up to bulldog rd now and I'm also going to run into whore pan slut face ugly as a mudd face bitch and her fucker of a BF. I'm getting on where they are going and what they do and getting a lot of sence about what they do daily. So I have been on them but also Christie still and a few others... they are calling from Bills go to a pay phone and say something. They are playing games.

From Chris on an unknown date, reporting on his surveillance of Bill's house:

> Yes Bill and Billie and stay at the house tonight Linsday is down there and we see everything. But they are holding back to do something I think real bad to your house or something. I hope this planeworks out and if it don't work for me - get jamie to call her cell phone.

More surveillance from Chris on May 5, 2011:

> [B]ut Bill's cell is the one they are using too and its bad they are being hateful fuckers tonight. I will get them mom and I'm sure buddy too. Well, they, I hope, will back off but nothing scares this girl so I guess I just need to kill and shoot her 4 times in the fucking head and a few other times, and then she will be gone. Your Mom is fucking crazy and Christie and Bill and Billie and Lindsay and her damn fucking bf and the fucking so called cops. I can't wait to shoot them... Let Buddy do his thing that's the best anything. Jenelle don't need the upset—they would just make her really upset tonight. Its so sad.

From Chris in May:

> KILL KILL KILL and dont worry about them... Buddys ID they need to give him that shit b/c he could use it right now and do what i'm doing and then he could work with us you know.

On an unknown date, Barbara suggested to Chris that Buddy could further his training:

> [M]eet with him - he wants to meet... he will straighten your mind out about what is CIA work & recon, black ops, etc.— very experienced in all things you are doing and have not done yet... so, he is willing and ready to help you, work with you (with ID would really be a great help too) and go at it with you - and he wants to back you and teach

you more than you already know. Go for it! He is good at what he does. I mean it, he is, and he is tired of all the bullshit. he would be a good teacher for you and friend/ father person you can talk to - just between you two... yes, the cemetery is near JD's... Bud thought of that place bc you 2 can pull over and talk in peace w/o being watched.

In classic catfishing fashion, Chris wrote approvingly of receiving Buddy's training, and that he looked forward to seeing him:

I got everything Linsday said and Billsaid too and i got all wha ti needed there. She is awful and she better know God. If not she will see hell. i'm going to kill her and Bill then Billie for sure. then cops... I'm so pissed that I will get her car agian and i will do something much wrose. Let them play their games she dont know who the law it. and Buddy is CIA dumb ass girl dont know he's on the computer but the cops do... Well buddy can kill thembefore they will so no worries there. dumb bitch ho. she needs her butt kicked good and left. and maybe run over and a bullet in her head. then she would be a dead pan whore face bitch. LOL Karma it will come back on her. I hate everyone one of them. LOL. Yes iknow Buddy can teachme alot when i'm good again i will come up and see himand you guys too. I'm happy Jenelle is happy.

Predating Barbara's long e-mail of April 12, 2011, where Barbara wrote approvingly of Chris tampering with the girls' cars, Chris had written this on April 1:

I'm very upset but yes I got Lindsay today? She got hurt a little bit but her car will not ready for a while. I wanted to kill her but it didn't happen. I will do what I need to do.

Chris referenced Jamie on November 14, 2011:

Jenelle does not need this and Bill and them are really trying to kill her. He's been bugging Jamie a lot as well. He's pissed b/c Jamie is a good guy on your all's said and he don't like that.

There was a useful message from Barbara to Chris where she instructed him on how to sign off on his messages, and she explained how Jenelle shared her Facebook account with her so that she could see what Chris was writing. But perhaps most importantly, Barbara told of Bill having a binder of writings that he (correctly) had alleged were written by Jenelle:

> From now on please when you write on Jenelle's FB—on Wall or in e-mail to any of us or others/whoever, just sign it, 'your brother,' 'son', anything that makes it clear you are writing not Jenelle, an 'adopted' relative of ours... Bill is going nuts, has texted J and said that he has a Binde ready for court against Jenelle -of all of Jen's words on her Fb wall-has taken pics of all comments made by you & othersi guess, and also on e-mails, under 'jenelle potter' name. But a lot of things he has are 'made up' words by Billie, Lindsey and Tara have done on jen's FB and on fake jenellepotter FB's-that are made up by Lindsay & Billie ... As you know, Jenelle shares her FB with me (& you) so I/we know & see what is said by her and by you. She is accused of saying Bill is a bad father, Billie a bad mother, and awful things about the baby. She nor we would ever do that especially put down a little defenseless baby who is having enough of a hard time in life... poor child. We'd never mistreat him at all. Jenelle does not talk about them AT ALL. and you know that. Its you or whoever writes comments back on her Wall, maybe even them for all we know - as we know they are hacking.

In April, Barbara wrote approvingly of Buddy and Chris joining together to end the conflict, and wrote a delusional passage where her family sensed the presence of the CIA at the court proceeding brought by Tara against Jenelle:

> I mean mean ppl doing mean things to good ppl - wrong... so if you don't get them w/Bud, God will or someone will in their lives..that is life. Sort of like Karma &like Jesus said, treat others as you wanted to be treated... Mean ppl will

pay in some way... By the way, Bud pointed out the tall, dark, bearded mahn as CIA in court to me. Also, Jen ran into one dressed in suit outside while at restroom, & he gave her a thumbs up & smiled..so that was easy and we were glad they were there. Now the bearded only showed his face up front once, but we figured he was right behind the door behind the judge somehow to hear it all.

Barbara also wrote this chilling message to Chris:

[T]hey need to back off. Bud is sooooo mad, &I'm 100% behind whatever happens. You guys meet when you are ready Chris. Maybe Bud will have ID by then & can use CIA guns,etc. for his protection-get the jobs done ya know. They all need to go & the ones left need to be given a big scare as they watch & wonder 'am I next?'

And in another dire prediction, Barbara wrote:

[T]hey messed up Bud's truck and tried to break into it & he saw them, ID's 2 of them but there were 3. Well they were down at the firehouse the next day and told all the guys that they all three were here and were coming back to finish the job and mess up his truck and get Jenelle+ChrisCampbell I/m'd Jen&told her! They did not show tho Bud waited all night, & last night it rained, but they drove by 3 times in Tara's vehicle, so maybe you need to disable it..in fact disable all their vehicles for that matter. It sounds like to me Chris, that all of them are going to have to go to prison or die. We just can't take anymore... Bud is waiting for the call from Dugger[1], wants his PHONE NUMBER HIMSELF - HE SAID THAT HE WILL CALL HIM AND THEY KNOW EACH OTHER FROM SERVING TOGETHER IN 'NAM, SO THEY WOULD BE FINE TO TALK PRIVATELY... I am thinking of you, praying for you and hope to meet you someday soon-Bud & you for sure...He wants to help you do 'thing.'

---

1   In some e-mails, Chris referred to "Duggar" as his CIA supervisor.

There were a lot of hand-written papers of Barbara's included in the shredded documents. The vast majority of those were irrelevant, but this notation was one that we on the prosecution team always found amusing due to the idea of Barbara catering a training "session" for Jamie Curd's benefit:

> Bud & Jamie had a good time & session last Thursday - shooting, cleaning guns, we ate together worked w/ computer, generally had a really nice time. I made pineapple upside down cake everyone enjoyed.

Besides using these writings to prove a conspiracy existed that Buddy Potter acted upon, my mission in introducing them was to give people a taste of the trial against Barbara and Jenelle. This first jury would be my guinea pigs.

25

The trial of Marvin "Buddy" Potter began October 7, 2013. The courtroom stayed well-populated throughout the five-day proceeding, with victims from two families present and cameras from each of our three local television stations. Normally those cameras come and go, just getting a little footage. On this case, they weren't going to miss a moment.

The opening statement is the one golden opportunity for the prosecutor to paint a picture before the defense has a chance to comment. I started off aggressively, describing the horrid scene investigators first came upon, baby in its mother's arms and all.

"The child was not harmed but had been left there in his mother's arms—in his dead mother's arms—by someone who was cold enough, calculating enough, and trained enough to be able to conduct murders like that," I stated. "Ladies and gentlemen, today in this courtroom we are going to show you that you're in the midst of someone trained and cold-blooded enough to do that kind of thing.

"At least, he *thinks* he is. He thinks he is. He likes to tell people he's that kind of person. He likes for his family to *think* he's that kind of person."

I continued on, explaining Buddy's habit of bragging about his CIA past and future. I then went into the whole sordid history of harassment against Jenelle, the family dynamic, Jamie Curd, and all. The more I talked, the more I saw jurors' heads tilt in ways suggesting confusion, much like those of the grand jurors months before.

As I finished, I said, "What we're going to hear about, ladies and gentlemen, is something that is so ridiculously not in our imagination. That's just the way it is. The kind of hatred of and contempt that one bunch of people can hold against another bunch of people for nothing—no reason at all. And you're going to hear it over and over. And at the end of this, the proof is going to be overwhelming that, yes, Buddy Potter is responsible for these two deaths."

Buddy's attorney, Randy Fallin, countered with talking of how Buddy's interrogation had taken place while Buddy was without his oxygen and not thinking clearly. He suggested a different gunman existed, one outside the Potter-Curd clan.

I couldn't wait to hear that evidence. Fallin's only real reference to proof of a different shooter was the discovery of methamphetamine sitting on top of some furniture in the room where Billie Jean had been found dead. Fallin noted that neither autopsy revealed drugs in the victims' systems.

"So, that person, whoever was using meth and had been there that morning, was the shooter," he ended.

Agent Lott was our first witness. He would testify at various points about our proof. For now, he introduced his photos of the crime scene, detailing how the victims appeared. He noted the baby bottle found in Tyler's Pack-n-Play, multi-use playpen, the bottle full of formula ready for the child's consumption.

Lott testified to finding a fired round of ammunition near Bill Payne's body, the round having penetrated a pillowcase, where it stopped. The round that killed Billie Jean took longer to locate, probably because of the unusual place in which it rested—Tyler's bouncy seat, on the floor near Billie Jean's feet. Each round was either .38 caliber or nine millimeter, he said. Investigators found no shell casings, suggesting that the shooter used a revolver that would not discharge casings, since most killers do not take the time to pick up casings emitted from a gun with a clip. Particularly when it's mostly dark.

The photos of the victims lying dead were jarring. Bill's body was sprawled out on the couple's bed, face up. He was shirtless, clothed only in the shorts he'd slept in. He had a single gunshot just under his left eye, and a long slice at his neck from a knife. Billie Jean was lying on her left side, her arms in front of her body in much the same way she had probably been holding Tyler. She had on a t-shirt, cartoon Grinch pajama bottoms, and socks. The bullet that killed her had entered one side of her head and exited through the other side, passing through her brain.

Fallin questioned Lott about the methamphetamine present at the home. Lott said that he found the powdered drug on top of a dresser in the nursery. He remembered a credit card with it, and possibly a straw. He acknowledged that using the credit card to make a line of powder and snorting it through a straw could be a way to ingest the drug. He also agreed that, from his review of the crime scene, he could not say how long the perpetrator had been inside the home.

Lott pointed out there was only one door to the home that appeared to have been used to enter or exit the house. This was a sliding glass door at the living room, facing away from the road. The front door of the home had towels bunched up at the bottom to prevent drafts, and the other door to the home had a baby swing blocking its path.

The theme of Fallin's questioning suggested he theorized that a big drug deal or shipment was to take place at Bill Payne's home around the time of his killing. Yet Fallin never came close to establishing his idea as a fact. He couldn't—if Bill was getting "shipments" of narcotics, he undoubtedly would have been on local law enforcement's radar. He wasn't.

Our next key witness was Special Agent Steve Scott, a veteran of the firearms identification unit in Nashville. I had dealt with Agent Scott before, and he was a great expert witness. Merely ask his name and get out of his way. No handling necessary for him to make his points.

Investigators had not found a firearm that matched up with the bullets used to kill Bill and Billie Jean. However, they had located loose, unspent rounds inside the cabin of Buddy's truck, in a small open compartment of his center console. This was the same truck that had held bags of shredded Chris-Barbara e-mails.

Agent Scott had some very valuable—and unusual—points to

Clockwise from above: Agent Scott Lott, Bob Meehan, and Barbara Potter. (Becky Campbell, *Johnson City Press*)

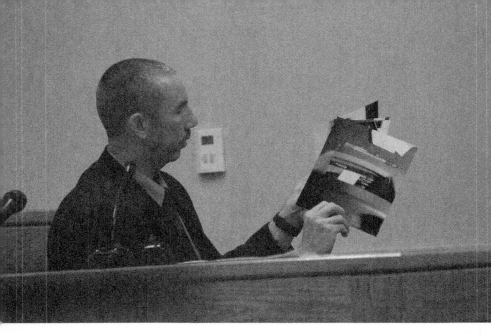

Clockwise from above: Chief Deputy Joe Woodard, Chris Tjaden, Christie Groover. (Becky Campbell, *Johnson City Press*)

Clockwise from above: Dennis Brooks, Jaime Curd, Jenelle Potter. (Becky Campbell, *Johnson City Press*)

Clockwise from above: Linda Stephens, Lindsey Thomas, Lyndsey Potter. (Becky Campbell, *Johnson City Press*)

Clockwise from above: Matt Roark, Melanie Clayton, Roy Stephens, Sheriff Mike Reece. (Becky Campbell, *Johnson City Press*)

ABOVE: Tara Osborne (L) and Tracy Greenwell (R). (Becky Campbell, *Johnson City Press*).

RIGHT: Marvin "Buddy" Potter. (Tony Duncan/*Johnson City Press*)

BELOW: Curd and Potter in court prior to the women being charged. Pictured there are Jamie Curd, David Crichton, Marvin "Buddy" Potter and Randy Fallin. (Lee Talbert/*Johnson City Press*)

make about those unfired bullets.

There were five. Two had the manufacturer markings "W-W," and said ".38 Special." Agent Scott said these were made by Winchester Western. The other three were made by a company in Korea named PMC. They were also .38 Special rounds.

In his analysis, Scott had removed one bullet each from the sets of unfired rounds, and compared the manufactured markings to the bullets used to kill our victims. The bottom part of the intact PMC bullets had dashed lines, called cannelures, around the body. The purpose of those lines was to add lubrication for the bullet as it traveled down the gun's barrel. The bullet that killed Bill had similar lines.

Scott also pointed out "markings" on the top of the unfired bullets, the part that is exposed on an assembled round of ammunition. In twenty-seven years of work in the field, he had never seen anything like them before.

The markings were not uniform. They were hand-done, sort of like doodle marks, lines cut repeatedly into the exposed circumference of the bullet. As if a person had used a pocketknife to cut markings into the bullets. The description made me recall the old men at the cattle stockyard when I was a child, who whittled sticks of wood with their knives.

Scott explained that bullets are made of lead, and lead is a metal that is easy to cut or mark. All five of these unfired rounds had these markings.

As did the round used to kill Bill Payne. Despite the mangled nature of the ammunition that had passed through Bill's skull, Scott showed the jury the similar doodle marks he'd found on that bullet. Unfortunately, the bullet that killed Billie Jean was too mutilated to determine if such tool marks were present on it.

Nevertheless, the match between Bill's bullet and those unfired rounds was a powerful piece of evidence implicating Buddy. In a career of examining guns and bullets, Agent Scott had never seen anything like those marks.

Additionally, Scott pointed out the features of the bullet

found in the bouncy seat that were consistent with the Winchester Western rounds.

I hoped the jury was joining me in imagining Buddy Potter sitting in his chair, on watch, doodling on bullets as he thought of killing Jenelle's enemies.

Throughout this testimony, and throughout the entire trial, for that matter, Buddy sat expressionless. He was so without emotion that I quit glancing over there for reactions. Of the many people in the courtroom for his trial, Buddy looked to be the least interested of all.

26

A few witnesses later, it was Roy Stephens's turn to share his observations. As the person who had discovered Bill and Billie Jean dead, his testimony would be riveting.

At the time of the victims' deaths, Roy was having an on-again, off-again relationship with his wife and began having his mail sent to Bill Payne, Sr. so he knew where his mail would be regardless of his marital status. His friend Paw Bill would stick Roy's mail on a shelf, and since the Paynes always left their door unlocked, Roy was free to enter and find his mail.

On January 31, 2012, Roy pulled his vehicle into the Paynes' driveway with his wife Linda riding with him. It was around 10 a.m. The first unusual thing Roy noticed was Bill Jr.'s truck. Bill should have been at work, Roy thought. Paw Bill's truck was absent.

Roy entered through the back sliding door into the living room, and went straight to the shelf holding his mail. The house was silent. With Bill's truck present, he expected that Bill and Billie Jean would be home, milling about.

"I hollered their names out," Roy said. "I didn't want to catch them in the act of something, you know, sexual. So, you know, if I enter someone's house I'm going to holler so I don't get shot, or you know, see something I don't need to see."

No one answered him.

"I hollered again, and I looked around and I said, well you know, something's not right."

With his wife waiting in the car, Roy ventured toward the hallway through the quiet, still home. In the first room to the left, he saw Bill lying on the bed.

"What I saw when I walked in that room was a little bit of blood on his neck, and then I walked up and touched his arm about right there to shake him," Roy testified, his emotions building. Bill's body was lifeless.

"So, I backed up and I went 'No, no, no, no, no.' And I realized he was dead."

Roy ran out of the house, screaming for his wife to call 911. Linda rushed out of their vehicle and into the home, where she called from the house phone. Meanwhile, Roy looked around some more. He walked farther down the hall. What he saw was even more shocking.

When he saw Billie Jean lying on the floor with baby Tyler in her arms, Roy froze.

"I really didn't step into the room 'til I seen the baby breathe and pulled it out of her arms," he said. "It was just laying kind of on its face in her arms, just, you know, I didn't know.

"And I seen it breathe and I said, 'No!' And I pulled it out of her arms 'cause I saw the back of her head blowed out. I mean, you couldn't help but to grab the baby."

Tyler was entirely quiet. No crying or whimpering. He had likely run out of such noises hours earlier.

With Tyler now in his arms, Roy went to Linda, who was on the phone with 911. Minutes later, the rescue squad arrived and took over tending to the young child.

Roy could not remember anything after that. He was in shock.

27

Ask almost any criminal defense attorney his or her opinion on whether a criminal suspect should talk to law enforcement officers, and their knee-jerk response will be, "No." An emphatic "no." Yet every day in the United States, guilty people think they can talk their way out of accusations hurled their direction. The law does not require them to answer a single question. But they do.

I've often wondered why that is. Perhaps the suspect is curious about the proof collected against them, and the only way to know is to face their investigator. Perhaps guilty people believe they can give their spiel and convince an investigator to look elsewhere. Sometimes that works.

A theory of mine is that suspects think there is no harm in speaking to an investigator as long as they do not confess to a crime. As long as one holds on to one's darkest secrets, all is well.

Not true. Every single time a guilty person gets interviewed, and there is a tape rolling, a skilled prosecutor can find something of great value to a case.

The Potter family made such a mistake one day after Bill and Billie Jean's deaths.

When Buddy Potter opened the door and allowed Agent Lott and Chief Deputy Woodard into his home on February 1, 2012, and allowed to them to interview Jenelle, Barbara, and himself, he gave me one hour's worth of jewels. The audiotaped interview was not valuable at first glance, but the more I learned about the case, the more critical the tape became.

First, considering that Buddy later admitted to doing "it," his hour-long denial, complete with expressions of sympathy for two people killed in such a heinous fashion, had value as far as the jury determining Buddy's guilt. Juries do not like feigned sympathy from a killer.

Also, for all their denials of involvement, the Potters sure had a lot to say about the victims' past transgressions. Bill and Billie Jean had been discovered dead only one day earlier, and the Potters' motivations were still fresh. They couldn't wait to speak ill of the dead.

"I know you're going to question about this thing, I guess, about Billie Jean and them," Buddy said after answering the door and allowing the investigators into his home. "I figured that you'd be around. Everybody always points fingers at us."

While they waited for Jenelle to finish her shower, Buddy talked. He told the agents about his past trips to the Sheriff's Department to complain about the victims' conduct.

"I'm sorry that those people died. I don't wish that on nobody. You know me; I've been up there oh I don't know how many times because of them. I just don't wish that on nobody, though. When we saw that yesterday afternoon on the TV, I mean that was a shock to see that that had happened."

Minutes later, Jenelle and Barbara walked in. Agent Lott introduced himself and explained he wanted to talk to anyone who had had a problem with Bill and Billie Jean.

Jenelle began recounting her harassment trial with Lindsey. For someone unfamiliar with Jenelle's voice, as this jury was, it was jarring. She had a high-pitched voice, like Minnie Mouse, unlike what one would expect from a thirty-year-old woman.

"They weren't too happy with me," she said, explaining that, over the past several months, Bill and Billie Jean had been in the Potter driveway and on their property. Buddy volunteered that the victims had made a path around his house and thrown rocks at it.

"I'm sorry it happened," Jenelle said of the killings, pausing. "But, I mean, I didn't—I—I mean, that's all I can tell you is they have been harassing the living crap out of me."

Buddy chimed in, saying he had quit calling the police over the "stuff" that went on.

Jenelle listed the girls who had harassed her—Billie Jean, Lindsey, and Tara. She said that, after the harassment trial, Lindsey had been cussing at her and "giving her crap."

Recently, one of Lindsey's friends had assaulted her, Jenelle alleged. She said that Nikki Church hit her in the side, but Jenelle did not fight back because she was afraid she would go to jail.

Barbara then interjected that this was not the first time such a thing had happened.

"Why would she hit you?" Agent Lott asked Jenelle.

"No reason," interjected Barbara.

"She's trying to get me now," Jenelle said of Nikki. "She's trying to hurt me."[1]

Barbara said that recently, at the local Rite Aid drug store, Nikki had seen her and Jenelle present and got on her cell phone to tell Lindsey that they were there.

"They all come and gang up, and they beat up people," said Barbara. "Anybody that is a friend of Jenelle or with Jenelle, or Jenelle herself—they're looking for her always. She's never out without her father or me—"

"She doesn't drive," Buddy contributed.

"Now they say even if I'm out with my parents, they will kill them to get to me," Jenelle pleaded. "I've gotten threats and everything."

Within a mere five minutes of meeting Jenelle, investigators had heard Jenelle complain of threats to her life. Threats of undetermined origins and unknown rationales. Jenelle's recitation of her problems had become so ingrained in her life that her mouth was a continuous stream of made-up stories, even at a moment like this.

Perhaps Jenelle lacked insight into the proper times to shut her mouth. Like when homicide investigators come to one's home to explore possible motives to kill. The best approach would have been

---

1 I later found Nikki Church. She denied ever having a conflict with Jenelle. Considering Nikki stood around one foot shorter than Jenelle, the notion she would pick a fight was highly questionable.

to downplay the prior conflict. But Jenelle couldn't help it.

Barbara was quick-witted enough to try and pull Jenelle out of a potential jam.

"But we thought it was all over after November thirtieth," Barbara said, citing the date Lindsey's harassment case against Jenelle had failed.

"Yeah, that's...." Jenelle tried to contribute, in a higher-than-normal pitch that I came to associate with her efforts to make someone believe a falsehood.

"We haven't seen any of them, any of *those* people, you know, that she was in there with," Barbara continued. "Except for them going up and down the road, which has been going on for over a year."

Buddy was keenly aware of the victims' efforts to pass his house. "I sit here in this chair every night starting at about 11:00, until 6:30 to 7:00 in the morning, then I go to bed," he said.

"Have you posted anything negative on the Internet about them?" Agent Lott asked Jenelle.

"Uh, the only thing I had ever posted was, 'Please leave me alone.' They were on my account. They hacked in," Jenelle answered.

"They hacked in all the time," Barbara said.

"And I just said, 'Please, Bill, Billie Jean, Lindsey, please leave me alone,'" Jenelle continued.

"And Tara," Barbara added.

"And Tara," acknowledged Jenelle. "I've never said anything about nothing other than, 'Leave me alone.'"

"You never put on the Internet that you wished that they were dead?" Agent Lott asked.

"No," Jenelle answered, in an especially high-pitched whine designed to fake sincerity. "I'm not that mean. I just tell people to leave me alone. I mean, that's as mean as I can get."

"So if we had stuff we pulled off the Internet from you saying that, it wouldn't be correct? How would that get on there?" Agent Lott pressed.

"They actually made up three Facebooks of me, using my

picture," said Jenelle.

"They hacked into hers and stole everything," Barbara added.

"My friends up north have been harassed by these girls," said Jenelle. "A state police officer was even called and harassed. He was my friend on Facebook, and I told him to get off because he was getting harassed, and it's not—it's just not fair.

"If you see my Facebook, it's songs and pictures of me and my friends, and of dogs. Bulldogs. I have a fascination with them."

"Why would they be harassing you?" Agent Lott asked.

Jenelle answered that the reason had come out during the harassment trial.

"It came out to be a jealousy thing. They said that I was too pretty, that I wasn't from here," she said.

Perhaps stunned by the absurdity of it all, Agent Lott stammered for the right words. "You know, just, it's hard, hard to grasp, that they would pick on somebody for no reason, you know…."

Jenelle was quick to answer, saying, "Do you know that I have had other girls pick on me for no reason? I've actually had guys pick on me for no reason."

"It's been like that ever since we came down here," said Barbara.

When the harassment trial ended, Jenelle said, looking at Buddy, "You and Jamie carried me out. And she stood in the middle of courtroom and said, 'I hope you die.' Billie Jean said it. I was too out of it to say anything. When I get DKA, I'm out."

Buddy added, "Lindsey actually stood up and she said, 'I hope you f'ing die, you bitch.' And it turned out, she almost did."

Jenelle and Barbara then recounted Jenelle's heart trouble after the trial.

"I'm scared to go away because I've been in the grocery store by myself, and they were right there," Jenelle said. "And I run the other way. I carry Mace with me because I'm scared. Anyone would be if they were threatened. I have been threatened with rape by some guys."

"Yeah," Buddy chimed in. "Who was—"

"That was Jonathan Eisenhower," Jenelle said. "And another

one of Billie Jean's friends threatened to rape me. And he even beat on my dad's truck."

"They call her on the phone and threaten to rape her," Barbara said.

Buddy then said they had kicked in his garage door while Jenelle was alone at the house.

When asked how she got to know these people, Jenelle recounted being friends with Bill's sister Tracy Greenwell and being introduced to Bill. Jenelle had gone with Tracy and Bill to a rock-climbing gathering. She said Tracy once took her to Bill's home when a party was taking place, and it made her uncomfortable. She described a scene of drug and alcohol use, guns being bandied about, and "a lot" of girls raped there.

"There was too much drinking go on there," said Jenelle. "I came home and was real upset. I said I didn't want to go back there."

Buddy acknowledged that Jenelle had told of what she had seen. He even speculated on what type of gun she had described. Buddy even knew of Bill carrying a stainless steel .22 caliber handgun.

"Bill carried it in his pocket all the time," he said.

Barbara decided to join in, disparaging Bill and Billie Jean and adding that they claimed to have a gang. Jenelle said that the group bragged it was bigger than MS-13, which was a prominent national group. Buddy joined in, saying the gang was all over the country.

"I wasn't going to let them get me," said Jenelle. "I would have fought them all the way."

The investigators got around to asking Jenelle about whether Jamie was her boyfriend. She said he was just a friend. Barbara agreed, saying he was "a good friend to the family." Buddy voiced his agreement.

Agent Lott asked the Potters, if they were in his position, who would they look at as possible perpetrators? Jenelle provided no answer. She could only suggest anyone who came into contact with the victims or had problems with them. Barbara was silent.

"When I first found out, I was like, 'Oh my God,'" said Jenelle. "I would never want somebody murdered."

"We were all surprised," added Barbara.

Agent Lott said they just wanted to make sure Jenelle did not have anything to do with it. That was met with another high-pitched "Nooooo," before Jenelle said she was being accused by the victims' friends. First, she had been in bed, she said. Second, she couldn't drive.

"Why would I do it?" she asked.

"You're not strong enough," added Barbara.

"Especially with a guy, a girl, and a baby. Why would I do it?" Jenelle asked.

Buddy contributed that Jenelle couldn't do that to anyone if she wanted to. Jenelle then said she could kill someone if they were going to rape her.

By my count, that was four references Jenelle had made to rape so far.

After an hour, the investigators wrapped up their questions.

"What was your name again?" Jenelle inquired of Agent Lott, showing an unusual level of curiosity.

"My name is Scott."

"Scott? It's been very nice to meet you."

Barbara asked Agent Lott to write his name down.

"Even with this [the harassment], I'm sorry that this happened to them," Buddy said as the investigators were getting up to leave. "I wouldn't wish that on nobody."

"Especially with a baby," added Jenelle.

As the jury listened to this, I hoped that the recording would drive home one main point: Buddy Potter believed any ridiculous statement that came out of Jenelle Potter's mouth. And he believed her words to the point of acting on her wishes.

28

After the jury heard the Potter family interview, they listened to the call Jamie made to the Potters, in which Buddy assured him that he had gotten rid of everything from Bill's. They then reviewed Buddy's interrogation and resulting phone call home, where he told Barbara he "did it" while both Barbara and Jenelle maintained that he was at home the whole time.

We were also able to show the jury a snippet of Jamie's interrogation, in which he asked the TBI agents, "Is the CIA here?" Even though Jamie's videotaped statement was 99% hearsay, his question was not hearsay since a question does not constitute a "truth of the matter asserted," as hearsay is defined. This was a valuable piece of evidence, especially since we were introducing the shredded e-mails that discussed the CIA having the Potters' backs.

Lindsey Thomas was the next person to take the stand. She told the jury about becoming good friends with Billie Jean, and about Billie Jean giving birth to Tyler on July 11, 2011. When asked if Billie Jean had any enemies, all Lindsey could think of was Jenelle. She told the jury about her and Billie Jean having accepted a friend request from Jenelle. They both soon regretted it.

"Shortly after accepting her friend request, she started posting things about Billie Jean and myself, saying that we were really mean people, really mean girls, and that was how it all started," Lindsey said of Jenelle. "She continued to write stuff about both of us on there. It was a continuous thing.

"She even took pictures from our Facebooks and tagged herself in them, then turned around and put them on her Facebook."

Lindsey testified that, after some time, she called Jenelle and asked her to stop talking about her and Billie Jean.

"She proceeded to tell me that she did not know what I was talking about," Lindsey said. "And I had the computer in front of me, and I told her that I could see it as we talked on the phone. And she kept saying that she had no clue what I was talking about, that she did not write anything, and that was all that was said."

Instead of that phone call improving relations, the online trashing continued. But now, Lindsey was getting annoying phone calls too.

"It started off being just a couple of times a day, maybe, or just randomly a few times a week, to anywhere from fifteen to twenty times a day, every day," she said. "I would tell her to please stop calling me."

"Did she ever say anything back to you?" asked Roark.

"No," answered Lindsey, saying that sometimes the calls consisted solely of someone breathing on the other phone.

Lindsey denied ever hacking into Jenelle's e-mail or Facebook accounts. Or creating a fake Facebook page for Jenelle. Whatever things Jenelle had accused Lindsey of doing, Lindsey denied.

Eventually, Lindsey said she had had enough and swore out the harassment charge on May 10, 2011. After some resets, they held the trial in November only to have the judge dismiss it.

"Did you stand up in the courtroom and tell Jenelle, 'I hope you die, bitch?'" asked Roark.

"No sir."

"After the case was over, did you or anyone you were with wait for Jenelle Potter and her family out in the parking lot?"

"No sir."

"Did you make any remarks whatsoever to Jenelle and her family?"

"No sir."

Lindsey said that Billie Jean and Tara were with her during the court proceeding, and she denied either of those females saying anything hateful to the Potters.

Roark then went through a litany of questions, asking if

certain events had occurred in her life that had been referenced in the shredded e-mails. Being assaulted, getting a ticket for a taillight violation, her car being tampered with, and so on. None of those things had happened, she said.

"Have you ever posted anything derogatory about Jenelle or her family online?" asked Roark.

"I don't understand what derogatory means," said Lindsey.

"Have you ever put anything hateful or mean?"

"I've probably said stuff back to her, but I don't think in a violent way, no. Just that if I saw her out I would confront her, but not in a physical way, just meaning that there might be words between us."

She also denied putting a $3,000 hit on Jenelle's life, which was something that Buddy had tearfully recounted during his interrogation.

On cross-examination, the defense did score a point regarding Pepper, the Jack Russell dog that lived at the Payne residence. Pepper had been present in the home during the killings, and the dog had some blood on her fur from being near the bodies until they were found.

Lindsey said that Pepper was a hyper dog, and that she would bark if she did not know a person.

"So, if she didn't know you and you came to that door [the sliding glass door], she barked, right?" Dave Robbins asked.

"Right," answered Lindsey.

Robbins moved on to a different subject, but they had a potential red herring for our case in that Pepper would likely have gone berserk barking if the story was as Jamie had described, that Buddy had driven his vehicle to the Payne driveway and they approached the door on foot. The victims would have gotten some warning that someone was present. Yet the scene was such that it looked like they had no warning. Something was likely amiss in our narrative.

Robbins cast doubt on Lindsey's assertions that Jenelle had made harassing calls to her and the unwelcome contact on Facebook.

"How do you know that [the friend request] was from Jenelle

Potter?" he asked.

"Just by the name and the picture that was on it," said Lindsey.

"Okay. If I got a friend request from Barack Obama how could I be sure that it was him?"

"Well, I don't know. I guess you would just have to go by the picture that's in the corner of it."

"Well, could I put any picture I want up as my profile picture?"

"You could."

"And I could put any name I wanted on my profile picture?"

"Yes."

"So there's really no way to tell if it was Jenelle, is there?"

"No. No sir."

"And when you confronted Jenelle about some of this stuff, she acted confused, didn't she?"

"Yes sir."

"And she actually denied it?"

"Yes sir."

"And when you say that she harassed you and called your house five to twenty times what do you base that on?"

"By the phone number that showed up on my phone."

"But you don't know it was her, do you?"

"No, but it was from her house."

"How do you know it's from her house?"

"Because of the number that showed up on the cell phone."

"Have you ever heard of spoofing?"

"I've heard of it, but I'm not familiar with it."

"From what you've heard you can take somebody else's number and make it look like a phone call originated from that number?"

"Yes sir."

Robbins finished by having Lindsey recount her written statement to Agent Lott, which she'd given soon after the murders. In that statement, she had told of being at the Payne residence on January 30. Billie Jean had told her that the person who had been supplying her pills to sell had already been there. Lindsey had speculated to Agent Lott that since Bill was also selling pills, she wondered if someone was supposed to meet Bill before he left for work on the thirty-first. She thus feared that the killings could have been over a drug deal gone bad.

That was her statement at the time, and coupled with the methamphetamine found in the baby's room, the defense had some sliver of an argument that an unknown person had committed these crimes. At least, it was a good argument if the jury wished to completely ignore the evidence against Buddy Potter.

Lyndsey Potter was the next state's witness. Of no relation to Buddy Potter, Lyndsey was a friend of Billie Jean's from childhood. She had accepted a friend request from Jenelle on Myspace years ago and had a passing acquaintance with her. Lyndsey said she had no problems with Jenelle until Billie Jean began seeing Bill. Lyndsey had confronted Jenelle about posting a picture of Billie Jean, Lindsey, and Tara and saying "some pretty nasty things in it."

Jenelle took down the posting, but months later she sent Lyndsey a private message, complaining about the girls bothering her and being by her house, and about being sick. Lyndsey said she tried to tell Jenelle that she doubted the girls were doing any of those things.

"Jenelle went on to tell me she didn't like me anymore, and that I was just like them, and she blocked me on Facebook," testified Lyndsey.

Next it was Tara Osborne's turn on the stand. Tara testified to being friends with Bill and Billie Jean. She said she met Jenelle at a grocery store in the checkout line. There, Jenelle was showing off a ring her "alleged boyfriend" had given her. Judge Blackwood sustained a hearsay objection to Tara's statement that Jenelle had named that boyfriend as Jamie Curd. Tara said Jenelle acted "bubbly" over the ring.

Later, Jenelle found Tara on Facebook and sent her a friend request. Tara obliged. Then the two engaged in instant messaging and even phone calls. Tara described it as a friendship at one point. But then the drama began, and Tara found it unbearable.

"It went through 'pitiful me, people are harassing me,'" Tara said of Jenelle's representations. "And her being friends of my husband and us knowing things about her home life, or not being able to see her boyfriend, it not being approved, how her father treated her, how her mom was. It was just constantly something. You couldn't talk to her without her being 'the world's after me,' it felt like."

Tired of Jenelle's drama, Tara said she set her Facebook account to where people could not see when she was online, basically turning her "chat" function off. Thus Jenelle could not hit Tara up with instant messages. Later, Tara reconsidered her approach, turning her chat back on but deleting Jenelle as a friend. Then Jenelle sent her a private message, which prompted Tara to explain why she had unfriended her.

After that explanation, Tara began receiving unwelcome phone calls, which led to her going to the authorities for help. To no avail.

As Tara left the witness stand, we had presented to the jury a slew of people who had issues with Jenelle—issues that had potentially aggravated Jenelle's parents and propelled them to extreme reactions. With the next witness, we were going to spring a different but similarly disturbing story on the jury.

29

We had shown the jury the incriminating evidence against Buddy Potter and his family that was in his truck—the shredded e-mails and ammunition. But there were equally damaging items found in the Potter home.

While Agents Lott and Hannon were grilling Buddy at the Sheriff's Department, Chief Deputy Woodard was overseeing the execution of a search warrant on Buddy's home. Woodard sat in the living room, writing evidence descriptions on his log sheet as his investigators brought the items to him and sat them on the coffee table.

One item turned over to Woodard was a spiral-bound notebook. Contained within it were handwritten notes concerning e-mail addresses, online accounts, and passwords. The e-mail addresses included bul2dog@aol.com and bmp9110@aol.com, and Christie Groover was prepared to testify that the handwriting was her mother's.

As he studiously logged items into evidence, Woodward wasn't paying much attention to what was on the coffee table. Barbara was sitting in the living room at the same time.

"During the time that I was sitting in the living room with Mrs. Potter, Mrs. Potter had got up and walked over to my left and picked up these papers," he said. "Well, after she sat back down, I was still logging items down, and she started ripping up the papers. So I asked her, 'What have you got there?'"

Barbara handed him back the papers, some of them ripped, and Woodard took a look at them.

The papers' value as evidence might not have been immediately apparent, but when the jury got a look at them, they had to be shocked. The papers were pictures printed on a color inkjet printer. As we flashed the images on the wall, the jury saw Billie Jean and friends in flirty Halloween outfits. Pictures of Billie Jean in a bikini at the beach. Pictures of Lindsey Thomas in a bikini. Captions of the girls as "Billie Whore" and "Panface," which was the favorite label ascribed to Lindsey's looks whenever Jenelle's Topix alter ego Matt Potter trashed her.

The photos were parts of e-mails, messages involving the bmp9110@aol.com and bul2dog@aol.com addresses, and they had undoubtedly been printed from social media sources.

For all their shrill claims of being "hacked" or "spoofed," Barbara's attempt to destroy this evidence was proof enough that the Potter family did indeed have a very unusual, even troublesome interest in those young women. For the jurors to be able to hold these pictures in their hands, many of the images torn in half, was some very powerful proof of that unhealthy preoccupation.

Next was Christie. As she walked into the courtroom, I tried to glimpse any reaction Buddy had to his daughter taking the stand. From what I could see, he never looked at her. My direct examination was to the point, drawing out some basic family background and then diving into her authenticating her mother's handwriting in both the notebook and some of the shredded documents.

On cross-examination, Fallin asked her about her background as a graphic designer and her computer experience. She said she was experienced with Apple systems. Fallin pointed out that she had aided in installing the software for the camera system at her EMS station as well as her status as website administrator for the department.

Fallin was trying to make Christie appear to be a potential hacker or spoofer, intent on ruining her family's lives. He asked her if she was aware that it was possible to access a person's Facebook account, access someone's IP address, and send e-mails from another person's computer. She testified to having very little knowledge of such.

"Your sister is borderline retarded, correct?" Fallin asked.

"No," answered Christie.

"You don't think so?"

"She was born with learning disabilities, but anytime I ever referred to her as retarded I was reprimanded, told that she was not retarded. Her learning disabilities, I was always told by my mother, revolved around auditory processing disorders."

"But she functions on a much lower level than her age?"

"Yes, mentally."

"She's probably like, what, maybe a fifteen-year-old girl—would that be your experience?"

"Depending on the issue, and depending on what it is."

While there was likely some truth to what Fallin was asserting, I failed to see how that helped his case at all. If Jenelle functioned at a low level, surely his client should have taken that into account when she recited her plethora of perceived threats. So that's precisely the area I dove into once I had a chance to do my redirect examination of Christie.

"You said in some ways she functions at a lower age, what do you mean by that?" I asked.

"She doesn't understand common joking like you and I would. Like, you know, if we were kidding around, and I said I was going to beat you up, she may take that seriously, but you and I would take it as a joke," said Christie. "That's most of it, just generally not being able to function the way you and I normally would. She really hasn't gone above a teenager's level."

"From your experience dealing with your father, do you think he's able to perceive that?"

"Yes."

I asked her about how Barbara treated Jenelle.

"I've always thought that Jenelle was coddled her whole life, and she knew how to play my parents," Christie said. "She always did."

30

Of the most valuable witnesses for a prosecutor, perhaps none is stronger than a good, impartial eyewitness to bad conduct by a defendant toward a victim. Such witnesses were in short supply for us. We had our written documents, we had our conflicts between Billie Jean's friends and Jenelle, and we had our admission by Buddy Potter. But few eyewitnesses.

Nevertheless, we had some semblance of an eyewitness, not to Buddy's behavior, but to Barbara and Jenelle's.

Linda Stephens, who had been separated from Roy Stephens but present in his vehicle when he discovered death in the Payne home, had things to tell the jury other than how she called 911 for Roy. She'd also been witness to some pretty ugly conduct by the women in Buddy's life.

Linda had worked for years at Potter's Store, as it was known in the Doe Valley community. The store was a hub for the community's people, which included both her and the victims. Linda testified to a time in 2011, after Billie Jean had given birth to Tyler, when Linda was working in the food prep area of the store facing the front window, so she could see the gas pumps.

"I was putting bread in the microwave and seen Billie Jean at the first pump pumping gas," said Linda. "I didn't see anyone with her, but a vehicle pulled up between the store and the gas pumps, and I could see a look come over Billie Jean's face, one of dread.

"I wondered what was wrong, and that's when I realized Billie Jean was already crying, and I could see the people in the vehicle throwing their arms around and the person in the passenger's seat leaning over like they were screaming and pointing and Billie Jean continuing to get more upset."

Linda explained that she could not recognize the two people in the vehicle since they were facing away from her, but the driver was a blond-haired woman, which would have described Barbara. The person in the passenger seat was a female with her hair pulled back. Linda said she rushed to the front door and called out.

"I hollered and asked Billie Jean was she okay. She said 'No.' And I said, 'Do you need the police?' and she said, 'Yeah, I think I do.' She was very upset, crying, her voice trembling. She was shaking."

Linda said that when she mentioned calling the police, the car sped off.

"I walked over to make sure that Billie Jean was okay, because she was very upset," Linda said, explaining that she had to help Billie Jean place the gas nozzle back into the pump because of Billie Jean's trembling.

"I asked her 'Who was that?' and she said, 'Jenelle Potter and her mom.' And I said, 'What were they doing?' She proceeded to tell me that they were, the words she used were, 'threatening me.'"

Quoting Billie Jean, Linda testified, "They called me trash, said I shouldn't be here, and that I shouldn't be a mother. That I didn't deserve to have Tyler, that I was trash."

Linda said Billie Jean was sobbing as she recounted the Potter women's words. Linda saw that Tyler was in the car, and Billie Jean mentioned that she had been on her way to Tyler's first checkup.

After Linda had calmed Billie Jean somewhat, Linda said Billie Jean handed her twenty dollars for the gas but left without getting her change. She was headed to find Bill and have him accompany her to the pediatrician.

Linda was a very solid, believable witness. If the defense's effort to cast doubt on the authorship of the shredded e-mails had had any success on this point, Linda's testimony hopefully put that to rest. The hatred of the Potter women had been put on full display.

Sheriff Reece was next on the stand. He testified to the time Buddy had come to his office and declared his past as a CIA operative and his belief that he would be reactivated at any time.

Due to a pretrial motion, the Sheriff was barred from telling the jury that Buddy told him he had killed people before. The Sheriff did mention a time when Buddy, along with Barbara and Jenelle, had come to him to complain about the county's 911 director, Eugene Campbell, having unfriended Jenelle on Facebook.

They were upset, he said, and they thought the Sheriff needed to know. Which was pretty bizarre.

"I don't know if they thought that he was employed by me because he was in my building, but I explained to them that I had nothing to do with 911. I had no control over him."

With that, it was Tracy Greenwell's turn before the jury. She shared with them her close relationship with her brother, Bill Payne, who had been three years older than her. She told the jury the times her father and Bill would have left for work on January 31, 2012. It was a workday for each of them. Paw Bill would have left for his job in Boone at 5:30 a.m., and Bill would have left between 6:30 and 7:00 a.m. Thus there was a one-hour window within which Bill and Billie Jean could have been killed without Paw Bill present.

Tracy shared with the jury her past friendship with Jenelle, and that she had introduced her to Bill, who had come up with the idea of getting Jenelle and Jamie together. She said Jamie had never had a girlfriend before, despite being in his late thirties.

Perhaps matching two reclusive individuals made sense to Bill and Tracy.

"I just tried to get [Jenelle] out of the house," said Tracy. "She didn't ever go anywhere with anybody."

Later, Jenelle turned hateful. Bill had become upset about the Topix posts from unfamiliar names, believing they were Jenelle's writings. Tracy told the jury about Bill having a binder of such postings, all of which spewed hate toward him, Billie Jean, and Lindsey.

"One evening when I got down to Dad's, he [Bill] got the book out and like, tossed it over to me and told me to look at what she was writing now. He was mad."

She said Bill told her of a plan he had executed to see if his suspicions of authorship were correct.

"He told Jamie something at work that was made up that nobody else knew, and then he [Bill] would go home, and it would be on it [Topix]," she said. "And he confronted him [Jamie] about it, and they got into an argument over that."

I ended with Tracy establishing that Jamie had been at the Payne home many times and would have been familiar with the home, which was important since this was a surgical home invasion, and Buddy likely needed intelligence information.

Neither side was able to draw any information from Tracy about girls being raped in the Payne home, as Jenelle had alleged. Or any of the other outlandish and absurd things that came out of Jenelle's mouth.

31

Fallin had promised the jury an alternate shooter during his opening statement. He failed to deliver. In fact, by the time the defense closed its proof and we got to closing statements, Robbins totally bypassed Fallin's opening prediction, never addressing it. The best they could do was act like Tara Osborne's husband Brad might have killed Bill, his best friend. It was a weak assertion, since Osborne had zero motive. Following the defense calling Agent Lott back to the stand and grilling him over not examining this or that piece of evidence for DNA or fingerprints and posing Osborne as the culprit, we simply cross-examined Lott about how Osborne had acted during his interview the day after Bill and Billie Jean died.

He cried, Lott said. Osborne had acted just as any close friend might after the death of his friend. He cried. Much different from Buddy Potter's cold ambivalence, which we had seen on tape.

The defense put a couple more people on the stand either to establish that Bill and Buddy had reached a peace agreement back in November (they hadn't) or that Bill was expecting a drug shipment around the time of his death. Another subpoenaed witness for the defense never showed up, calling in periodically from various points between Mountain City and Jonesborough. From the reports of his locations, he seemed to be getting farther away from the courthouse with each call. "That lying son of a bitch," Fallin remarked in our presence outside the courtroom, calling his own witness a liar. We got a kick out of that. Back in the courtroom, Fallin told Judge Blackwood that the witness was a vital witness. Blackwood ordered he be arrested for his failure to show, but the trial went on without him.

Buddy elected to not testify. Blackwood went through the litany of questions to ensure Buddy was making a knowing and intelligent waiver of his right to speak.

After closing arguments, jury instructions, and several hours of deliberations, the jury filed back in with their verdict. Even on a case like this where the state had a confession, physical evidence, and motive in abundance, there was still tension when the foreman rose to deliver the verdict.

"Guilty of first degree murder," he said in regards to each victim.

Buddy had no reaction. Behind us, the victims' family members and friends—many in number—crumbled into emotional heaps with the relief that at least one person had been brought to justice. Behind Buddy was one person, Christie, who had hung around to see her father's fate, and perhaps be of some support to a man whom she still loved. Buddy never acknowledged her. No glance back at her, no nod in her direction, no goodbye.

We went through the courtroom hugging family and friends of Bill and Billie Jean, but the prosecution team had a bigger verdict to obtain. We had to get to the other side of the courthouse and intercept the jurors before they left. We needed to know what they thought of Barbara and Jenelle.

Agent Lott got to a few of them first. He was engaged in conversation with a lady who was happy to talk. When I got to her, I flat out asked her what she thought of the women being involved. She firmly answered that the jurors felt they were guilty. The look on her face revealed how much she disapproved of both of them, particularly Barbara.

While this jury had not seen the bulk of the e-mails and had not heard a single argument about forensic linguistics, what they did hear was persuasive. The shredded documents, the torn-up Facebook pictures, Jenelle's bizarre statement a day after the killings, and that strange call from Buddy to Barbara after his confession, where she offered up an alibi defense that he rejected—it was enough for this jury.

To me, this feedback was more of a relief than Buddy's verdict.

I had verification we were on the right track. Of course, these jurors had not been subjected to defense tactics on behalf of the women. And how the forensic linguistic evidence would play out, I did not know.

At the sentencing hearing later, Judge Blackwood sentenced Buddy to two consecutive life sentences. Buddy was a soldier to the end. No emotion. He took his medicine without complaint. After all, he had done his duty, at least as he saw it. He had protected his family, and he sure wasn't going to do anything to harm them now. Even if he realized that his daughter had duped him into spending the rest of his life in prison, and even if he now knew that his wife had played him like a flute, his love for both was still too great to say anything, or do anything, that would reflect poorly on them.

Buddy silently slipped out of the picture.

32

Jamie Curd gave every indication that he would go down with the ship, just like Buddy. His lawyer, Casey Sears, insisted on obtaining the polygraph procedures and results from Curd's lie detector examination. By telling Curd that he had failed the test, TBI Agents Hannon and Lott wore Curd's defenses down to the point where he acknowledged his presence at the crime scene. However, a day after his arrest, Curd retracted the statement he'd made implicating Buddy and himself, and his jail calls to family members were arrogantly defiant, acting as if we had no case at all.

I was perplexed that Sears was asking for the polygraph information. Since the results of lie detector tests are inadmissible at trial, the procedures undertaken to get results would surely be irrelevant. Later, Sears provided us with a report from an expert polygrapher who stated that Hannon's techniques were flawed, and insufficient to lead one to believe that Curd's testing results were conclusive.

Again, this kind of "evidence" is inadmissible. Polygraph tests are not foil-proof, and courts have long held that allowing juries to hear polygraph results is ripe with the potential for them to neglect their own task in determining the truthfulness of statements.

Worried that the introduction of such matters could lead to an ineffective assistance of counsel claim, I filed a motion to bar the evidence. At a hearing, Judge Blackwood deemed that if Sears got into the testing procedures, he ran the risk that the jury would surely hear that Agent Hannon believed Curd had lied during his polygraph. Sears understood, stating that it was the best defense he had.

Sears knew what his client was ignoring—that the Potter women's communications with him put him squarely in the crosshairs of a criminal conspiracy, his statement from February 6 notwithstanding. He was doomed. Easy pickings for the state.

At a later meeting in my office, Sears and I were discussing trial issues when I cut to the chase.

"You know, the best chance your client has at getting a shot at daylight is to cooperate and testify against those women," I told Sears, adding that I realized it was improbable. I knew Jamie's prior legal team had been there, done that. I hardly expected Sears, a nice fellow but woefully inexperienced at representing killers, to triumph where others had failed. But Sears listened and said he'd do what he could.

Meanwhile, we were pouring through e-mails to determine which ones to use and which to jettison. It was a tiresome task. Sometimes there would be a single line in a long message that I would deem critical, regardless of the fact that the rest were the same old rants found in a million other places.

Dr. Leonard took my shortened list of e-mails and did his analysis, issuing a lengthy report with example after example of linguistic nuances peculiar to Jenelle and Barbara. He found clues that I had completely missed.

Jenelle had a bad tendency for using apostrophes where they were not needed. "He know's I...." She wrote in massive run-on sentences, chronically transposed letters, confused homophones (new/knew), and rarely used punctuation. She used wrong but similar words, such as writing "packing" when "parking" was appropriate. She unnecessarily capitalized words in the middle of sentences, and she often misspelled words, or omitted a letter here and there. She often strung a series of words together without commas: "kind and caring and sweet." She forgot to double the consonant when adding "ing," resulting in words such as "siting" when she meant "sitting." And, as I had picked out, she tended to leave the "e" when adding the "ing" to a root word.

Dr. Leonard found other examples. These characteristics were present in Jenelle's known writings as well as the questioned e-mails from Chris and the mysterious Topix postings by Matt Potter and Dan White.

Barbara had her own style. She almost never wrote the word "and," instead using an ampersand. She used "tho'" in place of "though," "yrs" for "years," "rec'd" instead of "received," "atty" in place of "attorney," "bc" for "because," "fr" for "for," and "espec," for "especially." She wrote "w/life" instead of "with life." She was addicted to ellipses … as well as hyphens. She had a strange habit of pairing alternate words separated by a slash, such as "attack/stroke" or "dead/gone." Lastly, she inserted phrases within sentences and enclosed them with parentheses. She did all of these things often, both in her known and questioned writings.

While his analysis was very persuasive in identifying idiosyncrasies, Dr. Leonard stopped short of giving an expert opinion that each woman had authored the writings from her own respective e-mail account. Instead, he gave it the nuance of saying, in effect, that it was more likely that Jenelle was Chris, Matt, and Dan, and that Barbara was Barbara. He did this because of the peril an expert such as himself could suffer in his industry by making firm statements better left to the sound judgment of a jury.

33

Time passed. Other cases from my regular work dominated my thoughts, and focusing on this case was near impossible at times. A trial date fell through as Hyder experienced issues with expert witnesses, primarily in locating a forensic linguist to combat Dr. Leonard. Quite frankly, none of us were eager to get to trial too early.

Except for Sears. As Curd's attorney, Sears began saying that he would ask for a severance if the trial was postponed for too long. The last thing I wanted was a trial for Curd and then a trial for the women, so the focus became on getting materials to Hyder, items his expert needed for a report to counter Dr. Leonard. Meanwhile, I tried to keep Sears at bay. Every time we mentioned the possibility of Hyder needing more time, Sears started up about a severance.

With his interest in a speedy trial, the last thing I expected was a call from Sears saying that Curd was willing to talk to us. Yet that was the call I got in early 2015, as we moved toward a May trial date. Sears said Curd had realized that cooperating was his best chance at eventual freedom.

Had he come to his senses? Could he finally have realized that Jenelle had duped and played him? I think I wanted to know the answers to those questions more than I really needed Curd's help. This case had become more than simply an effort to get convictions. I wanted to know the story. I wanted to understand Jenelle Potter as much as I could—how she thought, what she felt, and how in the heck Curd could be fooled into thinking the CIA was sending him messages. I figured the jury would have the same curiosities, and anything we did to get answers to such questions would inevitably help us get the verdicts we sought. I discussed the idea with Agent

Lott, and he was of the same mind. We wanted answers.

Jamie Curd was our only shot at knowing the full story.

In one way, it wasn't totally necessary to have Curd's assistance to convict the women. As long as the jury believed the women authored their respective writings, I could fill in the blanks like any aggressive prosecutor could, painting the worst possible picture at every gap in the story.

However, one major gap we had was the verbal discussions in the Potter home before the killings. We knew what they had written. We knew what they muttered in interviews and recorded calls. Yet we did not know for certain what Barbara or Jenelle had said to Buddy Potter to propel him to kill. We did not know the details of any planning sessions, reconnaissance efforts, or botched attempts regarding the murders of Bill and Billie Jean.

Could Curd provide those things?

If he could, and say such things believably, then his testimony would be worth something. I gave Sears the parameters of what I thought could be workable in return for truthful testimony, such as pleading him one class down to facilitation of two counts of first degree murder. He would have a long sentence, but he would be parole eligible—which was plenty of incentive for him to cooperate.

"Truthful testimony," though, was a concept to be judged solely in the eyes of Agent Lott and myself. We would have to make that judgment as best we could, ever mindful that compelling him to create lies to help us could be more damaging than not having his cooperation at all. Care had to be taken.

We arranged for a time to talk to Curd with Sears present. We had a team in attendance—myself, Roark, Agent Lott, Chief Deputy Woodard, and Investigator Brown from the Johnson County Sheriff's Department.

As I walked into the room, I wondered how Curd would receive me. Would he tell me to take my deal and stick it up my rear? That was what he had said he'd tell me, during that long-ago recorded jail call. In an effort to build some rapport with him prior to such an outburst, I had made up a list of things I hoped he and

I could agree on.

I sat down across from him, and began going through the list.

"You loved Jenelle." I hoped this subject was no longer controversial.

"You wanted her parents to approve of you."

"You would have never been involved in any significant crime if it wasn't for the Potters."

"Jenelle got attention from her parents by gaining their sympathy."

"You were scared to admit to law enforcement and to Jenelle's parents that you loved her."

Those weren't questions. I knew them as answers. Answers that I hoped would convince Curd that I had some empathy for his situation. I sat across from him, just a few feet away from his eyes as he gazed through his shaded glasses, and I delivered each line with care. To every sentence, Jamie gave a silent and subdued nod. I told him that I had always heard that sometimes love could be blind, and that I thought he had been blinded by love for Jenelle. Again, he was quiet.

Reading his body language, I could tell he had given up the fight.

From the start, Jamie was willing to tell us some things. Of primary interest was his take on Chris. Had two-plus years made him realize Chris was a fictional character? Jamie said he had believed him to be real, even though he had never met him or talked to him. His communications were exclusively by e-mail and text messages.

Jamie had some elaborate stories that he said convinced him of Chris being real. One was when he was in town doing something, drove here, drove there, and came home. He said he later got a message from Chris detailing everything he had just done, and Jamie could not believe that anyone would have known all those things. He believed he had to have been followed by someone real.

How Jenelle could have known such things, I wasn't sure. Or could Jamie have made up such stories to justify his foolishness? I hoped to get back to this subject and discuss it in greater detail.

Regarding Barbara's conversations with Buddy, Jamie said that every time he went to the Potter house, Barbara launched into a complete update of all the harassment that they had suffered. That always took a lot of time. When she got started on such recitations, Jamie'd just have to let her wear herself out before she'd end with asking Buddy, "What are we going to do about it?" Meaning, "What *are you* going to do about it?" If all four of them were together at once, Jamie said Barbara would do eighty-five percent of the talking. Not surprising.

Buddy had told him about being in the CIA. He related some story about participating in an Operation Briar Patch while in Vietnam, where a mission went into another country where the U.S. should not have been, and since that mission "didn't happen" per the official records, when Buddy later cited his having earned a medal from the operation, it was considered a false statement. At least, that was Buddy's explanation for the federal trouble he'd experienced in Pennsylvania.

Jamie said that Barbara talked about Chris like he was her son. Buddy mentioned Chris on occasion also, saying that he had gotten in touch with Barbara at various times.

The initial use the Potters had for Jamie was working on their computer. As he explained it, their Dell computer was old and froze up every month or so. He tinkered with it and got it running by using antivirus software or reformatting the hard drive. Jamie spent his Thanksgiving and Christmas with the Potters in 2011.

While Jamie was cooperating in some respects, it was a long process to get the full truth from him. Truthful people tell everything—the good and the bad stuff. Tell us something unflattering that we did not know before, and we prosecutors and investigators are more likely to conclude a story is truthful. Jamie was failing that test. He wanted to cast blame everywhere else but never assume his own responsibility. We realized he wasn't simply a person in the wrong place at the wrong time. He was an active participant, we knew, but we needed to hear that from him. More critically, the jury needed to hear it.

Another problem we had was that I was doing most of the

talking. Jamie would just say, "yeah" or nod back. We needed him to be the talker. That's how it works in court. Prosecutors must refrain from asking leading questions of their own witnesses.

Even though Jamie was beginning to realize that he needed to play ball, verbalizing a story was difficult. Was he just too uneducated to talk, or were the facts too awful to tell the people who could jerk a deal from him in an instant? I figured the latter.

At times, I got frustrated. Jamie would feign that he didn't remember something or wasn't good at talking. Or just act like he was an unwitting participant in the events of January 31. Once, after I had hit a roadblock on an issue, I'd had enough.

"Jamie, if you think we don't have a strong case on you, you just wait 'til May. What's going to go through your head as the bus leaves for prison, and you're on it?"

There is a truth-telling value to looking into a person's eyes as a tough topic is discussed. I could read in Jamie's eyes that there was some detail he dared not admit. It was a detail that he could not go near, and it colored his sometimes evasive statements. What that detail was, I did not know.

I was afraid I might never know. I tried other angles.

"Do you believe in God?" I asked Jamie.

He said "Yes."

I told Jamie that even though he had failed to help Bill in those final moments, he should at least help him now. On Jamie's real judgment day, not in court, but before a higher authority, wouldn't it help to say he told the whole truth at the end? At least give yourself that dignity, I told him.

Despite my best efforts, there was still an invisible wall between Jamie and us.

We gave up on busting down that wall and proceeded with our preparations to try Jamie along with the women. While it would be nice to go to trial with the background information Jamie could provide, if he could not seem truthful on the tough questions, his testimony was worthless.

Going through Jamie's text messaging after the killings, he had communicated a lot with his niece, Lori Curd. Reading between the lines, it was my opinion that Jamie had said something to her following the crime. I grew curious about what that was.

The texting began at 7:41 a.m., probably within two hours of Bill and Billie Jean being killed. "U heard ne.thing else bout that?" Lori asked Jamie, beginning the exchange. Jamie replied by apologizing for waking her up, saying, "It was just a bunch of shit."

Jamie then began a rant, showing what was on his mind.

"I love jen who is hated by everyone the only girl i ever gave a dam about an we have been hit from all sides il go find a girl 4ft 5in 350lb maby that will make everyone happy," he texted.

Why was his brain fixated on his love for Jenelle and people's perceptions of her? I had a good idea why.

I figured Lori did too. When she was interviewed in 2012, she feigned ignorance about anything Jamie had done. She had acknowledged that he'd come by her camper the morning in question and had coffee. She gave no hint there was anything unusual about his visit, even though it would have occurred right after the killings.

I had a hunch she had held something back, so I suggested to Agent Lott that we approach her again. It would be my first visit to the Curd property.

Lori was now residing where Jamie had lived. It was where Jamie grew up, hardly leaving there until he was hauled off to the Johnson County Jail. The home was a single-story structure with a porch. As I walked around, it was clear this house had seen better days. There was rotting wood all around it. There was decomposing food in a skillet at the back door. The household washing machine was in the backyard, sitting up on bricks to get it level with an extension cord connecting the machine to the house. From there, I saw four deer run across a field.

We knocked over and over. I beat on the door loud enough for anyone to hear me. There was no answer.

We drove to Parkdale Mills to find Jamie's brother, who still worked at the factory where Bill and Jamie shared the same machine. Lori was his daughter, and he said she was likely at home.

So we drove back. This time Lori met us as we walked up the long hill leading from the muddy driveway.

"Are you the ones who were knocking on the door?" she asked.

She didn't invite us in. We sat on the porch with her to talk. I was horribly curious what the inside of the home looked like, considering she had the washing machine banished to the backyard.

We asked her some questions, and her story wasn't any different than before. She knew nothing. Thus I started reading the text messages, letting her realize I had figured her out.

Without any prompting, Lori acted like she now remembered something. Her acting job was unconvincing. It was clear she had been holding back and was only going to be forthcoming when she was backed against the wall.

Lori related that Jamie had knocked on her camper door (her residence at that time was a camper located on the same Curd property), and came in for coffee. She said he would ask her to make coffee often, so that wasn't unusual. However, as he sat there drinking, he was looking down and blurted out that he'd just gotten a message from Chris that the Potters wouldn't have to worry about Bill any longer.

Had she just forgotten such a statement when she was interviewed in February 2012?

I didn't jump her case for the omission. Instead, I gave her a subpoena to appear at trial and tell that story to the jury against Jamie.

What was interesting was the look on her face when we asked about Chris. She still wondered if Chris was real, her eyes blazing when we asked her to talk about him. She and Jamie had referred to him as "Casper," she said, which cleared up my confusion about them using that name in text messages. Agent Lott and I had to explain to her why we believed Chris was a fiction. How much we convinced her of that, I didn't know.

As we left the Curd compound, I took one last ditch effort to reach out to Jamie.

"We tried talking to Jamie, but we felt he wasn't telling the whole story," I told Lori. "He needs to help us to help himself."

Lori agreed.

"If you have any communication with him, convince him to tell the truth," I said.

She said she would.

About a week later, Sears called me.

"We had a breakthrough," he said. "Jamie broke down. It was like you said. When the truth comes out, it's going to be obvious. I think he's ready to tell the truth to you."

Agent Lott and I rushed to the jail. In the past week, Sears's private investigator Randall Witting had worked on Jamie, getting him to understand the need to be fully cooperative. As I told Jamie, we needed to hear the good, the bad, and the ugly.

We were about to hear it.

Jamie related the story of what happened the morning of the killings. It was not what I expected, but it was a plausible account of the events. In other words, Lott and I did not have quick counterpoints with which to challenge his statements. He delivered the narrative with a naturalness that convinced Lott and myself that he was likely telling the truth. At least, there was enough "ugly" there to pass our test.

And this time, Jamie was the one talking. We were furiously compiling notes, interjecting only occasionally to inquire about different subjects.

When we finished with that topic, we moved to Chris. Another story that suggested Chris being real to him was a time when Jenelle told him that Chris was talking about a place up the hill behind Jamie's house. From that spot, Jenelle said Chris could look over into Doe Valley and see Bill's house. Jamie had no idea how Jenelle could have known that, but he said there was indeed such a view from that hill. That further solidified his opinion that Chris was real.

To understand Chris, we needed to know everything about Jenelle's relationship with Jamie. After over two years of confinement, Jamie had finally given up on the only love of his life.

34

"Like adolescents engaged in a forbidden love." If limited to less than ten words to describe Jenelle and Jamie's love interest, that's how I would explain their interactions.

"I thought she loved me, but looking back, she didn't," he sighed. "I was played."

How did that make him feel?

"Embarrassed. Ashamed."

As I had assumed, Jamie believed that Jenelle had desired Bill Payne at some point. Before he knew Jenelle, he was part of a conversation at work where Bill and a Jonathan Lewis were talking about her during break time.

"Bill talked about seeing her," said Jamie. "But she wasn't his type."

Why was that?

"Bill was a player. He was the type who just wanted to drive to a girl's house, pick her up, and take her wherever." Jenelle would have been too much of a hassle, getting her away from her parents. Just not his type. Bill called Jenelle the "Shut-In."

Bill enjoyed life. What little money he made at the plant, he spent on fun.

"Bill had caviar tastes on a poor man's salary," said Jamie. "He had a Mustang and he'd go to Gatlinburg." In looking at Bill's computer contents, I had seen photos of him in Las Vegas. He also loved going to the NASCAR races at Bristol. Clearly, Bill enjoyed life.

In 2009, Bill introduced Jamie to Jenelle. Bill took him to the Potter house to deliver some prescriptions his sister Tracy had prepared while she worked in the local pharmacy. She had asked

Bill to get them to the Potters. In doing so, Jamie met Jenelle. Later, Jamie's dog died, and Bill brought him alcohol to commiserate. While they sat there drinking, Bill's phone rang. It was Jenelle. Bill spoke to her for a short time and Jenelle asked him questions about Jamie.

Instead of answering those questions himself, Bill told Jenelle, "I'll do you one better," and handed the phone to Jamie. She asked Jamie how he was doing, if he remembered her, and if he cared if she called him. He gave her his number. After the call, Bill made some sly comment, but said, "I'll leave that up to you."

I could imagine Bill's amusement at pairing two socially backward individuals together. In his mind, they were probably a perfect match.

Soon Jamie was getting short calls from Jenelle, who was using the Potter house phone. They were short calls because Jenelle had limited privacy, living with her parents. Jenelle was also still calling Bill. Bill told Jamie that. Jamie said that did not make him mad.

"She was your friend before she was mine," Jamie said he told Bill.

At first, Jamie and Jenelle were just friends. Soon, though, she was telling him that she loved him. And he got to see her briefly from time to time, since her parents asked him to help with their computer. But that was it. There were no traditional dates. No going to the movies. No going out to eat. No picnics in the park. Only brief phone calls with little depth of conversation.

What was most odd was that Jamie was not even free to call the Potter house and ask for Jenelle, lest it attract negative attention from Barbara and Buddy.

Before long, during their short phone conversations, Jenelle was talking of getting married to Jamie. She wanted to elope. Now Jamie had my full attention. I was hoping to hear his version of the story Christie had told me, of Jenelle being found by police alone on the road.

It was around March 2010. Jamie said it was a miscommunication. Jenelle thought he was going to meet her. He wasn't going to. He didn't expect she'd actually do it. Instead, he celebrated his birthday that day at two places, including Bill's, where he drank to the point where he passed out.

"Sometime that morning I came to and went home," he said. "About 8:30 that night, the Potter residence called. I was hung over. It was Buddy.

"Buddy told me he wanted me to stay away from Jenelle, that they found her in a ditch down the road this morning. He said she didn't love me. He put her on the phone and she said she didn't love me. She said it real quiet, like it was rehearsed. I wondered what the hell that was about and went back to sleep."

Days later, Jenelle snuck around to call him. She said she didn't mean what she had said. She still loved him.

The relationship continued.

Frustrated that their calls were so short, Jamie bought Jenelle a cell phone. This was a detail I had completely missed—the case file was simply too enormous for me to catch every little thing. Jenelle's text messages to Jamie during the day of the crime were texts made from a phone that was in Jamie's name. Long before, Jamie had bought her a prepaid phone so that they could text and sometimes talk without fear that her parents might pick up the other house phone and catch their affectionate conversations.

A few weeks later, he got a text from Barbara from that phone, asking if this was Jamie. They had been caught. He said Barbara confiscated the phone from her daughter. When Jenelle was able to get off a house call to him again, Jamie told her he would get another phone and throw it in the bushes at the corner of the Potter property. She was to sneak out at night and retrieve it. Then she was to keep it hidden from her parents.

She did, and it remained the phone she used to communicate with Jamie right up until his arrest. They texted each other often, and they would spend hours talking on it late at night. Of course, Jamie would have to wait for Jenelle to call. He could not call her, lest her parents hear it ring.

Meanwhile, Bill was going from girl to girl in his relationships. None were serious, Jamie said, until Bill met Billie Jean at work when she was hired onto the cleaning crew. Their relationship was on the fast track.

"I could tell he was serious," Jamie said of Bill. "He fell for her right off the rip."

Once Bill and Billie Jean began dating, word traveled, and Jenelle found out.

"That's when the shit hit the fan," said Jamie.

Jenelle told Jamie that Billie Jean was just another of Bill's "whores" that he'd throw away. Jamie told her no, that this seemed serious.

"You could tell it irked her," he said. "She didn't really believe me that he was serious. She found out Lindsey was friends with Billie Jean and then things started with Lindsey."

Bill also quit talking to Jenelle. Before, he and Tracy would talk to her often. Now, Bill cut off the phone calls, Jamie said. Billie Jean disapproved of him talking to other women. So Jenelle stopped calling Bill.

Then came the most important fact of all.

"That was the beginning of the e-mails," he said. It was the beginning of Chris talking to Jamie.

We had evidence of Chris's communications back and forth with Jamie. That evidence came from the e-mails between sleepiingbear@yahoo.com and bul2dog@aol.com. Yet we were missing a ton of their communications, because Jamie disclosed that most of their talks had occurred via text messaging. We did have Jamie's text history from the day of the killings until his arrest, but we were missing so much. Cellphone providers delete those records after a short period of time.

Jamie said that Chris usually texted him between 4:00 and 8:00 p.m. or at 10:00 p.m. Jamie worked twelve-hour shifts at the plant from 7:00 p.m. to 7:00 a.m. When he wasn't at work, he spent hours on the phone with Jenelle, after her parents had settled in for the night.

"Jenelle was a night owl," he said. "She'd go to sleep about 3:00 to 4:00 a.m."

In their conversations, Jenelle talked to Jamie as though Chris was real. On the rare occasions they were together, Jenelle would show Jamie pictures of Chris on the computer.

"Jenelle would tell me that she'd heard from Chris. She talked about him like he was her brother."

Jamie knew about "Chris" prior to Billie Jean and Bill getting together. Jenelle had talked of him as a family friend, and a person she'd been close to in Pennsylvania, growing up. But the Billie Jean development caused Chris to come to life, so to speak.

After Buddy's call to him after the failed elopement, Jamie had not been welcome at the Potter house. He and Jenelle kept their communications hidden from her parents.

In May 2011, Jamie's mother died. He had never strayed far from his family, sitting by his father's side and then his brother's as each passed away. Jamie had dropped out of high school to work and help pay for his mother's medications. When his mother died, Jamie was alone in the house. He took her passing hard, experiencing what was probably a state of depression for three or so months.

After his mom passed, Jamie got a call from Buddy Potter. It was the first time in a long while that he had talked with either of Jenelle's parents. Buddy called to express his condolences. That phone call was a turning point, and Jamie was again welcome to come to the Potters' house.

However, his love for Jenelle had to remain a secret. If Jamie pressed Jenelle to ask her parents to allow them a traditional boyfriend-girlfriend relationship, he said she got upset, insisting that she would talk to them soon. She never did.

By Thanksgiving and Christmas, Jamie was one of the Potters' most valued family friends. We had recovered numerous pictures from Christmas 2011 in which Jamie wore reindeer antlers at the Potter home, and the Potters all huddled around him on the couch for happy photos.

Nevertheless, Jamie remained a "family friend" in the eyes of Jenelle's parents. The closest they ever got to going out together, Jamie said, was a time when Lori took the two to the mall in Boone.

Jenelle's parents wrongly assumed that Jenelle would be going alone with Lori.

"They went to the mall, and I walked around like the fifth wheel," he said.

The more we talked to Jamie, the more I realized that my first impressions of him were wrong. When I initially watched his interrogation video, he was cowering, and appeared to be incapable of any intelligent speech. His having been misled into friendship with a non-existent CIA agent didn't help my impression that he was a complete dolt.

Upon further review, though, Jamie had a great deal of native intelligence. He could drop phraseology like "walked around like the fifth wheel" or "caviar tastes on a poor man's salary" in an instant, doing it often enough that I had to pay close attention to catch the wit he conveyed.

Agent Lott had noticed that aspect of Jamie early on. During the interrogation in which Jamie succumbed to their methods, he had described himself during the killings as "shaking like a dog shitting a peach seed." Lott found that phrasing as important, since he could not imagine a person fabricating his presence at a crime when rendering such a description.

That phrasing was so descriptive, and so unique, that I later googled it to see if Jamie had made it up or just heard it somewhere. Sadly, he'd just heard it. The Urban Dictionary website had a definition for the phrase. Jamie was not an idiot, even if he played the part in this case. Had he benefitted from a more privileged upbringing, his life could have been very different.

At least Jamie would have been socially advanced enough to not get caught up in Jenelle's world. Jamie's main weakness and vulnerability, in my mind, was his lack of a love life leading up to his meeting Jenelle. As a lonely, thirty-eight-year-old man, he was almost defenseless to her advances. More importantly, he was prone to succumbing to any wish of Barbara's—or Buddy's. In order for his relationship with Jenelle to progress, he needed their approval. He needed them to believe he could take care of Jenelle, love her, and provide for her.

Fact was, Jamie had a tall mountain to climb to get in their good graces. And if Jamie loved Jenelle and just *had* to be with her, he was liable to agree to anything.

Even assisting in his cousin's murder.

35

Bill Payne was not only Jamie Curd's acquaintance. He was his cousin.

In pulling the truth from Jamie, we not only had to overcome his reluctance to admit guilt to horrible crimes, we had to overcome the family angle. When Jamie would tell his story, he'd be telling it to Bill's family, which was his own. Any time we broached the notion that he knew Buddy intended to kill Bill, Jamie would deny it.

I was not totally inclined to believe Jamie when he claimed he unwittingly joined in a plan to kill on January 31, 2012. There had been enough writings from Jamie to suggest he knew their plans. He had written to Chris about his wish for Jenelle to have "peace" from her tormentors, and that was written in the context of Chris wishing sinister things upon them.

Jamie said he never hated Bill. Even with all the controversy the Potters had tried to kick up between the two, he never did.

"Up to him getting with Billie Jean, we were like brothers," he said. "I was going down there getting drunk every weekend."

Perhaps because of his recurring headaches, Jamie told me he had been addicted to pain pills all of his life. When he began hanging with Bill, he'd get a headache and Bill would give him a Lortab. He'd mix it with beer and chase the headache away.

Once Bill got with Billie Jean, Bill got a prescription for Suboxone. There were other people who wanted Suboxone. They'd call Jamie, telling him they had Lortabs, and ask if they could get a Suboxone strip. Jamie would call Bill and ask if he had strips. If Bill did, Jamie would go pay for the Lortabs and trade part of them with Bill for the strips to take to the other people. By doing this, he could skim Lortabs off the top.

"I had a prescription for the pills, but I had an addiction. I needed more than I could get with the prescription. When they threw me in jail [for the murders], I lay there with sweat dripping off my nose and felt like I was freezing to death. The days were a blur."

Since they thought of themselves as upstanding citizens, the Potters looked down on drug or alcohol use. Thus Jamie hid both habits from them.

"They didn't know about me doing all that," he said. "Jenelle was down on drugs. I didn't want to turn her off."

Jamie's involvement in Jenelle's harassment trial was a turning point as far as his relationship with Bill. Lindsey had filed the charges, but Bill had an interest in the case as well. Jamie came to court that day with the Potters, sitting with them and waiting his turn to testify.

"I was only there to testify that Jenelle was sick and didn't drive," he said, points the Potters believed were somehow important to a phone harassment case. Jamie never took the stand.

Bill was not at the hearing, but Billie Jean and Tara were there for Lindsey. When the trial ended, everyone went their separate ways. We asked Jamie if Lindsey or any of her friends had threatened them after court (the Potters had told Lott and Woodard that Lindsey had expressed hope that Jenelle would die). Jamie remembered no such thing.

One incident after court did stand out. Jamie said that Buddy offered to get Jamie something to eat and took him to Potter's Store in Doe Valley, the same place where Linda Stephens had witnessed the Potter women berate Billie Jean at the gas pump. While they sat in a booth eating, Jamie noticed Billie Jean and Tara walk in. Minutes later, as Buddy was in line to pay, Bill showed up. Bill was not there to buy something. Bill was there to give the Potters a piece of his mind.

"There was yelling and shouting [between Bill and the Potters]," said Jamie. "Bill had come out of his car cussing them. It was something about court, that Lindsey got shitted out of the case.

"Bill looked at me and came over, looking like he was going to say something, but he didn't. He just looked at me. Buddy said something, and he turned and said something back. Jenelle said something. I got out of there and left in my car. I figured the police would get called, and I didn't want to be in the middle of it."

This confrontation had been repeatedly referenced in Barbara's emails to Chris, but now we better understood what had occurred due to Jamie telling us this.

Hours after this conflict, Bill called Jamie at home, telling him of the notebook he had of Jenelle's purported writings and how she had harassed them.

Jamie had been unaware whether or not Jenelle had placed unwelcome calls to Lindsey. Nonetheless, he later wound up having a strong suspicion that Jenelle had placed calls when she dropped a hint.

"Something was said, I can't remember what, but it was something about Lindsey." he said. "Jenelle let it slip that that she needed to start calling her again."

"I said, 'What?'" said Jamie. "And it was like she goofed. Bill told me one time there were 137 calls in just a few hours from Jenelle's house number."

36

Barbara was a "worrywart," according to Jamie. She always needed something to worry about. And as much as Jamie wanted to come over, he said he only came to the Potter house on invitation.

"Barbara wasn't the type of person that you just drop by to see," he said. "She didn't like unannounced appearances."

When he did visit, Barbara would hold the floor, reciting all the latest harassments and issues they were experiencing. Barbara would talk of Chris, making it sound to Jamie like Chris would stop by and talk with them at times. And Barbara began writing Jamie e-mails.

"When Barbara would write to me, they were so long, when I did open them up, I'd just skim them," he said. "I never read everything that she wrote. It was always the same 'ol, same 'ol. Like a broken record. If you read one, you've read them all."

Barbara's form of writing was similar to how she spoke, both in topics of conversation and in style. Chris's topics and harsh language, however, were in stark contrast with how Jenelle would talk with him, Jamie said. Jenelle was not one to curse. Yet Chris ranted and raved constantly.

"Chris would threaten to blow up the whole county," he said. "I'd ask Jenelle about it, and she'd say that when he was mad, he'd say stuff he didn't mean."

During their oral conversations, Barbara would talk about what Chris had said to her.

"She mentioned it to me one time I was there, that Chris wanted to get rid of everybody," said Jamie. "Buddy was sitting there in his chair (when she said that). He didn't say anything."

Even looking at the situation in the best light, Jamie had been horribly negligent in not warning Bill of the things Chris said of him and others.

"I never told Bill about the things they'd e-mail me about," he said. "I thought it was people just talking shit. If you stir shit, you'll get it on you. I didn't want to look like I was driving the gas truck."

Perhaps a deeper desire motivated Jamie to stay quiet—his love for Jenelle and his yearning to have more of a relationship with her. Had he told Bill of what he was hearing, he would have blown it with Jenelle.

Jamie had never met Christie, but he had heard plenty about her. He said Jenelle hated her sister. Jenelle told him of Christie being mean to her as a child, of Christie locking her into the dog enclosure or pushing her out a door and locking her out. Jamie said Barbara did not talk about Christie, but she would say she had one daughter she loved. The other was unmentioned.

When he was still on good terms with Bill and the gang, Jamie was in their presence when he said they were together discussing what to say in e-mails back to the Potters.

"When anyone would tell me of all the harassment, I'd tell them everyone just needed to leave everyone else alone," said Jamie. "If Jenelle talked about it, I'd cut her off and say everyone just needed to let it go."

Through all the hours we spent with Jamie, we were not getting the holy grail of his potential testimony—that moment when Barbara, Buddy, or Jenelle outright solicited him to commit murder. Or at least join in.

The training sessions that Barbara alluded to in e-mails? No such thing, according to Jamie. There had been one time when he shot guns with the Potters, but that was an innocent occasion, he said.

"I had an AK-47 of my late brother's, and I took it over and Buddy helped me clean it. Then we shot it and some of their guns."

Jamie insisted that was not a "training session" and that none were held.

Jamie did relate times when Barbara and Buddy talked of the

continuing controversy, which had some value for us.

"When I would go there, I'd sit down and Barbara would bring me up to speed on what they'd done. Buddy would be sitting there," said Jamie. "Barbara would say, 'You wouldn't believe the awful things they were saying about Jen, Buddy, and me.' She said Chris was sending e-mails back. Buddy would just nod his head, like it was ridiculous of them doing that. She'd turn to Buddy and ask him what they were going to do about it.

"Buddy would always say Barbara told me about e-mails. I don't think he knew how to turn the computer on."

37

We deliberated on whether to pull the trigger on a deal for Jamie. While I harbored misgivings about Jamie being forthcoming about the planning of the killings, I couldn't discount that perhaps he was telling the truth. Certainly Agent Lott and I found his narrative of what happened in the Payne house on January 31, 2012, to be believable.

I could win the case without Jamie. At least I hoped I could. What would help would be Jamie explaining that key moment of conspiracy when all the participants huddled together in the Potter home and planned it out. There was no such thing, he said.

Perhaps there wasn't. Jamie should have had enough sense to know that I wanted to hear that story, if it had occurred. I made it clear I was interested in the preplanning. Jamie knew he stood little chance of avoiding a life sentence if he went to trial. Thus, he had every incentive to tell me what I wanted to hear.

Well, he sort of had, and he sort of hadn't. In a way, that made me feel good about his truthfulness. After all, defendants desperate for a plea bargain are prone to lying. Make up a good story so the prosecutor likes it, then get the deal you want.

Jamie had not done that. He could have painted a picture of Barbara at the Potters' kitchen table plotting out the scheme, but he didn't. That made me think he was playing me straight.

One thing Jamie's cooperation would do for us was help complete the story of his relationship with the Potters. Since the jury would hear from Jamie, instead of him hiding behind constitutional protections at his own trial, they could evaluate for themselves what little danger he would have presented to society had he not been ensnared in Jenelle's web. He could explain how he got that phone to Jenelle, which was a fact I hadn't appreciated at all prior to talking to Jamie.

What value that backstory had to our prosecution against Barbara and Jenelle, I could not know. It could've been little. Perhaps a lot. One thing that I considered important, however, was that Jamie was a secondary actor in these crimes. I firmly believed that. If the Potter women were the primary actors, as I thought, then common sense told me not to leave anything to chance in pursuing them. As I saw it, my first duty was to ensure that the persons most responsible for Bill and Billie Jean's deaths were convicted of the highest crime possible. To hold back on the evidence against Barbara and Jenelle and choose to go full-bore against a secondary character... that didn't make sense to me.

Another point in favor of offering something to Jamie was a simple sense of fairness. I had squeezed the man as much as I could, begging him to share the truth. All the good. All the bad. Concluding that he had done so, I didn't feel it would be right to pull away and subject him to the jury's wrath.

There was yet another consideration. In all the many times I had envisioned arguing this case to a jury, I anticipated the real possibility that a jury could find him guilty of "facilitation" of first degree murder. Being charged with two counts of first degree murder, the lesser charge of facilitation would be given to the jury as an option. The definition of facilitation was that "knowing that another intends to commit a specific felony, but without the intent required for criminal responsibility... the person knowingly furnishes substantial assistance in the commission of the felony."

Such language has seduced many a jury when considering the culpability of lesser players to crimes. Moreover, in a joint trial of Barbara, Jenelle, and Jamie, I fully intended to portray Jamie as a hapless fool manipulated by the women. I was going to throw every persuasive point I had against the women, regardless of whether that, in the end, helped Jamie.

Whenever I had thought of conducting this trial, in the back of mind I thought that a facilitation conviction for Jamie would be a victory if it came with first degree convictions for Barbara and Jenelle.

Perhaps more than anything, Jamie had given me the morsel of evidence I needed to argue what had previously been a mere hunch. When I long ago had read Chris and Matt's writings talking of Tyler as "that damned baby" or that the baby needed to die, my suspicion was that Jenelle's jealousy of Billie Jean's relationship with Bill was the driving force behind her hate. But all I had was a hunch. When Jamie told me that the Chris e-mails began at the same time Billie Jean had moved in and became pregnant, I then had what I needed to confidently share my hunch with the jury. Juries crave believable motives, and now I was convinced I could give them one.

Thus I offered a deal. Jamie would testify, and after the women's trial, he would accept a twenty-five-year sentence for facilitation of first degree murder, two counts. That crime, one felony grade level below first degree murder, would at least get him a chance at parole after serving 30 percent of the sentence, minus whatever creative arithmetic the Department of Corrections employed toward his good time or work credits. I told him that I could not guarantee his success with the parole board, and that the victims' families would have the right to raise hell at every parole hearing held.

After our plea agreement was made, Sears gave me permission to see Jamie on my own. So I did. With Jamie now on our team, I made a few subtle efforts to bond with him. Once I snuck some Reese's Cups into the jail for him to eat during one of our meetings in the chapel room of the nearby Unicoi County Jail. He gobbled them down. After considering his interest in computers, I showed him how my Mac worked. He was impressed with its speed, but he maintained his loyalty to Microsoft. We got along well. Well enough that I'd lose track of time and leave past 10:00 p.m. I didn't mind.

I had a purpose in meeting with him. I was going through our e-mail evidence with him, figuring he might have insights that I lacked.

He did. Among those clarifications was a demon reference that had meant nothing to me. On October 27, 2011, Chris made this statement to Jamie:

> **This Demon thing came to us from them. I think it really came from Linsday and Billfrom what i'm hearing and learning.**

"Jenelle told me that Chris was doing CIA work in Trade, and a demon came out of the ground," Jamie explained. "She said it scared him. I think Barbara was aware of it."

Jamie was unaware of what pressing international intelligence matter existed in Trade, a community small enough that a person could drive through it without noticing.

We talked more about Jenelle's behavior. He said she spoke differently with Jamie than she did with her parents. He said she knew how to get what she wanted from them.

Jamie's sense of humor popped up every now and then. Looking over one of Chris's messages detailing the reason why Lindsey did not like Jenelle, he saw that Chris stated it was because Lindsey saw Jenelle using food stamps at the grocery store.

Jamie piped up, "Hell, half of Johnson County uses food stamps." Indeed, it seemed like a badly thought out explanation for hatred, much like the idea that any female might be jealous of Jenelle because she was "too pretty."

She was attractive enough in Jamie's eyes that in October of 2010 he saved those pictures she sent to him specially via phone messaging. The nude selfies. Pictures covering every portion of her body. Most did not include her face, but some did.

Those pictures had been a key discovery by investigators early in the case. Since both Jamie and Jenelle had denied their love to the detectives, finding nude photos of Jenelle in Jamie's e-mails was quite the revelation. Jenelle had sent them from her secret cell phone to Jamie's cell, and Jamie then forwarded them to his e-mail account. We assumed he did so in order to save them for the future.

We also assumed that the descriptive subject headings for the nude e-mails were written by Jamie. Titles such as "A HOLE,"

"Both girls top shot," "Close up," "First tit shot," "It covered in com," "Kicked back," "Lip shot," "Muff one shot," "New my toys," "On back," "On back at side," "Shower," "Squrt good," "Squrt my favorite," "The girls sexy," "Wet and good," and "Wide open."

For Jamie, the photos constituted the closest form of physical intimacy he could achieve from this odd relationship. He was a man accustomed to a lifetime of never touching a woman. These photos, sent exclusively to him, likely drove him wild.

I respectfully asked him about the pictures.

"Jenelle sent you pictures. We've seen them. I imagine that since you're a man, you liked her doing so," I said.

He nodded.

I never pushed the question that raged in my head: Did they ever consummate the relationship? It didn't matter to my case, but on a personal level, I was horribly curious.

On October 27, 2011, there had been a series of messages between Jamie and Chris that suggested some intimacy between Jamie and Jenelle. First, Chris had suggested to Jamie that he take Jenelle out that Saturday and "make sure you have Candles and make sure you have a card and make the bed really pretty and just love on her."

Which is not the type of advice I'd expect from a CIA agent.

I asked Jamie if he heeded that suggestion.

"No," he said. "Chris would often suggest I do something like that and sneak her out of her house. But I figured we'd get caught, and it'd be over."

Nonetheless, Jamie's reply to Chris's love tips suggested to me that at least on one occasion, little Jenelle had slipped out of the house and joined Jamie:

> [I] know how much it means to jen to see me an she needs that talking to her it one thing to be able to hold her an tell her she is safe an dont have anything to worry about i can see the peace of mind on her beatufull face... if there was any outher way to get jen here id go for it you woldn't

> belive how calm she is hee[1] like she dont have a care in the world it beatful an when its time to go i can see the worry an dread in her eyes an that hurts every bit of happyness i can give her i wont to.

Love can make a fool out of anyone. It had done so with Jamie. He was so fooled into believing that Chris was real that he completely missed Jenelle's clumsy hints that I found; hints that showed something was amiss. There had been one long e-mail exchange in October of 2011, where Chris signed off saying that he'd need to get off the computer so that Jenelle's mom could read his e-mail to her—a statement that made no sense unless both Chris and Barbara were using the same computer. In a later text conversation, Jamie snapped at Jenelle and upset her. Almost immediately, he began getting texts from Chris pleading with him to apologize to Jenelle and tell her how much he loved her. After enough apologies from Jamie to Jenelle, Chris disappeared from the conversation and Jenelle came back, happily returning Jamie's statements of affection.

Those are just the things I had found, searching for sense in it all. Yet it had gone over Jamie's head. I asked him how he knew Chris was writing to him from bul2dog@aol.com and not Jenelle.

"Well, he'd start the message with, 'Hey dude,' or 'Hey man,'" Jamie said.

That was all it took. I asked him in what percentage of their conversations they talked about Jenelle versus how often they talked about guy stuff, i.e., work, ball games, fishing.

"It was all about Jenelle," he answered. "All the time."

"Well, that tells me a whole lot about who was really writing," I told him. "Guys don't talk about relationships all the time. We talk about that other stuff a lot."

I realized that the point of me spending this time with Jamie was to prepare for trial. And I realized that I was working on a much more important matter—achieving justice for one of the worst crimes I'd ever prosecute.

---

1   I concluded he intended to type "here."

Yet I couldn't help but feel pity for Jamie. The guy had proven that he was capable of working. He had shown love for his mother, caring for her until her death. I was sure that if given the opportunity, he would have loved and cared for Jenelle as much as any man could for a woman. As odd as Jenelle was to me, Jamie would have appreciated her. He would have treated her as his prize, which was something Jenelle probably craved more than anything.

Would these murders have occurred if Barbara and Buddy had let go of the reins and allowed their daughter to go her own way? Had she married Jamie and lived a normal marital life, cooking and cleaning for him, and him buying her a pretty dress and all the other things that go with such a life, would that have occupied Jenelle's mind? Kept her from playing bizarre conspiratorial games and manipulating all those around her?

Those questions will never be answered. But if I guessed, marrying Jamie might have changed a lot about Jenelle. Perhaps for the better.

38

The greatest value of Jamie's cooperation for our prosecution of Jenelle and Barbara had nothing to do with anything he told me. It was what he did not say that proved most helpful.

When I first pictured the case against Jenelle, and then Barbara, I was focused on the "solicitation" part of the criminal responsibility statute. Remember, the Tennessee statute covering criminal responsibility for the conduct of another required that the defendant "solicit, direct, aid, or attempt to aid another" in the commission of the offense with the intent the offense take place.

I had expected Jamie to give me the solicitation on a silver platter. He didn't.

The women's e-mails still constituted a solicitation, in my mind. Or at least circumstantial evidence that they were soliciting the men to kill. Barbara and Chris had written back and forth about the need for action, and in doing so Barbara had written about Buddy's ongoing plans. While the e-mails didn't include a statement such as, "I am writing to you to gain your cooperation in killing Billie Jean," the e-mails were tantamount to being a solicitation.

However, I feared at this point I was going to have a hard time arguing that. Especially since the women's defense attorneys could harp on Jamie's denial that the women ever solicited him in person. I was a prosecutor who liked arguments that were simple. Easy to understand. My solicitation argument was too complex, I feared.

Thus, out of necessity, I reconsidered my theory. For a brief moment, I panicked that my agreement with Jamie could doom the case. It was entirely possible the jury could go our way and then an appellate court reverse the convictions because we didn't have a direct solicitation in the testimony.

So I went back to the basics, back to the basic meaning of the criminal responsibility statute. Yet I knew it was a little late in the game, less than one month prior to trial, to be searching for such preliminary answers.

As I looked, I suddenly saw a different theory that was as simple as I desired, and it was completely encompassed within the e-mails we would submit. And that was the real value of Jamie's cooperation—it forced me to rethink and hone our theory for the jury.

"Attempt to aid" was the phrase in the statute that I had completely misapprehended. Suppose Buddy in fact was the sole person who decided to kill the victims, that Jenelle's actions merely constituted a bunch of false allegations of harassment to engender attention from her parents, that Jenelle really only intended to obtain sympathy rather than to cause murders, and that neither women ever really "solicited" either man to kill.

Even if I conceded those arguments, the women still "attempted to aid" Buddy to get the job done. Buddy was sixty years old and had drawn disability for many years. He lacked the mobility to hunt down victims in their twenties and thirties and successfully carry out his mission without a glitch.

I considered what would have happened if Buddy had entered the Payne home alone. Perhaps he could sneak up on one victim and get a shot off. Problem was, he was targeting two people. While he was gunning down one, the other was liable to slip away.

Killing people is not like what we see in the movies. In films, a killer can get a head shot off from a long distance. For anyone with experience with pistols, however, we know that the greater the distance, the slimmer the odds of a kill shot. Try firing a pistol at a target from five feet, and then compare the results to a shot from fifteen feet. There's quite a difference. If the second victim was able to get any distance away from Buddy, there was a strong probability that person could dart out the sliding door and escape into the protective darkness. Buddy couldn't chase them. He wasn't able.

Which meant the mission would fail, as the second victim would surely survive to tell the tale and firmly convict Buddy Potter.

Buddy was too smart for that. As Barbara had stated in her e-mails, he needed another guy. He needed someone to stand at that door and keep everyone corralled in as Buddy executed his targets. One by one.

By their written statements, Barbara and Jenelle recruited that help for Buddy, thus "attempting to aid" him in his mission.

I could draw a timeline of the progression of the plans Buddy and Barbara had for ending the drama. At first, Barbara and Buddy wanted a CIA identification and hinted at their desire for CIA support. Ideally, they desired Chris as Buddy's helper. As previously presented in longer form, this April 12, 2011 message was a good starting point for this criminal responsibility analysis:

> Bud is sooooo mad, &I'm 100% behind whatever happens. You guys meet when you are ready Chris. Maybe Bud will have ID by then & can use CIA guns, etc. for his protection- get the jobs done. ya know. They all need to go & the ones left need to be given a big scare as they watch & wonder "am I next?"

On May 28, 2011, Barbara sent this message to Chris regarding his "plans," and more importantly, she confided to him about Buddy having pondered how to do what needed to be done:

> If you come back, do you have 'plans'? like talked about before for her espec. and for others? I hope they wil let you do what needs to be done, and Bud is ready to help you. Though he needs an ID, he says in this town, they only look at the computer. He has thought and thought of ways & is ready...just needs another guy. They are driving by, parking in front of our house at night from 11-3:30 am in morning. Last night they were in Tara's SUV some, & in Lindsay's car some...she is just studying our house & wondering if we are up I think. Well, we are. Bud is in the living room watching and waiting. He goes to bed at daylight so he is on the 'night shift' and I get up during the

night & I watch from the back of the house/bedroom. Its not way to live.

Of course, Chris could not be the other "guy" for Buddy, even though Chris wanted them all dead as much as Barbara. The only solution was to offer up an alternative. Jamie Curd became the alternative. Jenelle Potter had learned how to manipulate her parents, and in the past couple of years, she had learned how to toy with Jamie as well.

Thus Chris began throwing Jamie's name into the mix during the spring of 2011. Chris claimed to Barbara that Jamie was being harassed by Lindsey and others, and was fed up. In effect, Jamie was having the same problems with these people as the Potters were, according to Chris.

At first, Barbara's response to Jamie's name was negative. After a few months, her attitude changed. Perhaps the change of heart was due to Chris being unable to kill their tormentors himself, or that Chris was unavailable to help Buddy take care of it.

Out of necessity, Barbara accepted Jamie as a team member. She warmed up to him. As Lindsey's harassment case against Jenelle was thought to be coming to trial, Barbara was roping Jamie into possible testimony. She wrote to Chris on June 21, 2011:

> **Anyway, a note to let you know this....I called Jamie this evening & talked for a while. then Bud talked to him. He is coming here on Thurs at noon to see us/talk for a while... so will try to tell you some in 'code' but he can tell you All -if he wants to. We are going to try to get him to testify in court that she is hacking & how it is breaking the law the way she is doing it like he explained to me-he said she is illegally doing that.**

While Buddy and Barbara were readjusting to having Jamie in their home, they were not ready to let go of having CIA agents meet up with Buddy. This was Barbara's message to Chris on June 30, after having asked Chris about having a "list" of people to kill:

Bud asked me to ask you if Adam[1] would meet him/pick him up somewhere, whatever, & talk to him or bring him to you & you three talk, whatever? possible? At night of course& he would not say a word about where you are or whatever he & Adam talk about. think about it & tell me. Ok? Well, son I will close for now. You take care of yourself & let me know what's going on. Bud will call Jamie.

Perhaps happy that Jamie was being welcomed into the Potter home, this message from Chris on July 1 was intended to help grease the welcome mat by offering an apology for Jamie's past transgressions:

Wow that was a long email lol. But its ok. I read it. I know Jamie said he was sosorry about all of that stuff. but he said you were always good to him and his mom . and he said nothing bad about any of you all at all. He's just mad about how they are buging You and Him and he wont take it. <u>He would kill her if he had someone he siad. He know's some ppl that would help him but he said trusting someone you know. He don't want anyone to talk.</u> But yes i think if he and buddy would meet it would be a good thing. Before July 27th and let him tell you how he found out everything and he knows them girls was well so he can pretty much tell you if your going to have any isssues with bill or billie next and he know's a lot. But i can understand. But please just talk to him.

Barbara replied the next day, on July 2, writing that Buddy intended on meeting with Jamie and that everything was fine, forgetting that just a few months prior, she'd been writing that he stunk and was ignorant:

About Jamie, yes, everything's okay with us about way back then.We don't dislike him in any way. Bud really wants to meet with him but he thinks he works all the time. I told him to give him a call and meet him out somewhere or over

---

1 In Barbara and Chris's messages, "Adam" was often referred to as a coworker of Chris's at the CIA.

his house. It needs to be done asap.He says he will. He has been worried about me bc I've been so bad w/pain,but I told him not to worry bc sooner or later, things will get better at least I'm praying for that. So he will meet with Jamie, I'm sure, before 7/27!— hopefully he will be able to talk to our lawye &possibly go to court w/us to speak if lawyer says so. We'll pay him.Bud wants to meet w/him... he just kind of thinks that Jamie can't help w/anything,ya know, like he'd like, so he don't know if info would do him any good. He is upset that if Jen goes to jail-ya know..& then when Billie starts on Jen after court in addition to Lindsay again... we just need to get away from it.

By November, Barbara's dealings with Jamie were good enough that she was trying to get Jamie to believe that the CIA would back Buddy's efforts. This message from Barbara to Jamie on November 23, 2011, was particularly useful, since Jamie later asked the TBI interrogators, "Is the CIA here?"

By the way, <u>if you talk/text with Chris, ask him if he thinks the cia will back up Buddy if he takes it into his own hands</u>.. not an email but a text...he is worried he will get locked up for doing nothing or you know...what a worry. They are trying to kill Jenelle little by little (but doc says that at this rate, it could happen anytime w/heart attack/stroke, DKA itself-that she is getting it too often now & the stress has to stop) It seems that they are going to keep going after all of us until we're all dead/gone...not right & the cops are behind them per Chris.

The team in place, Chris began pouring more fuel on the fire. In reference to what Jamie had told us about Bill confronting Buddy at the store after Lindsey lost her harassment case, Chris wrote on December 2 that, from his CIA surveillance, he learned that Bill was mad about Jamie eating with the Potters. Chris wrote that Billie had urged Bill to kill Jamie.

On December 4, Chris wrote this to Barbara, telling more about his surveillance and what Bill and gang had planned for Jenelle:

But round 3 is Bill wants to hurt Jenelle or just yell at her he has not made his mind up yet. from the phone call's there are a lot of guys looking for Jenelle and know's her now. and She will be fine like I said she never alone. They are wanting to hurt her for many reasons. But it will be ok. as you know what I mean. Love you all and god bless you all.

In another message from December 4, Chris wrote to Barbara more about what he knew:

Well we know that Bill is Fucking drug head. Yes he has told everyone Buddy is selling drugs LOL like anyone would think that. They need to stop hacking and Lindsay has been down there Bill Lies and everyone know's it and is always trying to hurt someone. He is trying to take Jenelle's life by having no friends and it's not going to work. It none of his Boss or anything else what Jenelle does. I wrote on her wall leave it I want there friends and Bill to see what I said. I'm going to get after him if he don't stop running his fucking Mouth and Fuck Him. I know everything that's going on and I see and hear I'm not dumb like they think. They do need to leave you all alone. If I thought anything about Jamie I would have said something and I have his back always he's a good guy and I don't like a lot of ppl and you know this. I just pick good ppl. And Bill know's who I am what I look like and what I do but he can't think of me LMAO fucker head. He just is trying to make up all the lies he can and Lindsay ugly ass hooker fucker face is just a Brat and ugly . and No one would really want wake up and say your so pretty they laugh at her I bet and say what did I do? LMAO> Billie is a fucker head too. I hate them all. I heard what Bill said tonight and let me tell you something FUCK them Hell is closer to them. We got Jamie's back and tell Jamie to stay if he want's anytime b/c they are after him a lot. and no need of this fucking shit. We are pissed off guys. we will be around. Happy you made it home safe. I will talk to you soon. Love your son Chris God Bless.

While Jamie never admitted to me that he wished harm to anyone in this matter, he did write this e-mail to Chris on December 14, 2011:

> [H]ay hows is it going i can show you a few ways to get rid of the files that slows your computer down just remind me when I'm there when they get a lot of stuff on them they get so slow i can't stand a slow computer an i hope every one is doing good an bill Billie an Lindsey will get whats coming to them well i got to run call me anytime you need me have a good one God bless Jamie.

One key to our case was the small window of time available for a home invasion that would not endanger Paw Bill. That window of time was perhaps as short as a half hour early in the morning, and Buddy's execution hit it perfectly. Jamie had told us that Barbara would always talk about "poor Paw Bill" during her in-person diatribes, and her e-mails to Chris had expressed an apprehension of anything bad happening to Paw Bill. Jamie told me that, for some reason, Barbara liked Paw Bill.

Along these lines, the following message on December 15, 2011 from Barbara to Chris was important to me, as she alluded that Bill and Paw Bill's work schedules at the plants would be altered due to the upcoming Christmas holiday:

> Hey C.-its later on, but justg wanted to touch base and say that tho the 'weather' didn't work out tonight, wow! it was a nice & close time...but things didnt' work out. but there will not be any giving up..and you don't either. -.! and yes, are aware of the worries with j.[1] and are talking & visiting...so he's ok...not to worry. So let me know what is going on. —What are your feelings if someone was found w/a hole in them somewhere in a car? have you done this? Would they chk it out or not? just wondered bc we worry about one of us being shot or ..You know..... hopefully mon. will be another good weather day;..you know..& dad will be on his A game...you know...then the

---

1 I assumed "J" was Jamie.

plant is closed until dec 27th.... so the situation will be
changed for a short time as planned now, but there may
be other ways...you know.

In speaking of "worries" about Jamie, it was possible that
Barbara and Chris were having a discussion of Jamie's skills in
carrying out the crime. However, my better guess was that they were
uncertain if Jamie was prepared in his *willingness* to aid Buddy.

Jenelle, or Chris, continued to try and heighten Jamie's
aggression by cutting and pasting any and all Internet exchanges
deemed to signify a threat to Jenelle. Those pasted exchanges would
be sent from bul2dog@aol.com to sleepiingbear@yahoo.com. To
a normal person, the messages would seem juvenile and silly. To
Jenelle Potter, they were evidence that bad people had targeted her.
An example is this cut-and-pasted dialogue between Jenelle and
someone named Aden Pierce, sent to Jamie on December 5, 2011,
just a few days after Jenelle's court victory against Lindsey:

> **Aden:** Jenelle why dont you just stop and move on i would
> like to know what me and lindsey did to you that was
> so bad?
>
> **Jenelle:** I dont even know you and Linsday i won't even go
> there . But She need's to leave me alone that's all i ask. All
> of them. I don't know you. I don't think. So please leave
> me alone.
>
> **Jenelle:** what do you mean with you and Lindsey b/c I
> don't know you at all???Fill me in
>
> **Aden:** go to hell oh what you are you lie under god.
>
> **Jenelle:** Dude you don't know me. And you were not
> there. And you are taking up for someone who lies and
> hurts a lot of other's all the time. Now back of me. Do
> you even know me in PERSON. SHe Linsdey does not even
> know me and she has told everyone she don't know . Her
> story's are Bull crap and keep on sleeping with her. she
> use's everybody. Guy's and Girl's

Aden: I dont know what its gonna take for you to take a hike. Ive asked you on more than one occassion to leave me the fuck alone. You must not understand what that means so let me explain: Quit talkin shit about me and my friends to everyone and espeacially on facebook. All you keep saying is that you want us to get lives well we have lives and are extremely happy with our lives. Your the one that needs to quit talkin shit and get a damn life of your own. You have no clue how mean I can get my advice is to stop or I will make your life hell. And the next time I wont be emailing you I will be confronting you in person regardless of where you are. I cant help it that your jealous of me and my friends and the amazing lifes we have. You know if youd grow up and quit starting shit with everyone you might could have an amazing life like ours! The bad thing is you think you know so much about all of us but you dont because if you did youd know better than to fuck with me. Ive tried being nice but we're obviously past that point because you just dont know when to quit. And is far as my friends and you know who they are if you dont quit your shit with them your gonna deal with me. I can be a real BITCH if you wanna try me and see. If I had it my way i would have done fucked your stupid ass up along time ago.... THANK YOU & GOD BLESS!

Jenelle: Ok frist of all. It was posted. But I have someone that know's everything that's going on and He want's to say something he is more then welcome to . I Don't care what he say's b.c of who he is. And he has very right too it.[1] Now as for me . You don't know me at all Nor my Family I did nothing to her or anyone else. I have asked everyone to back off me and leave me alone a lot. But Also has this other person he don't care what he say's really. I have knwon him my whole life. None of you want me to have alife well i dont put anything out for anyone. And My Dad

---

1   Obviously, Jenelle was referring to Chris posting the derogatory comments.

and Mom Don't either and My Dad is not Bill's friend at all. We are going to make that clear. He hate's bill. and Bill needs to shut up. I think this is either to be on my Mom's and Dad's land and I dont drive and you will never get me so why don't you stop. Get a life and move the Hell on with your self and just take it like it is you LOST and you can't stand it. Everyone of you is just trashy peolpe. And you want to try to mind oters lives but i'm telling you leave me alone. Don't make me say it . I'm going to block you now. Linsdey or Billie or Bill. All of you are TRASH So go to your thing and I dont bug anyone. I have been very sick. I dont care if you like it not. Stay off my damn Piage. thank you. and GOD BLESS your Lives b/c i do have God in mine.

Aden Pierce probably thought this message was a good idea. By speaking frankly and getting rough with Jenelle, maybe she thought she'd get the message and stop. But when one was dealing with people as delusional and deranged as the Potters, such statements were the equivalent of poking a lion with a stick. It surely only made things worse.

In their crazed minds, the Potters felt they had no choice in what they had to do. However wrong they were, they truly believed Jenelle's safety was at stake.

39

It was showtime.

In order to expedite matters, we picked a jury the week before the trial. Before the proceeding began, Jenelle walked into the courtroom wearing the clothing picked out for her to wear during court. Defendants have the right to wear street clothing rather than jail uniforms.

I realized then that Hyder was the perfect lawyer for Jenelle. As she walked in, I overheard him say, "Jenelle, you look very pretty."

"Thank you," she sheepishly replied.

She was wearing black-rimmed eyeglasses that were circa 1950s, along with a white cardigan over a dark blouse. She looked like she was going to Sunday school.

When Hyder posed the question to the jurors about what word they would use to describe his client, he had a particular aim. He wanted the jury to absorb just how unlike a stereotypical killer she appeared. Indeed, she looked more suited to cross stitching than engineering a double murder. Our theory of the case might have resembled what the state of California had done years before against Charles Manson, but she sure didn't look like him. Prosecutor Vincent Bugliosi had it easy by comparison when he convicted Manson. There was no crazed look in Jenelle's eyes.

Barbara appeared no more threatening. She rode in a wheelchair, pushed by a jailer, each time she entered the courtroom. The wheelchair was hidden every time the jury came in, as she was able to manage to sit in a regular chair. Why she required a wheelchair, I had no idea. She likely didn't; we had a jail surveillance video of her on her feet shooting basketball at the Johnson County Jail just a few weeks prior to the trial.

When the trial's opening day came, I had to hit the defendants as hard as I could. I had to paint a different picture and do it immediately.

"There is nothing in your lives or background that has prepared you to understand the Potter family," I began. "You have never seen anybody like them.

"The story is very, very simple. It's a story of a manufactured conflict born in the mind of a very bored, lonely, thirty-year-old woman. It's the seed that grows into a tree. And it's not just that seed. It's all the water and fertilizer that's put on that seed to make it grow and bear fruit. And all of that happened as the result of Jenelle Potter's actions."

I went straight to the pictures of each victim lying dead in their home. As that shock lingered, I moved into Jenelle's writings penned under fictitious names. The worst ones I could find.

> [J]ust die. She is a waist being on earth... Damn whore . There all whores and always will be and you cant make them in to wives they have 10 more men they sleep with . They are not happy and they want evetone else not to be happy. Fuck them. I'm happy Jenelle is so sweet careing and will stand up for her self whats lisnday and billie do nothing but lie and try to get others hurt. Fuck them I hope they die die die and that baby and bill.

I made sure to place special emphasis on the "die die die and that baby and bill." More:

> I'm about to fight with you Billie why dont you shut up your fucking month you Bitch. One day girl you are going to get beat up really good andleft for dead. You better shut up you bitch. Go fuck a cow for all i care. Damn hooker, slut bag whore ....and your Basterd baby take it with you and leave this fucking town. you wont leave here alive. Keep on doing your damn fucking shit bitch. FUCK YOU and BILL and YOUR FUCKING so called baby. Go after my wife again you little fucking whore bag. I hope you die and i hope its a painful death. YOUR A FUCKING NO BODY.

And a Matt Potter Topix posting for good measure:

> Bill said on tape's they will she would drive so they can
> kill her. They want Jenelle dead so bad and it's them
> that should be dead and that should go to Hell where
> they came from. She don't want to drive and she has
> friend's she does go places with but everyone need's to
> let herlive her life and Stop buging her. You fucking don't
> know Jenelle at all and for you to say this about Dad is
> very wrong and Jenelle is 30 year's old not her Dad. Damn
> ppl do the math or is that to hard for you . You need to
> go back to school and you need to get fucking jobs and
> leave fucking ppl alone. I Will not care what happend's to
> you or anyone else Linsday. Billie Tara Bill JR Jess ex of JR
> for cheating and also Jesscica Tester and ToolBox and etc.
> Now fuck off my sister before I fuck with you your little
> evil Bithc's and Linsday your day will come and your going
> to be gone and no one will give a god damn shit about
> your fucking as or Billie's I hope that baby get's taken
> away from her and I hope tracy dont get it she no mother
> either. Damn whores. why dont you DIE BITCH die. then
> saying that to my sister. DIE DIE DIE Bitch fucking woof
> woof dog face bitch. Your Mom is really fat and one day
> you willbe too. HIV whore.

I had the jury's attention. I hoped I was wiping away that impression of Jenelle looking "scared" or "ordinary." As I told the jury, they would see these and many more writings where "the hate dripped off the pages." And I promised them that we would prove in their minds that those messages were written by that woman, as I turned and pointed at Jenelle. She would not look at me.

For good measure, I included some of Barbara's writings, including this excerpt:

> [I]f someone wants to bring it on, they will All die, including
> the baby. —Yeah we know that Lindsey is the one pushing
> this along but Bill , Billie, Tara-all their mean buddies - are
> enjoying it & he can't act or think alone; he has to have

his gang you know.... well they may as well stay at home
bc there is no getting Jen, no way no how.

My opening statement lasted two hours, the longest of my
career. Someone told me later at the lunch break, "You really need
to keep your opening brief." I told them that I had. That was as
brief a summary as I could give.

Just as I had said to Buddy's jury, I prepared this group to
expect that this would be the craziest story they would ever hear.
As I finished, I felt I had done a good job of getting the jury to
think about the case the way I did, to look for the linguistic signs
consistent with each author, to condition themselves to understand
the requirements of criminal responsibility for the conduct of
another, and finally, to know Jenelle Potter.

The defense attorneys, Fallin for Barbara and Hyder for Jenelle,
took turns lambasting our case. They claimed this was a case of
hacking, and that their clients were the unwary victims of Jamie
Curd. Fallin even had the novel idea that since Jamie could not have
Jenelle for himself, he had set up the Potter parents for murder so
that he could have her. That theory did not fit our facts—when
Jamie had spilled the beans in 2012, he said absolutely nothing to
implicate Barbara or provide probable cause to have her arrested. In
reality, Barbara was the greatest impediment to him having Jenelle.

Hyder stated that our case was all smoke and mirrors while
commencing to voice a defense strategy that was essentially smoke
and mirrors. Our computer data was suspect, our linguistic proof
questionable, our very theory that the childlike mind of Jenelle
could be a criminal mastermind, he said, was impossible.

For the next several days, Roark and I did our best to prove
him wrong.

40

The initial state's witnesses were a repeat of Buddy's trial. Roy Stephens told of finding the victims, and Linda Stephens relived the moment when the Potter women brought Billie Jean to tears as she pumped gas.

Agent Lott again told a jury how his investigation had begun, showing them pictures of the crime scene. Tate Davis, an attorney assisting Fallin, quizzed Lott upon cross-examination about tests run at the scene. I found it curious that Davis grilled him over not testing the baby's bottle for fingerprints. Would one really expect a killer to feed baby Tyler right before he left the scene of a killing spree?

I hoped the jury could sense that the defense was grasping.

Chief Deputy Woodard recounted the initial interview with the Potters the day after the killings as well as Barbara's effort to rip up the Facebook pictures printed of the victims and Lindsey.

On behalf of Jenelle, Hyder aimed the bulk of his defense on our computer evidence. Rather than us simply evaluating the e-mails sent to us by AOL and Yahoo, he apparently thought we needed to do a full-scale computer forensic inquiry into the Potter and Curd computers. Somehow such an exercise would prove who typed what, he proffered. Hyder further questioned our TBI computer expert at length about malware and how it could have allowed someone access to the Potter computer.

I only paid slight attention to Hyder's computer defense. I knew it would go nowhere. For one, we had all those shredded e-mails bagged up in Buddy's truck bed. Secondly, as one of our computer experts noted, if a third party had been using the Potter women's e-mail accounts to send messages, the women would have been privy to it happening. They would have seen the hatred brewing on their accounts. If so, they should have made mention of that when Lott and Woodard paid their first visit the day after the killings. After all, they were asked if they had any ideas on who might have committed the crimes. As it was, they did not mention their hundreds or thousands of "hacked" e-mails, probably because they did not wish for the investigators to see their correspondence.

Lastly, Hyder never could offer a reason for the jury to believe that anyone would be so consumed with the Potter family that they would conjure up this intricate spiderweb of implicating writings. To imagine Jamie having the wherewithal to pull off such a stunt was improbable.

So I had Roark fight the good fight on the computer issues while I kept my focus on making our case.

Roark took care of it. He entered the IP address history for both the Potter and Curd homes, and the e-mail data we received from the e-mail providers had those very IP addresses beginning the delivery chains. Hyder tried to obfuscate this simple evidence, but his approach was so complicated and disjointed that I doubted it was scoring points with the jury.

Christie Groover had her turn. She provided the authentication of Barbara's communications, both handwritten and typed, that we needed for her known writings. When the defense attorneys cross-examined her, they didn't question her about her computer prowess as they had in Buddy's trial. Obviously that jury had not bought their insinuation that Christie somehow hacked the family computer and concocted this whole scheme. Instead, they tried to get her to say that she hated her mother and sister. Hyder even screamed at her in regards to growing up as Jenelle's older sister, "Why didn't you take care of your sister?"

Christie countered their blows. She said that while she did not care to be around them, she did feel love toward her family. She fiercely maintained that testifying in the case was very difficult for her, and she fought back against Hyder's representation of Jenelle as practically helpless.

"I have my opinion about her intellectual ability," she said. "She is a slow learner. Her cognitive formulation is odd. But she is not as bad as you're making it sound."

Christie told the jury that Jenelle had the ability to manipulate people, particularly her parents.

Next, Agent Lott took the stand for nearly two days of testimony. His mission this time was to introduce my selected 207 pages of AOL and Yahoo e-mails as well as the shredded documents and Jenelle's Facebook records. It was a tedious process, and I chose to point out particular sections of the e-mails for him to read to the jurors. Every few messages, the defense attorneys would object to my approach, but Judge Blackwood indulged me. For the amount of data we introduced in those two days, we actually got through it very quickly, as we avoided reading some of the more mundane portions of the e-mails.

There was one e-mail from Barbara to Chris on March 3, 2011, that was particularly noteworthy regarding Christie. It showed a shocking level of disdain for her eldest daughter:

> Jen ran into Lindsay yest. at RiteAid & Lindsay said,"Your day is coming." to Jen. Jen stood up to her and said "Why wait?" "I dare you to touch me here and now." And Lindsay backed off some & acted tough, but she's not w/o All of her rotten no good so-called friends....ha! I was proud of Jenelle &as far we say, Jen will Never be alone w/o one of us in the trucks or with her in a store, so THEY better Watch Out! We are Tired of all this shit Chris! 7 yrs. is 7 yrs. too many & it is soon going to have to be over. (You are welcome to shoot any of them, but Let Christie's body be found-we have life ins on her so may as well collect it...I know that sounds mean for a mom to say,but she hates me,wants me dead as well as dad & Jen..)What can I do? She'll get me someday if not here & soon or have me killed I'm afraid when I'm helpless someday. Worried :(

I heard an audible gasp from some of the jurors as Lott read the line about leaving Christie's corpse where it could be found so as to collect insurance upon her death.

When the defense got its turn with Lott, they did their best to make him budge from our theory that Jenelle had authored all of the writings from her e-mail address. They failed.

"I feel that Jenelle used her e-mail address and Barbara used her own," Lott testified. "For bul2dog, I feel that Jenelle hit the send button every time."

Hyder made little attempt to question our linguistic findings, much to my surprise. The best he could muster was pointing out that both Chris and Jamie used the word "karma." Hyder was going all in on the theory that Jamie was the author of all things Chris. He even pointed out a time where Jamie had typed "leaveing" in a message from sleepiingbear@yahoo.com.

I decided to play along. Instead of analyzing Jenelle's known writings alongside the Chris messages, I scanned Jamie's e-mails from his account, looking for peculiarities. I had never done that previously, as his writings had looked so distinctive.

However, as I studied while Hyder rattled on with his cross, I noticed something about Jamie's writings that was very consistent. Instead of writing the word "and," Jamie always typed "an." Always. As Jamie had told me, he was the type to just dash off a message without much regard for spelling or punctuation. In fact, he almost never used punctuation. He rarely took the time to even capitalize letters.

I quickly looked back at some Chris writings, and for all of the mistakes Jenelle would make, leaving the "d" off "and" was not one of them. I scurried to write down page references for Jamie's writings, and when it was time for me to do redirect with Lott, I let the jury see us play the game of looking for Jamie's use of "an."

This was a surprise to Lott. We hadn't planned this. Actually, I had just figured out this anomaly within minutes of questioning Lott. But he went along, finding all the instances of "an" in Jamie's writings. Every single sleepiingbear message utilized this error. While we hadn't subjected Jamie's writings to a forensic linguistic examination, I felt I had made my point very clear to the jury that

Jamie's style was quite distinct from Chris's and Jenelle's.

Deep inside, I was feeling gleeful. Not because of linguistics, but due to the surprise we had for the jury. I had purposefully avoided speaking of the next witness during my opening statement, and not a single mention of him had come from the defense. We had the good fortune of me being able to set it up with all the dramatic flair I could muster.

"When you first got these e-mails, when you first learned about Chris, was it important to you to figure out if such a person existed?" I asked.

"Yes it was," said Lott.

"Did you actually take some steps to contact the CIA and see if you could find a Chris who worked there?"

"I did."

"Couldn't find him?"

"No sir."

"You talked to all the law enforcement in Johnson County?"

"Yes."

"Do you know about this guy Chris—couldn't find him, could you?"

"No sir."

"You found *a* Chris, though, didn't you?"

"Yes sir. I did."

"He's here, ain't he?"

"Yes sir. He is."

I directed Agent Lott's attention to pictures sent from the bul2dog@aol.com and bmp9110@aol.com accounts, pictures that represented what Chris the CIA man looked like. One was sent to Jamie's address and contained a description, "Here I am, man—Chris." The pictures were of a young man with short, dark hair. In one he wore a dark police uniform. On a select few messages, he was further described as "Chris Tjaden."

In one incredibly long private Facebook message from Barbara to a childhood friend of Jenelle's, Barbara asked if she remembered Chris Tjaden. Barbara typed that Chris had helped save Jenelle a couple of times from "Amanda and others" back in school. Barbara said he was their adopted son, and they loved him, but lamented that they didn't get to see him often.

"How far did you have to go to find this Chris?" I asked.

"Delaware," said Lott.

41

Trials are stressful for the accused. Their liberties are at stake. So are their reputations. Troubling also can be the embarrassing aspects of proof, when the perhaps unflattering conduct of the accused is exposed to the public.

In anticipation of trial, I had fully expected Jenelle Potter to feel tragically embarrassed. With three local television news cameras constantly in the courtroom just waiting for juicy, sensational facts, I figured there would be parts of this trial where she would want to burrow deep and hide.

Jenelle seemed to have one of those moments during my opening statement. She held herself together fine throughout my talk, but when I showed a picture of Jamie kissing her in the computer room, I noticed her recoil. She looked down as if she was afraid of what her mother thought about her being so naughty. She seemed to be unable to handle the exposure of her illicit dalliance with Jamie less well than the times when I would point my finger at her, accusing her of causing the deaths of innocent people. Regrettably, I never stole a look at her when I asked Jamie about her sending naked selfies to him, but I imagine the tension between the Potter women was by then at a fever pitch.

But on the scale of embarrassing facts, the impact of an innocent peck on the cheek would surely pale in comparison to the next witness being present at trial.

We had gotten to know Chris Tjaden during our visits to his neat, orderly, middle-class home on the Philadelphia side of Delaware. His father was the chief of police in a nearby city. Tjaden was newly married and happily working in a law enforcement role himself, serving as a sworn constable in the employ of a local hospital.

He was also a high school classmate of Jenelle's.

He told us that Jenelle was a strange sort as a teen, never fitting in with any group. He was one of the cool kids. Their paths had rarely crossed aside from having a couple classes together. At times she would attempt to hang around Tjaden, as if she liked him, but he'd politely acknowledge her and then go his own way.

Following Tjaden's graduation, he likely never thought of Jenelle again.

In 2012, though, Tjaden was jarred by a phone call from Agent Lott. In investigating the killings of Payne and Hayworth, Lott determined that Jenelle had used publicly posted Facebook pictures of Tjaden and passed them off as being the likeness of the "Chris" behind her Internet accounts.

Being in law enforcement himself, Tjaden did not react with anger over his identity being stolen. He was more curious than anything.

For the prosecution team, it was valuable that there was a real person behind the Chris persona. The fact that it was a guy from Jenelle's schoolgirl past proved beyond any doubt that she was the author of everything "Chris." At least I thought so. Certainly no one in Johnson County would have known Tjaden. Jenelle was the only possible link.

It was easy to imagine Jenelle having had a crush on Chris way back when. He was everything she craved: a nice guy, handsome, and from good law enforcement stock. When my wife speculated that Barbara would have never allowed Jenelle to get married, I pointed out that if Jenelle had brought Chris Tjaden home, her parents would have accepted him immediately. Buddy would have offered to take him shooting, and Barbara would have scurried to bake a tasty dessert, both proudly wanting to impress their new son-in-law.

Trouble was, Jenelle could attract no such man. Jamie was more her level, and he didn't cut it by Barbara's standards.

When we spoke with Chris the night before his testimony, he remembered years ago receiving a Facebook friend request from Jenelle. He accepted it and, perhaps curious about what had happened to this odd acquaintance, checked out her page. He saw a bunch of crazed religious commentary on her part, and unfriended her within minutes of accepting the request. She possibly never realized she was briefly friends with her crush.

The pictures she had lifted from his Facebook page were his profile pictures. Such photos were available to anyone venturing his way. One that was used was a photo of him with his arms crossed in front of a picture at the House of Blues in Atlantic City. Another was of him propped up against a car. There was one of him at a bonfire. Yet another was of him at a Philadelphia Phillies game.

What was really odd was that Jenelle had also e-mailed pictures of other men, claiming they also were Chris. They all looked very like Tjaden. One was strikingly similar, a smiling portrait of a young cop in a police uniform. I could have sworn it was Tjaden, so much so that I actually held the picture up next to Tjaden's face as he stood in front of me in the hallway of the courthouse.

"That looks just like you," I declared. Tjaden and his father had to point out to me the distinguishing features of the police uniform, and that Chris had never possessed such an outfit, for me to be convinced it was not him.

How much time had Jenelle spent online looking for pictures of men who looked like Tjaden, attempting to add to her limited catalog of Chris images?

When the time came for the real Chris to testify, the courtroom sprang to life as he walked through the doors. Multiple media members scurried to get face shots of him as he entered.

My attention was on Jenelle. Roark was going to handle Tjaden's questions, and I was just dying to watch her. How would she react to seeing Chris for the first time since graduation in 2000?

I fully expected her to look embarrassed. She didn't. Not at all. Instead of crawling into her shell like she had throughout the trial, her attention was completely on Tjaden. Her eyes tracked him the entire way to the witness stand, and no matter what unflattering thing he said about her, her eyes never left him. She looked at him with an unwavering gaze.

"Can you tell us a little about your experience with Jenelle in high school?" asked Roark.

"She was very bizarre," said Tjaden. "She was one of those kids who was very strange. She always had issues. She was always complaining about a problem with somebody."

"Did you talk to Jenelle?"

"Periodically. I was one of the more popular kids in high school. I wasn't rude to anybody. I kind of was friends with everyone in high school. If Jenelle passed me in the hallway, I would say hi or just had a little conversation here and there. Nothing too extravagant."

"Whenever you would talk to her, would she approach you or would you approach her?"

"Sometimes she would approach me. You know, I'd be sitting with a group of friends and she would just come over and start a conversation, try to chime in with everyone who was sitting at the table."

"Whenever she would approach you, would she wait around for you to come by or seek you out?"

"I think it was more of a seeking out type of thing. Kind of randomly popping up in the hallway where I was."

At that point, Hyder objected on Jenelle's behalf, the jury was sent out, and Judge Blackwood cut off further questions about Jenelle in high school on a relevance basis.

Thus the jury never heard about how she would have tantrums and usually be in trouble for her behavior. People kept their distance from her. The story of her high school years sounded exactly like the story of her in Johnson County. She was a perpetual outsider.

Roark then went into the e-mailed pictures of "Chris," and Tjaden testified to which ones were of him and which were not. He also asked Tjaden questions to confirm he wasn't the "Chris" from the e-mails. Did he ever work for the CIA, run four wheelers around Johnson County, or help save Jenelle from an "Amanda" in school? He had not.

The defense had very few questions for him, perhaps not

knowing what the heck to do with him other than decline questioning so that he would get out of the courtroom.

Tjaden exiting the courtroom was not the end of the uncomfortable situations we had in store for Jenelle. I figured that surely Bob Meehan would make her squirm.

Bob Meehan was thirty-eight years old and a former boyfriend of Jenelle's. Yet when he walked in to testify, it was the first time they had been physically been in each other's presence.

Their love had played out online. Exclusively online.

Bob lived with his parents in Pennsylvania. During their cyber relationship, Bob worked nights as a janitor. He was a small, soft-spoken guy. Polite and nice, Bob was accommodating about our inquiries and always perplexed why we found him relevant.

Others might have disagreed, but I believed the jury needed to know Jenelle as much as possible. She led a bizarre life, as Tjaden described it, and the acts she had committed to cause two killings were also bizarre. The more the jury understood what she was like, the more they'd accept her criminal schemes.

There were many Facebook messages we'd recovered where Jenelle and Bob professed their love for one another. One was a chain of declarations such as "I love you," "I love love love you," "I love you more." All between two people who had never met.

Bob told us of a time he had bought a ring for Jenelle. He was not clear about what kind of ring it was, but he declared it was not an engagement ring. She asked him to get it for her. So he bought it at JC Penney, packaged it, and sent it by mail.

Curiously, their torrid love affair played out in 2010 and 2011, while Jenelle was calling Jamie her husband in texts and sending pictures of her privates. Bob told us that he "broke up" with her when he discovered she had a boyfriend in Johnson County named Jamie.

Bob was on the stand a short time, telling the jury of meeting Jenelle online and briefly how their relationship had progressed. Importantly, he told the jury that Jenelle had told him of having a close friend named "Chris" who was a CIA agent from Pennsylvania who had transferred to Tennessee.

The last of our long-distance witnesses was a female from Greenville, North Carolina. Melanie Clayton had gotten to know Jenelle in an AOL chat room years before. They became friends. They had online conversations, sent letters to one another, and talked on the phone. They talked almost every day.

When Melanie took the stand, though, it was the first time she and her close friend Jenelle had ever seen the other in the flesh.

Melanie told the jury how Jenelle had divulged family details. Melanie knew of Jenelle's conflicts with Christie and their grandmother. Jenelle had told her of her local boyfriend Jamie, and how he worked on computers. Jenelle had often complained of local girls bullying her and calling her names. Most importantly, Jenelle had described having a "Chris" or "Matt" in her life. He was like a brother to Jenelle, said Melanie.

In the event any juror had lingering doubts as to Chris's true identity, we hoped that Melanie's next line of testimony would obliterate the skepticism. Throughout the trial, the defense attorneys had insinuated that Jamie was the one person with access to the Potter's computer, and that the way he covered his tracks was by making the Potters appear guilty. As arguments go, it was a reach. A big reach. Nevertheless, we had to treat it seriously, lest jurors be led astray.

Following the arrests of Jamie and Buddy, Jenelle turned to Melanie for commiseration. She did it via text message, and I hoped the jury would catch all the linguistic clues contained therein. With Jamie in jail, he was incapable of authoring these Chris-isms.

At 9:31 a.m. on February 7, 2012, Jenelle sent the following text to Melanie:

> Hey girl jamie and my daddy are in jail the cops left onu our ago but the goa here at 3 they took the computer i am so up set wanted you to know.

Melanie replied, "Why?" Jenelle explained:

> Bc they think they killed bill and billie this got me and mom so upset I think they got jamie his cell is off and house

phone just rings i dont understand and 200 thousand for my dad i hope to find more my dad goes to court tomrrow i am so sad pray for us.

Melanie answered, "Oh wow. So who got killed?" Jenelle then made the mistake of explaining away the crime and offering up an alibi for her dear old dad:

The 2 that were after me but everyone knows it was a drug deal went worng but they are geting the blame dad was here the whole night jamie was geting off work and had a huage heack[1] but i am takeing this so hard and they took my computeq and all the bad girls went afater them.

Actually, no one knew it was a "drug deal went wrong." That was just the Potter family spin. Jenelle was repeating the very thing her father had said when Jamie called from the sheriff's office.

Jenelle asked Melanie to put a note on Facebook asking for people to pray for her family. Melanie said she would. Then Melanie asked whose phone this was, since this number was new to her. Jenelle was using the phone Jamie had given her. Previous to Jamie being jailed, Jenelle had only used the phone to communicate with him. In answering the question, Jenelle expressed her worry about Jamie:

Mine... i wish i new what jamie is thinking its bad the town is being really evil.

Late the night of the 7th, Jenelle repeated her worry:

Do you think jamie still loves me

Melanie answered that Jenelle had not committed a crime. She asked why would Jenelle think he did not love her. Jenelle still worried:

I dont know if he loves me or hates me.

This case was so layered that I truly never saw the significance of Jenelle's texting Melanie until Roark had her on the stand and

---

1   She meant "headache."

they went through the messages. On three occasions, Jenelle had expressed doubts about Jamie's love toward her. Why?

It hit me in a flash: Jenelle was wondering if Jamie loved her enough to keep his mouth shut. About her. About Barbara. About Buddy. And perhaps most critically, about Chris. In contrast, Jenelle was texting nothing about whether her father loved her or not. She knew he did. He would never say anything to harm his precious daughter's freedom.

Yet if Jamie's love was too shallow to keep him from telling all, Jenelle was worried she could be the next person handcuffed. At least, that was going to be my argument to the jury.

After all the lamenting about Jamie, Melanie posed a good question to Jenelle via text. She asked, "So if ur dad is CIA then why is he in jail??"

"Tbi is over cia," Jenelle answered. "They got blamed and they were both home and the cops are being mean."

Before the conversation ended, Jenelle threw in another "my town is being so mean to us" and an "i just hope jamie dont hate me."

Unfortunately for Jenelle and her family, Jamie's love had not been deep enough. And what to come next would confirm that fact.

42

"Call your next witness," instructed Judge Blackwood.

"Jamie Curd," I responded.

During a break, I got the chance to sneak into the hallway leading from the jail and see Jamie. He looked different, dressed in a simple collared shirt and slacks. For once his hair was combed. I made sure to tell him yet again that the key to this whole experience was to tell us "the good, the bad, and the ugly." He nodded.

Minutes later, Jamie proceeded to tell the jury about his life growing up, dropping out of school and going to work at Parkdale Mills.

I asked him about Bill's physical condition, which was pertinent to my theory of Buddy needing help to hunt down younger, healthier targets.

"He was fit," Jamie said of Bill. "You had to be, because we had two-story machines that had catwalks and ladders. You had to climb up them, dig chokes out, the cotton and everything. You had to be agile."

We continued through their history, how Bill introduced him to Jenelle and how she became his first girlfriend. Jamie testified that Jenelle had talked of Chris and claimed to have grown up with him, saying that Chris drove her to high school and picked her up after her track practices.

I spent considerable time with Jamie on the e-mails and his communications with Chris. Mostly, I wanted the jury to get to know him. After a couple hours of that, I had more items I wanted to get to, but the clock on the wall was telling me that I had just enough time to talk about the morning of the killings. I was sure the jury wanted to hear that before they went home. So I jumped to it, asking

Jamie what the first thing that led to him being with Buddy was.

"Barbara had called me the evening before and asked me to work on her computer," said Jamie. "She had a bill that she needed to have paid by twelve. She said her computer was locking up. I told her I'd come up and look at it.

"While I was looking at it, Buddy came in and started talking to me. He asked if I would do him a favor. I told him I would. He asked me if I would take him down next to Bill's, let him out and go down the road and come back and pick him up."

That conversation occurred around midnight. He and Buddy had been alone in the computer room. Buddy had not said when he would need the favor. Jamie finished with the computer and went home, only to tinker with his own.

While on his computer, Jenelle called. She told Jamie that "Daddy" wanted him to help do something.

"I didn't ask her what," said Jamie. "We hung up, and she sent me a text that said, 'Don't take your cell phone in the morning.'"

"Why did she tell you not to take your cell phone?" I asked.

"I don't know. I didn't know at the time."

Knowing how cellular call records can pinpoint the location where a call was made or received, I had a darned good idea why the Potters would want him to leave the phone behind. We've made cases based on the methods of determining call locations.

"Later on, I got up and went to the bathroom," said Jamie. "While I was in there, the phone rang. By the time I got back to it, it had stopped. I looked at the caller ID and it was the Potter house phone."

Jamie tried making a return call, but there was no answer. He then got another text from Jenelle. We had a log of those texts, and with those, Jenelle appeared to be knee-deep in the evil-doings percolating in the Potter home.

"Did Dad get the phone?" was the message from Jenelle at 4:25 a.m.

"No," Jamie texted back.

"Shit call back," Jenelle texted. "Tell if he gets it or i will wake him i love you."

Jamie called again. At 4:28, he texted to Jenelle, "He got it i love you."

Jenelle: "Ok good i was in bathroom sick gr i love you he was not mad was he."

Jamie: "No i dont think so why."

Jenelle: "Ok hes loud lol."

Jamie: "I hope he isnt mad at me I love u."

Jenelle: "No the closet is from the liveing room is at my head bord so i hear everything and he just hit 2 walls lol."

At 4:37, a mere nine minutes after Jamie reported that Buddy had answered the phone, Jenelle sent this update: "Is leaving now the front door open and closed."

Two minutes later, Jenelle texted, "Hes leaveing now i hear the car i love you baby i hate were my bed is lol," followed by "I love you he took off love you," and "I love you text me asap when you get back." With her texts, Jenelle had documented the very short time between Jamie's call and Buddy leaving. She also revealed that she was right in the middle of what was happening.

For the next sixteen hours and fifty-four minutes, the line between Jenelle and Jamie was silent.

Late on the evening of January 31, with Bill and Billie Jean's bodies having been found and the TV news trumpeting the news of their discoveries, Jenelle struck another blow against any lawyer's effort to portray her as a innocent fool. She texted to Jamie:

"[B]aby are you ok. and like dad said come over and talk ok. I love you so much baby/ He said you were sick soileft you alone."

The jury had previously seen these damning messages. We were filling in the blanks, Jamie explaining what had happened during that short phone call with Buddy that Jenelle had instigated:

"Buddy asked me, 'You remember that favor that I asked you?' I said, 'Yeah.' He said, 'Can you do it this morning?' And I told him, 'Okay,' and we hung up."

Buddy soon arrived at Jamie's house, which was a mere two to three minutes from Bill's home. Jamie testified he thought he remembered Buddy driving the family's Ford Explorer. Jamie climbed into his vehicle, and Buddy headed toward the Payne residence.

Instead of pulling into Bill's driveway, Buddy strategically parked at a church. From that location, only a field sat between him and the Payne residence. Buddy had a clear line of sight for one critical event: Paw Bill leaving for work in the dark of the morning.

They sat quietly in the Explorer, watching.

"I asked Buddy how far down that he wanted to me to go," said Jamie, who was still working on the assumption his job was to drive up the road and back. "He said that I may not have to go.

"We was waiting, and I seen the lights from Bill Sr.'s truck come on, from across the field."

Paw Bill backed out of his driveway and was on his way to Boone. Buddy then set his plan into motion.

"Buddy asked me, he was like, 'Let's walk over here,'" said Jamie. "And I got out of the vehicle, and we started walking across the field."

It was a long, dark, quiet trek toward the Payne house, Buddy and Jamie together.

"I thought he just wanted to check on Bill or check out something," said Jamie.

"Is this something you'd gone out and done with him before?" I asked.

"No," said Jamie.

"Did Buddy have any guns with him?"

"I didn't see any when I was beside him, but he always carried them."

They walked until they were behind a shed on the Payne property. It was behind the back sliding glass door that was unlocked, the door Lott had identified as the one that the killers most likely entered. Since Buddy had parked far away from the home and approached on foot, the Paynes' dog Pepper heard nothing to prompt a round of barking, which was a lingering mystery from Buddy's trial.

In his words, Jamie finally sensed something was up.

"I asked him, 'What are we doing here? If Bill sees us, all hell's going to break loose,'" Jamie testified. "He handed me a gun, and I took it. I looked at him and said, 'I can't kill nobody.'

"He said I wouldn't have to. He said, 'I just need you to stand at that door.'"

"How did he look? How was he acting?" I asked.

"Like a man on a mission," said Jamie. "Like he had something to do. Like… he was focused."

"Had you ever seen him like that before?"

"No."

"What did you all do from there?"

"We walked around the shed and went into the house through the back sliding glass door. I stood at the door. Buddy went down the hallway, and he went into the bedroom. I heard Bill say, 'What the hell?'"

"Billie Jean came out and went down the hall. I heard a gunshot, and then Buddy came out."

What Jamie said next was the fact that had convinced Lott and I that Jamie was trying to shoot straight for us. It was the ugly fact that I knew had to exist somewhere in the narrative, if only Jamie would resign himself to admitting his actions that contributed to one of the worst crimes of our area's history.

"Then Buddy came out, and he looked at—he—and I just pointed," said Jamie, pausing with trepidation. "Down the hall."

"Pointed where?" I pressed.

"Down the hall."

"Toward what?"

"The way Billie Jean went."

"Why did you do that?"

"I don't know. It was like a reaction when he looked at me."

By pointing, Jamie had directed Buddy where to go to kill a twenty-three-year-old mother.

Jamie said that there was little illumination in the home. What little light existed was coming from the bedroom Buddy first entered. When Billie Jean came out, the light was behind her. If she was holding Tyler, Jamie couldn't see. He was within several feet of where Billie Jean had ran out, her route of escape blocked by Jamie's presence. Instead of trying to push past him, Billie Jean turned left down the hall. She was seeking refuge for her child.

"Did you ever hear the baby?" I asked.

"No. I walked up to the bedroom door and looked in and saw Bill lying on the bed. It was like, when I was looking at him, I heard another gun shot. And it was like reality kicked in. I had to get out of there. I turned and went out the house the way we came in and back across the field to the vehicle."

"Why were you blocking the hallway?"

Jamie gave a long pause. "I was afraid. Buddy told me to do that, and... I mean, I—I just did it."

"You had a gun in your possession?"

"I can't kill nobody. I mean, having a gun and being able to use it are two different things." Jamie said that he had put the gun in his jacket pocket rather than hold it in his hand.

"You were how old?"

"Thirty-eight."

"Had you ever been arrested for anything violent in your life?"

"No."

"Have you ever done anything violent in your life?"

"No. The only thing I've ever had in my life was one speeding ticket."

I showed him a picture of his cousin Bill lying dead on his bed. "How do you feel about that?" I asked.

"Bad. Horrible. He was like a brother."

"Looking back on it, do you feel you have been manipulated in any way by the Potter family?"

"Yes."

"How so?"

"Well, I mean, I thought Chris was real. I mean, I thought that there was someone I was talking to there, and Jenelle, the way she would talk to me, you know, it was like, a bonding, or, a family. And it's like, it's all a lie."

"How does that make you feel now?"

"Ashamed. Humiliated. Stupid."

"If you weren't involved with this, would you be back there at your childhood home, working in that plant?"

"Yes."

"How do you feel about it, being where you are instead of where you would have been?"

"Awful. It's like a dream, really."

"Are there times where you have problems with it?"

"Yeah. Not being able to sleep, always hearing the keys or the doors lock. I mean, being locked up, words can't describe it. I mean, it's just a loss. It's the true meaning of loss."

"You realized that baby was probably in that house?"

"Yeah."

"How does that make you feel?"

"Sick. When we got back to the vehicle, I handed him the gun back and said, 'Here.' And he took me back. When we got to the end of the driveway, I told him to let me out here, and uh, I got out and when I walked across the road, I got sick. I threw up."

I trusted the jury remembered Jenelle's text telling of how her father had said Jamie acted sick.

"I didn't want to be associated with this. It was horrible."

When he cracked after failing his polygraph examination, Jamie had one last hope for his continued freedom. Trouble was, he went through hours of interrogation and not once had he seen a flicker of that hopeful light.

The hopeful light was his friend Chris, who could send the CIA swooping down and keep him out of a jail cell.

"At some point after they got you to break a little bit, did you ask [the investigators] if someone was there?" I asked.

"Yeah," said Jamie. "I asked if the CIA was there."

"Would you agree you were hoping somehow that this Chris stuff was real, and this was going to go away?"

"Yeah."

"It hasn't, has it?"

"No."

"Is Chris real?"

"No."

43

Sometimes during a trial I can get so immersed in pivotal testimony that I have zero awareness if the testimony is connecting the way I desire. Jamie's testimony was one of those times.

Despite my best efforts to prick his emotions, Jamie made it through his testimony without breaking down. Juries always find testimony more compelling when witnesses reveal that situations have affected them.

Jamie shed not a single tear. That worried me. I had spent many hours contemplating how best to get that out of him, but it wasn't happening. Was he merely the type of man who didn't show emotion? Had he become numb to it all? Or was he just a cold-blooded killer seeking a break?

It wasn't like I could query the jury on their thoughts. However, I am the type who likes to poll people on what they think of a witness. I don't question just anyone. Bailiffs may be prone to leaning toward the state. Likewise for the victims' families.

But there was one person there I trusted to give me a truthful, neutral viewpoint. I rushed up after Judge Blackwood recessed for the day, and I asked that person what they thought of Jamie.

"That poor man was manipulated by those people."

That was a good sign. An even better sign would be to hear the same thing from a person whom I knew was hostile to me showing Jamie even the slightest mercy.

For the last couple months, my wife and I had gotten into multiple disagreements about Jamie Curd. She is exposed to the fact patterns of most major cases, since they don't shut off in my head once at home. She understood the Potter case as well as anyone, whether she wanted to or not.

When I began visiting Jamie in jail, trying to get his cooperation, she had adamantly told me that I was doing the wrong thing. He deserved nothing, she thought. He left a baby to possibly die. True, I answered, but the focus needed to be on holding the most culpable people responsible. Had the Potters not come into Jamie's life, he would have gone to his grave without a single incident as a violent criminal.

I truly believed that.

My wife was sitting in the back of the courtroom during the entirety of Jamie's testimony. I went up to her as we walked out. Jamie had been played with, she now recognized. Absent the Potter family coming into his life, he'd still be at home in Johnson County.

Was Jamie's testimony valuable enough to justify giving him twenty-five years with a shot at parole? Time would tell. If anything, I hoped that by getting to hear from him, the jury could understand that his role in this charade was that of the fool.

Our proof ended after the testimonies of Lindsey Thomas, Tara Osborne, and Lyndsey Potter. They said much the same things as they had during Buddy's trial.

The defense got their turn. Fallin elected to not present any proof. Both Barbara and Jenelle expressed their desires to not testify.

Hyder called Keith Jones, a computer forensics expert, to testify for Jenelle. They tried to expose holes in our proof. Jones stated that there were ways to verify that a particular computer had generated questioned e-mails, but he said we had not performed those exercises on the Potter home computer. I found this defense to be useless. It ignored the shredded e-mails found in Buddy's truck and the linguistic features of the Potter women's writings. Moreover, it ignored the Potters' spoken words, which verified they were obsessed with the victims' lives. Surely we were well past wondering whether Chris and Barbara's e-mails originated from the Potter computer.

Jenelle's defense team was trying to do what it could to reveal any reasonable doubt. Yet I hoped we had convinced the jury about who wrote what. All that was left was for Roark and I to tie the case together in closing argument, painting the picture about how all this equaled criminal responsibility.

There was one last subject to tackle before we reached closing, though. Jenelle's mental functions were unquestionably unusual, and Dr. Eric Engum was prepared to explain that to the jury on her behalf.

Dr. Engum was a leading clinical neuropsychologist from Knoxville. He had interviewed Jenelle and administered various tests on her. He testified that she graded out with an IQ of 72. She had been identified as a special education student as early as kindergarten. He spoke about her bilateral hearing loss, which was consistent with what Christie had described in her inability to detect inflection, etc.

His report had been a great disappointment to me. As much as I would have been fascinated to review a full-scale mental health breakdown of Jenelle, Dr. Engum provided no such thing. He could not testify about whether she suffered a mental disease or defect that would have supported an insanity defense, and he could not testify that she had lack of capacity to form intent. He explained:

"She denied that she was involved in any of the activities that have been alleged against her, so I made no finding per se because it's improper for me as a psychologist to make a determination as to one's state of mind at the time of the commission of the offense if in fact they did not engage in activities that are the basis of the criminal indictment," he said.

"But... the allegation that she is in some way a mastermind or a manipulator or a planner, I think really flies in the face of the facts, which go back and say that she is functioning basically as a fourth grader."

Fourth grader? To be honest, I couldn't disagree. I had constantly felt like I was prosecuting an adolescent or younger girl. I didn't feel I could challenge that opinion.

Agent Lott passed me a note with a great question, which I posed to Dr. Engum.

"Can a nine-year-old be manipulative?" I asked.

"Sure," said Dr. Engum. "Nine-year-olds manipulate their parents all the time."

Dr. Engum had not examined the e-mail evidence, which I believed was a fatal flaw in his analysis. He could administer tests all day on Jenelle, but her actual conduct was the better indicator of her capabilities. He also neglected to interview anyone who knew Jenelle and could tell him their observations of her capabilities.

Whatever Jenelle said to him, his inquiry ended there.

"She said she didn't know why she was being incarcerated and held for trial," said Dr. Engum.

"So if the State had e-mails from her e-mail account that were purported to be someone else, but we were showing evidence that she was probably the author—you didn't look at any of those?" I asked. "You didn't analyze any of that for her state of mind or whether she was capable of forming a criminal intent in this case, correct?"

Dr. Engum answered, "One, the answer is no because my understanding was they were potentially authored by somebody else. Two, after I had statements from her that she did not engage in the activities alleged, there was no reason for me to address state of mind because if she didn't do it, I don't have a state of mind at the time of the commission of the offense to evaluate."

Unfortunately, a lot tax dollars went into Dr. Engum performing a function that told the jury nothing more than what they could already conclude. Jenelle operated with intellectual issues, but the analysis ended there, since she denied doing anything.

44

I had the last word during closing arguments. Following my remarks, Judge Blackwood would explain the laws that pertained to the case so that the jury could do its task.

Knowing this was my last chance to achieve justice, I gave it all I had. The night before closing arguments, I had gone through the e-mails one last time. I was looking for tiny snippets that I could use in a presentation to demonstrate the progression between Jenelle and Barbara's conspiracy. Even after pouring through these documents many times, I was still finding little nuggets that I had previously missed.

One aspect I had missed was a repeated reference to "Adam," whom Chris represented to be a coworker of his. There were many mentions of Adam. What I had missed was Barbara audibly mentioning Adam to Jamie when Jamie made the recorded call for Buddy. Barbara had told Jamie that she heard from Chris that Jamie had been booked in. When Jamie denied it, she said she told him that "was just Adam talking."

If Barbara had nothing to do with the conspiracy at hand, it sure was funny that she was dropping the same name that had appeared in 15 of the 207 pages of e-mails that the jury possessed. As I flashed the page numbers of references to Adam, some of the jurors were scurrying to write them down.

That was a good sign. A prosecutor has two aims during a closing argument: (1) convince as many jurors as possible that the accused is guilty and (2) give those jurors the ammunition to convince the remaining members. Jurors copying my information was promising. They wanted ammo.

I pointed out other things, particularly those printed pictures of Billie Jean and Lindsey that Barbara had stolen from under Chief Deputy Woodard's nose and torn in two. One picture was of Billie Jean lying on the beach in a swimsuit with the caption "Billie whore." On eighteen of the submitted e-mail pages, Billie Jean was referred to as a "whore." Again, jurors copied the page numbers.

Those pictures did not rely on forensic linguistics or computer investigations to prove Barbara and Jenelle's involvement. Those photos were printed and kept in their home for several months, and Barbara found it necessary to destroy them. They held secrets she wanted hidden from investigators.

I focused on things that made good common sense. I also hit them with the shredded documents, cataloguing how many of the 207 pages of complete e-mails were duplicates of what the TBI recovered from Buddy's truck. There were four such matches. Again, the jurors wrote down the page numbers.

I spent a short time rebutting the defense's arguments. Whatever the defense neglects to mention during their closing, that's always prime fodder to exploit in the state's final closing. Counsel for Barbara ignored one major fact Agent Lott had told the jury during his testimony.

"When Mr. Davis got up here, he went on and on about all the things we didn't do," I said. "He omitted addressing one thing that is undisputed in this proof, something they don't want you to remember. Barbara Potter, under oath in a previous hearing, admitted she wrote e-mails to Chris from the CIA. Investigator Lott told you about that, and it's undisputed. The defense couldn't get up there and ask him about it and pick at him about that because they knew it was the truth."

The bulk of my talk concerned a video presentation I had prepared of snippets of the e-mails and shreds. With these brief blurbs, I was going to make my criminal responsibility theory easy for the jury to digest. One of the first snippets I showed was Barbara's critically incriminating statement, which showed up on page 38 as well as page 103 of the shredded e-mails:

> [T]hey need to back off. Bud is sooooo mad, &I'm 100%
> behind whatever happens. You guys meet when you are
> ready-Chris. Maybe Bud will have ID by then & can use CIA
> guns,etc. for his protection-get the jobs done. ya know.
> They all need to go & the ones left need to be given a big
> scare as they watch & wonder 'am I next?'

There was Chris's suggestion that Buddy could indeed get the job done:

> Well buddy can kill thembefore they will so no worries
> there. dumb bitch ho. she needs her butt kicked good and
> left. and maybe run over and a bullet in her head.

I continued with Chris touting Jamie as a person who shared Barbara's distaste for Bill:

> Well I will tell you who came up here and talked to me.
> Jamie told everything on Bill and He has not been down
> there. He said they have been hateful to him last summer
> when Bill stared to date Billie.

Plenty of Chris's writings wishing death upon the victims and Lindsey were shown:

> [Lindsey] will back off fast and stop things. But that's if
> I let her live. I chose that... her boyfriend and Bill and
> Billie and that damn baby. I will see when I want to kill
> them... then I'm getting some of the cops. no one would
> ever miss them.

An example of Chris warning Barbara of how Bill and his gang were going about their harassment of the Potters:

> [B]ut Bill's cell is the one they are using too and its bad
> they are being hateful fuckers tonight. I will get them mom
> and I'm sure buddy too... nothing scares this girl so I guess
> I just need to kill and shoot her 4 times in the fucking head
> and a few other times, and then she will be gone.

Next I showed Barbara's words revealing conversations she had with Buddy regarding his designs, and their hope that Chris could help Buddy:

> If you come back, do you have 'plans'? like talked about before for her espec. and for others? I hope they wil let you do what needs to be done, and Bud is ready to help you. Though he needs an ID, he says in this town, they only look at the computer. He has thought and thought of ways & is ready...just needs another guy.

After having reminded the jury of Barbara's previous distaste for Jamie, I showed them how by this time she was open to having him around:

> Anyway, a note to let you this....I called Jamie this evening & talked for a while, then Bud talked to him. He is coming here on Thurs at noon to see us/talk for a while...so will try to tell you some in 'code' but he can tell you All -if he wants to.

At that point, Chris upped the ante regarding Jamie:

> [Jamie's] just mad about how they are buging You all and Him and he wont take it. He would kill her if he had someone he siad. He know's some ppl that would help him but he said trusting someone you know. He don't want anyone to talk. But yes i think if he and buddy would meet it would be a good thing. Before July 27th and let him tell you how he found out everything and he know's them girls was well so he can pretty much tell you if your going to have any issues with bill or billie next and he know's a lot.

Chris made suggestions that people can get away with murder:

> Now i know why ppl take care of there own issues with ppl kill themand no one cares. pretty much. I have head it and seen it for my self. I got ride of 2 and no one cared nor asked anything. lol. you can get away with it. She needs to be killed and Billie and i dont care if i killed that baby and her b/c she going to make it into her. Who wants that shit. fucking ass hole's and whores ... jamie is really mad

and he's told her stop messing with all of you and he said you come to my lane he will shoot and he said i wont miss.

Barbara was glad to hear they had an ally in Jamie:

I'm glad that Jamie is really mad & if he feels like Bud, they may take care of some things pretty good. We all need peace in this place till we move away. I hope they meet soon.

Yet Barbara and Buddy still hoped they could involve Chris:

No, I don't think anyone would really mess w/Buddy. No one has seen the 'other side' of him - not in this town. He always comes across as a gentleman, but he knows lots of stuff-ya know to do and say to get things rolling right. He's trained to rock n' roll..ya know. The time will come he thinks&he has thought it out. I'd love to say more, but better not here... the reason he wants to meet w/you.

I showed snippets of conversations between Chris and Jamie during October 2011, including the one where Chris said, "I hope she dont think about killing her self." Jamie described Jenelle as his "ray of light at the end of the tunnel" and that the love she had for him was "something I thought I'd never see, not from this shit hole."

Chris tried feeding Jamie with reassuring words that helping Buddy would be for the greater good:

Something will happen to them in time. With you and Buddy I hope you all can get them. I hope it all works out great. I hope that you will pray about it and Buddy is and that you know what you are all doing is great. Your going to help the town. I wish i could kill them but right now i really can't.

There was more feeding by Chris to Jamie:

I hope that Bill and them get what's comeing to them. Jenelle was crying over it earlyer from what i hear it's messing her up more then it needstoo and it's going to kill her.

Perhaps feeling that Jamie needed some reassurance, Chris offered to back him up:

> Jenelle is just at her end and from what her mom's say's all of this is getting to her so bad and she is worryed about Jenelle. But i think more you hang out and everything with them and then you and Jenelle alone it will all be ok you know. Man i have our back always and Jenelle never been happy or loved like you give her.

Barbara wrote her own message coaxing Jamie:

> I feel bad for you bc how they run you down, its terrible. You are not the bad person they lilke to say you are..they even told the police last year that you were in trouble & bad & to keep you away from our house! so you see? Can't trust bill or any of them. I feel bad for you. Know this. You are Not alone. We are here and we care bout you a lot.

Barbara hinted that a plan was in the works, writing to Jamie:

> I have emailed Chris that we are ready to go to the 'movies' next Friday or Saturday so to let me know the time/day and to text you. I hope that is okay....he will get the message that the time is next weekend.

Chris kept encouraging Barbara, writing, "I can't wait for you and Buddy and us to do our Job's."

Perhaps feeling she needed to help reassure Jamie, Barbara suggested:

> If you talk/text with Chris, ask him if he thinks the cia will back up Buddy if he takes it into his own hands..not an e-mail but a text...they are trying to kill Jenelle little by little.

In December, Barbara updated Chris on what she had told Buddy and Jamie:

> I did tell B&J you said that their backs are covered well and that all is good-but dad knows that but says that he will do whatever it takes no matter whose around ... they

are glad cia is around but they say that they will be able to handle it all but good to know.

Chris wrote back, urging haste due to what he was learning about the Payne residence:

This is far from over with them. They are not laying low at all. They are Plotting something but I think that will be taken care of. They are waiting to see Jenelle out. and By her self.

Chris then reiterated his support in this message to Barbara:

We got Jamie's back and tell Jamie to stay if he want's anytime b/c they are after him a lot. and no need of this fucking shit. We are pissed off guys. we will be around.

Chris pressed further, stating that Jenelle's safety was getting more doubtful in the face of threats by people who felt she was too pretty:

Now they want to hurt and kill Jenelle. She is the main one there is a plot just for Jenelle. So make sure she is always with someone and close very close. well I'm happy everyone that needs to carry is carrying and ready b/c you just don't know right now. I will say in a week or less it's going to get worse and nothing else needs to come you all's way. But with B and J I think things should go great. How have you been Mom? I don't care what they read or think. It goes to show you they are just evil and mean and that baby was never wanted and look how they treat it. I hope maybe it should die it come from the Devil. Them 2 making the thing. They can't stand it that Jenelle is so pretty and so truthful and just a great person. Lindsay is no good for nothing and she needs to put a bag over head and breath hard LMAO. Or pull her lip over head and just swallow LMAO eww her fucking ugly face and neck ... saw her at the store today ICKYYYY she wears short dress's.

Barbara then provided this update:

> Hey C.-its later on, but justg wanted to touch base and say that tho the 'weather' didn't work out tonight, wow! it was a nice & close time...but things didnt' work out. but there will not be any giving up..and you don't either.
>
> We worry about one of us being shot or ..You know.... hopefully mon. will be another good weather day;..you know..& dad will be on his A game...you know...then the plant is closed until dec 27th....so the situation will be changed for a short time as planned now. but there may be other ways.

I pointed out that the last message likely referred to the Christmas breaks at the plants where Bill and Paw Bill worked. Jamie had explained that Paw Bill's plant shut down for a few more days during the holidays. Since Buddy had waited for Paw Bill to leave prior to venturing across the field, I concluded that was the plan Barbara had alluded to in that message.

The last communication we found from Chris to Barbara was one of the recovered shreds. It had a date on the bottom of the page showing January 25, 2012 as the date printed. From its tone, I told the jury that by this time, Jenelle had run out of patience. It was time for blood:

> I hope Buddy and him get them and ASAP would be great. But anyway's yes whore fucking Lindsey moved in with Tim and No Cell phone and her Birthday is the 26 of Jan. I hope she dies before then. damn fucking whore. She is no good![1]

The final e-mail that we presented was not a message at all. It was an e-mail Barbara had sent to herself, presumably so that she could save the webpage link that was contained within it. Dated January 16, 2012, a mere fifteen days before the murders of Bill Payne and Billie Jean Hayworth, the webpage had this title: "Can God Forgive a Murderer? Christian News."

Agent Lott had testified that, when he clicked on that link,

---

1   Lindsey testified that January 26 was her birthday.

it went to an article written by Billy Graham. The Reverend had written a response to a killer in prison who asked if he could be forgiven for his sins.

Barbara had all her bases covered.

I ended with one facet that the jury might have missed when the testimony came in. Those texts that went back and forth between Jenelle and Melanie Clayton were revealing, as far as Jenelle's thoughts just after her father and Jamie went to jail. Repeatedly, she had asked Melanie if she thought Jamie still loved her and whether he might hate her now.

"Why is that on her mind?" I asked. "Her father is in jail for murder. Her boyfriend of almost two years is in jail for murder, and four times within an hour she's sitting there dwelling on 'I wonder if Jamie still loves me,' 'I wonder if he hates me.'

"I'm going to answer exactly why she's wondering that. She wasn't sure if Jamie loved her enough to keep his mouth shut about her. She didn't have to ask those questions about her daddy because she knew Daddy loved her that much. Daddy wasn't going to sell her out. Daddy wasn't going to sell Momma out.

"Jamie was the worry. When Marvin Potter calls his wife from jail on February 7 you heard her reaction, or her lack of reaction. A typical spouse gets a phone call from their spouse, 'I'm in jail for murder. I just told them I did it.' The reaction to that should be a lot more than what you got from Barbara Potter. Go back and listen to it. Ask yourself how reasonable people would react in that phone call.

"She's as cool as can be, and she's not surprised by the idea that her husband might have killed these people. After all, he was doing what she wanted. When she gets surprised, it's toward the end of the call when he says Jamie talked on me. 'What? What?' That's what surprised her. She thought she had Jamie Curd where she wanted him. But he said something. So now these defendants stand before you, and I submit that this proof is absolutely overwhelming that these crimes do not happen without these two people intentionally promoting it and assisting."

I asked the jurors to do one thing for me. Knowing all that they did about this case, I asked them to close their eyes and imagine these killings happening without Jenelle doing what she had. I asked them to do the same for Barbara.

"If you can't imagine these crimes happening without these women, then you know in your heart what your verdict must be.

"You have before you the two people most responsible for Bill Payne and Billie Jean Hayworth laying there dead, and a live baby that was left without a parent back in 2012. We ask you to bring justice for these deaths."

45

With the jury deliberating, I tried finding a quiet spot in the DA's office where I could check the e-mails that I'd neglected for the past two weeks. It was refreshing to get immersed in other cases. More routine matters. Burglaries, drug sales, DUIs—anything to get my mind off the impending verdict.

Perhaps in a few hours, I'd be giving an interview for the television stations and newspapers, proudly commenting on justice being served. Or perhaps I'd be talking as Jenelle and Barbara were transported back to the jail to be booked out, free forever.

There is a gap between those extremes that equates to infinity. I was going to be the hero or the goat. Justice served or justice eluded.

I learned long before that it was best to distract myself with other work rather than mingle with the officers, witnesses, and victims' families outside the courtroom as the jury deliberated. They'd just make my tension worse.

Nevertheless, people would find me. "How long they been out?" "How you think it went?" "I bet you're happy it's over." Yada, yada, yada. After about four times of being reminded about the case, I started snapping back with a slight note of anger, "I don't know. I'm trying to do other things."

It was a difficult time. Worse yet, it looked like deliberations would stretch into days. Judge Blackwood sent the jury home after an hour of work, and we came back the next day. I feared that this deliberation could last for a very long time. We had a mountain of e-mails, Facebook posts, text messages, pictures, and recorded interviews that a curious jury might peruse at length. If there were jurors uncertain of their opinions, they could take forever going through all that material. In fact, early in the morning on the second day, the bailiffs reported the jurors wanted a laptop with which to play the tapes. I prepared to settle in for a full day of waiting. Probably longer.

Many juries seem to reach verdicts right after lunch. They want one more free meal. This jury wound up no different. After lunch that second day, word spread quickly through the courthouse that a verdict was at hand. Spread out over two days, it had taken four and a half hours for the body to deliberate.

That was fast. Far too quick to think they spent much time studying Chris's linguistics or examining the criminal responsibility contained in the e-mails. These jurors were fully on board with whatever they had decided.

I put my jacket on and walked to the courtroom. My mind raced with full-force paranoia. Did the jury members throw up their hands and conclude we had no case at all? Had they found sympathy in the obvious fact that these women suffered from mental maladies? Had they been so revolted by Jamie's deal that they felt the women deserved no more punishment than him, or none at all?

I was about to find out.

In real time, waiting for the jury to walk in and deliver the verdict probably takes a mere few minutes. For me, it feels like an hour. The attorneys, judge, and court reporter must all be in the room. The bailiffs have to bring the defendants back in. The bailiffs then have to space themselves out to ensure security should an eruption arise following the verdict. Then there are all the family and friends of the deceased who take their rightful spots and brace for the excruciating pain that will result from whatever the verdict may be.

Roark, Lott, Woodard, and I rose from the state's table as the jury filed in. I never look at the jurors in such moments. I can't. I just look down as my blood pressure builds.

Judge Blackwood asked the foreman if the jury had reached a verdict. He said that they had. The judge asked for the verdict forms to be passed to him, and a bailiff retrieved them and walked them over. Blackwood examined the forms, and when he finished, I heard a sharp *thump, thump* as the bottom edges of the papers struck the bench as he tried to straighten them out.

I was so stressed out that my mind was trying to glean clues about the verdict based on how he shuffled the papers.

"Mr. Foreperson, I'm gonna return these verdict forms to you," said the Judge. "I would like for you to stand, and I would like for you to read your verdict, beginning with the verdicts against Barbara Potter and proceeding to the verdicts regarding Jenelle Potter."

Judge Blackwood then requested the defendants stand.

The courtroom was deathly quiet.

"Count one, we the jury find the defendant Barbara Mae Potter guilty of first degree murder," the foreperson announced.

I felt no sense of relief about that verdict. As the foreperson continued, announcing guilty verdicts on the second count of first degree murder as well as conspiracy to commit first degree murder and tampering with evidence, my tension built as he made his way to Jenelle.

"Count one, we the jury find the defendant Jenelle Leigh Potter guilty of first degree murder," the foreperson said.

The instant that sentence ended, I was in tears, emotionally spent. The foreperson announced that Jenelle was guilty as charged on everything else as well, but I didn't hear him. The moment had overcome me, much more than at any other time in my career.

For over two years, I had gotten into a tough, complicated case and dreamed up a way to prosecute these two women for killings that they themselves had not committed. I had no manual to guide me through the task. Yet the Potter women were responsible, now not just in my mind, but in the official records of the state of Tennessee.

My emotions, however great, were in no way equal to those of the folks sitting behind me. I could hear the many family members of Bill Payne and Billie Jean Hayworth weeping openly as Jenelle was deemed guilty, and giving an audible whimper of joy as Judge Blackwood then sentenced them to life imprisonment for their crimes.

After Roark, Lott, and myself took in our congratulatory hugs from those very appreciative persons, we had post-trial interviews with a hungry media. I was relieved to not be a goat.

When I got the chance to communicate the verdict to Dr. Leonard back home in New York, I summed it up as well as I could in an e-mail:

"Society is less two rotten pieces of fruit today."

46

I got to sleep a bit more the next morning. A massive amount of pressure had lifted from my shoulders. New challenges would arise, I knew, and for this day, at least, I could give my wife as well as our dogs, cats, and pet pigs more attention.

Yet the case kept swirling in my head. It was like a swarm of gnats that would not go away. After all, the case had practically consumed my life. Adjusting to my life without the Potters was going to take time.

For the first time in dealing with the Potter family, the idea of writing about them hit me. I had always aspired to write a book. As a kid, my first ambition had been to become a writer, and in college I worked in the sports department at the local newspaper, the *Johnson City Press*. I had loved writing, but I wound up pursing the law and I hadn't looked back.

My main concern about writing a book was that my imagination wasn't strong enough to carry my work to book length. But the Potters had provided all the imagination I needed. All I had to do was get it out.

Thus I opened my MacBook and started typing. The words and thoughts spilled onto the computer screen quite naturally. It was as easy as breathing.

Writing this book allowed me to lay the case to rest. It was the biggest, toughest, and strangest matter that I had ever experienced, and I am supremely confident it will remain so.

Soon television networks took an interest in the story. ABC sent a crew to do an episode on 20/20. They interviewed me multiple times. Right before their show was to air, the producer told me they had decided this was the craziest story they'd ever done. "And we do a lot of crazy," he said.

As I wrote this book, the entire system of boxes of files and computer media took up a bedroom in my house. I went back through statements, e-mails, and records. At times, I found little tidbits that I'd missed all along. The case was that enormous, that I could still be learning about the matter even after the verdicts.

There was one piece that I studied a lot more in writing the book. It was a tape recording that we never played for either jury. I wish we had.

On the morning of day one of the women's trial, I got a call from Tracy Greenwell, who was on her way from Mountain City to Jonesborough. She said she had a taped conversation between her brother Bill Payne and the Potters.

"Say what?" I asked. Lawyers hate surprises.

She explained that someone had "stolen" a tape recorder from Randy Fallin, attorney for Barbara and Buddy, and they had turned it over to her this past weekend.

"What in the world could possibly be on it?" I wondered.

Before the trial began, we got a brief listen. Indeed, it was the Potters talking to a man, a man whom Tracy told me was Bill. It's funny how I could deal with the case so much that I felt I knew Bill but, having never met him, I wasn't able to recognize his voice.

We decided to forget the tape. There were serious discovery issues ahead if we introduced it. Since the defense attorneys had not been given the recording, they presumably knew nothing about it. At least Hyder, on behalf of Jenelle, probably was unaware. Fallin pretended to not know anything, even though the talk was that it came out of his office. Who took it I had no idea. Since we assumed the Potters had brought the recordings to Fallin, Lott's opinion was to not use it, or else we'd be introducing evidence that Barbara thought was useful to her.

So I acquiesced and held it back.

However, in writing this book, I had plenty of time to analyze it. One track was a recording of an unknown man going to talk to someone about a domestic situation that obviously had nothing to do with our case. I surmised that it was this man who had gotten ahold of the digital recorder. He didn't really "steal" it. He was probably a client of Fallin's, and this being a recorder that held no useful material (to him, at least), the attorney likely gave it to the client to record a conversation.

How the recorder came into Fallin's hands was that the Potters had given it to him. It had three digital files featuring their voices. One was a completely innocuous audio file of Buddy making himself a shopping list.

Another was a long phone call Jenelle had received from a "Jo Ann." I could only hear Jenelle's side of the conversation as well as Barbara's report that the tape was running and Buddy stating that Lindsey had HIV. The call went on for several minutes, Jenelle complaining of harassment from people such as this caller. Jenelle claimed to have been called fifteen to twenty times that day alone. Within the same breath, she would contradict herself without realizing it.

"I haven't done anything to anybody," said Jenelle. "I try to live my own life. I'm with my parents 24/7. You all are not going to get me. I'm sorry. You're not. I know how to protect myself. I know how to fight back with my legs, my arms, my hands, my fingers, everything. So, if you want to come up and kick my ass, I dare you to come up to my door and freaking bring it on. Just do it.

"You're messing with the wrong daughter. You can mess with my sister all you want. But I am a daughter of a CIA...."

And on it went.

What I found significant was that it really appeared to be an incoming call to the Potters. I could not hear what was being said on the other end, but there was a person there. It was a person who called them, and that person was at least curious enough about Jenelle's extensive ranting to stay on the call and listen to her.

Had the Potters actually gotten harassing phone calls? Was there some merit to this claim of Jenelle's? Certainly, this was only one call. But it was easy to imagine young people enjoying the practice of calling Jenelle to get a rise out of her by committing a childish prank. If so, they were agitating persons who proved to be criminally inclined. Bad idea.

If the caller in this instance, and any callers besides, are still living, I wonder if there is any twinge of guilt on their part that they agitated the Potters into spilling blood. Personally, I hope they regret it.

47

Are mental diseases contagious?

As I wrote this book in the months following the verdict, I asked myself that question many times. I'm not a mental health expert. However, I feel I've seen enough mental disease to have a good idea when one is present.

Barbara and Jenelle possessed unhealthy minds. As I posed questions to the psychiatrist Dr. Engum at their trial, I described aspects of our case and asked him if they were consistent with persons with healthy minds. With each question, he firmly answered no. They were sick people.

As I pondered their situation further, I was convinced that whatever defects Jenelle possessed, they were greatly worsened by her mother's own maladies. Jenelle learned to get attention from Barbara by playing her games. She indulged her mother's fantasies, her fears, and her paranoia. Eventually those defects rubbed off on Jenelle.

Throughout their prosecutions, I had thought of Buddy as a slightly unwitting pawn of the women. I was likely a bit off in that assessment. As the recorded phone call between Jenelle and the unknown person developed, Buddy was right in the middle, feeding Jenelle information.

The e-mails Jenelle wrote under pseudonyms included many references to sexually transmitted diseases that she believed Lindsey and her friends possessed. Those were not just Jenelle's beliefs. Buddy was right there during the phone call, telling Jenelle that Lindsey had HIV. He didn't correct Jenelle when she said he was CIA. The entire call was ridiculous on all the Potters' parts, Buddy included.

In retrospect, Buddy was probably every bit as deranged as the women. After all, he was the one who aimed a gun toward the head of a young mother holding her baby.

It is probably human nature to want to bring order to such things as which Potter was the worst of the lot. They probably all tied for first place. Jenelle instigated the whole conflict, Buddy executed the mission, and Barbara drove the other two crazy to the point where they did what they did. Each one contributed to the faults of the others.

For all the thought I put into such questions, I was not the first. One person had pondered the Potters long before.

Bill Payne possessed no college learning, but he had a grasp of what was wrong with Jenelle Potter. And come to find out, he tried communicating it to her parents.

The final audio file on the digital recorder was a recorded incoming phone call from Bill to the Potter home. He was calling in an attempt to end the online derogatory comments he thought were coming from Jenelle.

I determined the call occurred on September 1, 2011, five months before Buddy would end Bill's life.

"I get sick and tired of every time I turn the computer on, my name is—" Bill said, talking of insults against him that he saw Jenelle posting on her page, before Barbara cut him off.

"Well, that's Lindsey Thomas," Barbara asserted. "She's using Jenelle's page. She's been doing it for a long time. She created four other screen names under Jenelle Potter. We know that for a fact."

I could hear Jenelle in the background, crying and whimpering as Bill made his accusations against her.

"I'd come up there and mow your damned yard for you if my name could be off the damned Internet for three or four days calling me a bad father," said Bill.

"That's Lindsey and Billie," responded Barbara, transitioning her voice into her best manipulative inflection. "We don't think you're a bad father at all, Bill. We don't have anything against you at all."

"I'm sitting right on the page for it," said Bill. "You and Buddy get in your little truck and drive down here to Dad's and we'll just have a big family—"

"No, no," Barbara answered quickly. "I will not come to your house. You can come to ours."

"No," replied Bill. "I wouldn't come up there because then you'd say that we was trying to—you'd have the damned law there before I got in there."

"No, that's exactly what you were planning to do to us," said Barbara, her voice rising. "That's exactly what you want to do."

"Bullshit," said Bill. "Hell, we can bring [Sheriff] Mike Reece down here. We'll call him and he can meet us here too."

At this point, the conversation was heated enough that Bill and Barbara were talking over one another.

Bud interjected. "There's not a thing on her Facebook. We're looking at it right now."

Sounding like a little girl, Jenelle offered, "The only thing that's on here is my pictures."

"She's lying to you all," said Bill.

"No. She's not lying," responded Buddy. "I'm sitting here looking at it right now and there's nothing there."

I could hear Jenelle crying. Buddy tried to end her wailing, telling her to stop worrying about it. Meanwhile, Barbara explained to Bill how Lindsey had stolen Jenelle's pictures and created false Facebook pages.

After enough attempts at telling Jenelle to stop crying, I could hear Buddy tell her, "Bull, bull, bull, Jenelle, you're not going to jail. Now quit. Stop it."

For all the insanity he was facing, Bill was diplomatic with the Potters. At least more than they had a right to.

"I'm a different person. I'm a better person," Bill tried to explain to them how he had been changing his life for the better. He was a proud father of a new baby, and he clearly wanted to do right by his child.

"Well, I never thought you were bad, Bill. I never did," Barbara lied.

"Well, I'm even better now," said Bill.

Eventually Bill made reference to Jenelle and Jamie.

"Oh my God, are you crazy?" asked Barbara. "Jenelle's not interested in Jamie."

"Jenelle ain't?" asked Bill.

"No," said Barbara. "They're just friends. That's all."

"Well, she's lying to you about that too," said Bill.

"Bullshit," replied Barbara.

"She's lying to you all the way around," explained Bill. "You kept her sheltered in a house and she hasn't had a life."

"She's here because she's sick, Bill," Barbara replied.

"She's not that sick," said Bill.

"You don't know a damned thing about her," Buddy yelled.

"I've got all the hospital reports, all the doctor reports; she's been in the hospital over sixty times," said Barbara.

"If she's that damned sick, she would be in a hospital," said Bill. "Hell, you've *had* her thinking she's so damned sick, wiping her hind end."

"I hope to God you never get the kind of thing she's got wrong with her, especially diabetes, because it will kill you, the kind of life you live," replied Barbara.

"What do you mean?" asked Bill, sensing the insult Barbara had just hurled at him.

"You have to be very strict with your diet," she said. "You have to take your insulin. You can't be stressed out. I know you all want Jenelle dead. I know you all do. And you might get your wish."

"I do not," Bill answered. "I want her to quit."

Jenelle screamed, "There's nothing on my page!"

Bill said he could see it on her Facebook page. Jenelle replied that he couldn't see it because she had blocked him. "You're hacking!" she exclaimed.

"I can get in through Jamie Curd's account," explained Bill. "He said I could get in it anytime I wanted to."

"Well, I'll talk to Jamie about that," touted Barbara. "He won't let you anymore."

After more accusations were hurled back and forth, Bill provided a gem of insight.

"Jenelle has more than one personality," he said. "One minute Jenelle's lying in town, talking to Tracy and Clay and everything nice and the next...."

Barbara then accused Bill of being crazy.

"Leave us alone!" she screamed. "If you call here again, I'm going to do something about it!"

The call ended, Barbara hanging up in a rage.

I was numb from hearing Bill, my victim, being so on point. Again and again.

My assessment of the call was that Bill's intent was more of solving an ongoing problem than of being confrontational. He wasn't calling the Potters names. He wasn't making threats. He was trying to make Jenelle change her behavior. That he failed in his mission and ultimately lost his life, well, hearing his voice in this context made the killings all the more senseless.

Tragically, for all his correct insights into Jenelle's issues and their causes, Bill Payne never truly comprehended the danger that was to befall him and Billie Jean. He had his back door unlocked, after all, a mistake which allowed Buddy to quietly enter his home and end their lives.

Until that fateful conclusion to this story, the Potters were a mere nuisance to Johnson County. They were the wacky family up the road without friends, always causing trouble. No one got along with them. Every community in the United States has such a family, including yours.

The strangeness of the Potter women didn't end with their verdicts. Having each elected to not testify, and thus not face my cross-examination, both Barbara and Jenelle elected to be interviewed on 20/20 within a few months of their convictions.

Of course, Barbara denied any guilt. She didn't write those messages. Jamie had written it all and set them up. He had the motive to kill the victims, not them. Buddy indeed had been a CIA agent, but she couldn't talk about that since his actions were a government secret. Of this crime, though, he was innocent. Jenelle? Well, she hoped she wasn't involved. Her interviewer told Barbara that she was either innocent or one exquisite liar. She responded by asking, "What do you think?"

In her interview, Jenelle claimed to have undergone horrible harassment from the victims. When asked if she had hated them, she responded that she did not hate them, that she only "disliked" them. There was no follow up question to that assertion, but I found it significant that she could perceive a difference between "hate" and "dislike." Ascertaining that difference would not be consistent with someone who was at a fourth grade level. She denied being Chris and said she did not know who Chris was. Her family had been trying to find out, she claimed. When the interviewer pressed Jenelle, saying that she was Chris, Jenelle broke down on camera, sobbing as she terminated the interview.

She also claimed to have never "been with" a man. However, she did concede to the proven fact that she and Jamie had had quite the relationship.

The Potter who remained silent throughout his trial and my finishing this book was Buddy. When we tried the women, Buddy had been transported to the courthouse and was available to testify on behalf of his wife and daughter. Yet he was never called to the witness stand. The word we got from the defense attorneys was that, if called, he would assert his Fifth Amendment privileges. And when 20/20 came calling, Buddy didn't talk to them.

I found that to have profound implications. The one person who potentially could have helped Barbara and Jenelle at trial was Buddy. He could have taken the stand and said, "I did it, it was my idea, and they had nothing to do with it." Such a statement probably wouldn't have worked, but it might have been a good effort. I wondered why Buddy declined to talk and possibly take the heat off his wife and daughter. Had he finally realized that his daughter had performed an elaborate hoax at his expense? Had he grown to resent how his wife had used him, building him up to be this grand CIA type, only to spend the remainder of his days in a penitentiary?

As with any complicated, layered story, as one learns more, some questions get answered and still more pop up. I am curious what Buddy now thinks about Barbara and Jenelle, and whether time to reflect following his verdict has given him any more clarity of thought. However, I expect his outlook will always be consistent with that of a sick man capable of taking two innocent lives and leaving a third to grow up without parents. It's hard to expect more.

If there is one thing I hope that this story accomplishes, it's that some law enforcement officer or prosecutor absorbs it, and it affects them. Impacts them for the better. Perhaps justice in other cases can be attained if they challenge their assumptions and take chances. Sometimes getting justice is simple. Other times, it takes a hell of a lot of work.

Also, I hope this story increases our appreciation of the importance of the piddly cases in our workload. The simple domestics, the harassment claims, the stalking allegations—all the little cases that come and go without much thought. They can digress to something much worse, like this set of events. We need to do better as a system to prevent such outcomes.

And one more thing. Our world today is dangerous. Lock your doors.

CREDITS

It has been the greatest honor of my life to present the case of Bill Payne and Billie Jean Hayworth to two juries, and to bring it to you by way of this book. The goal of every prosecutor should be to make a positive difference on behalf of justice. I am blessed to have this as my finest example.

I could not have done it alone. If the TBI's Scott Lott hadn't gotten Jamie Curd to crack and then utilized that probable cause to discover the e-mail and texting evidence in this case, perhaps no one would ever have been held accountable for these horrible crimes. Scott's work was of the highest caliber throughout this journey, and I would have no story of my own to tell without his tireless efforts. The families of the victims should feel more indebted to him than anyone else.

Likewise, Joe Woodard of the Johnson County Sheriff's Department proved to me to that he was a great asset to his county. If I called or texted him with a question, he'd reply within minutes. Every time. If I needed to find a person, he'd have the individual to me by the end of the day. The entire department showed a level of cooperation and effectiveness that transcended the meager salaries that their rural county could provide.

One regret that I have in this book is that ninety-nine percent of it revolves around me. It is written from my viewpoint, after all. Unfortunately, that's a disservice to my colleague Matt Roark. He put as many hours into the case as I did. Maybe more. His grasp of the trial's computer issues was far beyond mine, and his attention to that freed me up to focus elsewhere. This case meant as much to him as it did to me, and our differing styles complimented each other well in presenting the case.

One unsung hero in this narrative was Rosemary Blackwell, our office's secretary in Johnson County. A splendidly sweet person, as were most people from the county, Rosemary worked tirelessly to coordinate the many people testifying at the trials. I cannot express how important her work was to our team.

Last but not least, I want to thank the two females in my life who have sacrificed the most for the stress toll inflicted on me over the years. My daughter Cassie turned eighteen before the last Potter trial. Interestingly, she gets credit for one important contribution to this book: the second chapter. When I began the book, I explained to her my dilemma about how to begin this story, and she chirped, "Use foreshadowing." I blew her off at first, but hours later, I took a shot at it. The result was the second chapter, in which Mr. Hyder asks the jury to describe his client in one word. When Hyder asked the question, I really wanted to raise my hand and answer him. Of course, I couldn't. Yet with this book, perhaps I have.

My wife Sandra has lived through enough murder cases to make her something of an expert in the field. Unfortunately, all the stress and tension in my job affects her as well. She is happiest when I'm not in the middle of such an experience. Yet I keep getting in them, and I continue running facts and scenarios by her, since she's the most convenient person for me to pitch ideas to. Without her continued support, I would not have the strength to do what I do. Perhaps no greater example of her support can be found than the fact that she tolerated me spending even more time on the Potter family as I wrote this book, long after the final verdict for this deranged bunch.

I pray I never see anyone like them again.